A FEW LAWLESS VAGABONDS

A FEW LAWLESS VAGABONDS

Ethan Allen, the Republic of Vermont, and the American Revolution

DAVID BENNETT

CASEMATE
Philadelphia & Oxford

Published in the United States of America and Great Britain in 2014 by
CASEMATE PUBLISHERS
908 Darby Road, Havertown, PA 19083
and
10 Hythe Bridge Street, Oxford, OX1 2EW

ISBN 978-1-61200-240-8
Digital Edition: ISBN 978-1-61200-241-5

Cataloging-in-publication data is available from the Library of Congress and the British Library.

10 9 8 7 6 5 4 3 2 1

Printed and bound in the United States of America.

For a complete list of Casemate titles please contact:

CASEMATE PUBLISHERS (US)
Telephone (610) 853-9131, Fax (610) 853-9146
E-mail: casemate@casematepublishing.com

CASEMATE PUBLISHERS (UK)
Telephone (01865) 241249, Fax (01865) 794449
E-mail: casemate-uk@casematepublishing.co.uk

MIX
Paper from responsible sources
FSC® C011935

CONTENTS

ACKNOWLEDGMENTS

THE AUTHOR RECEIVED GENERAL and helpful advice on this book from Mark A. Stoler and Tony Whedon. John J. Duffy made a great number of suggestions for the text, both critical and constructive, and read extensive passages, particularly those on the Eastern and Western Unions and the Haldimand Negotiations. Without John Duffy's great help, willingly given and often unsolicited, this would have been a much poorer book.

Amani Whitfield and Frank Luce read and criticized the passages on Slavery and the Vermont Constitution. From Amani Whitfield I learned that the history of slavery in Vermont after the Constitution of 1777 was a far more complex matter than I had ever imagined, something which he pointed out to me with great courtesy. From Frank Luce, I learned that the phasing out of slavery in Upper Canada was less of a progressive matter than has been estimated and is, no doubt, why it has not been trumpeted by Loyalist historians.

I have to thank the archivists of Special Collections, University of Vermont, the Vermont State Archives, the William L. Clements Library and Library and Archives Canada for their great help in tracking down primary sources. For help in preparing the manuscript for publication, I am indebted to Nicole Adani, John Bennett and Susan Hall

It is fitting that much of the research for this book was done in the library of Carleton University, Ottawa and much of it written in Montgomery, Vermont, almost within sight of Hazen's Notch. Lieutenant-General Sir Guy Carleton and Major General Richard Montgomery are among the outstanding characters of this book and I could think about the project while walking the "right" of Ira Allen in the town of Montgomery. Passing regularly through the Notch and by the monument commemorating the furthest point of the Bayley-Hazen Road, reached in 1779, was a reminder that we live in the midst of a history which, in the minds of the advocates of the Second Republic among others, is still with us today.

A NOTE ON SOURCES

THE PRIME SOURCES FOR this book are the copies of original documents in the archives of the University of Vermont (UVM), the State Archives of Vermont (VSA), Library and Archives Canada (LAC) and the William L. Clements Library (WLC) at Ann Arbor, Michigan. A limited number of documents were also used, from the Connecticut State Archives (CSA), the Connecticut Historical Society (CHS), and the State Papers of New Hampshire. The author has made extensive use of collections of documents such as the Vermont Historical Society (VHS) *Collections*, the *Documentary History of the State of New York*; Peter Force's *American Archives*; the Henry Stevens Papers and Collection in the VSA, the *Records of the Council of Safety and Governor and Council of the State of Vermont;* the Vermont State Papers, including the *Journals and Proceedings of the General Assembly of Vermont,* and *Documents Relating to the Constitutional History of Canada, 1759–1783;* also the extremely valuable collections of the writings of the Allens by John J. Duffy et al., and Kevin J. Graffagnino.

Some of the documents in the Haldimand Papers (the "B" Series, LAC) also appear in the Henry Stevens Papers (VSA) but the selection is very limited and there are some notable omissions. Justus Sherwood's Journal of his meetings with Ethan Allen in October, 1780 is omitted, only to be drawn to the attention of Vermont historians such as Henry Steele Wardner in the 1920s. Stevens did include Sherwood's Journal of his meetings with Ira Allen in May, 1781. He did not, however, identify the Journal as such, suggesting that he did not realize what a crucial document he had come upon.

Up to the present, systematic study of the Haldimand Papers has been rare. After Canada acquired copies of the Haldimand Papers in the British

Museum, James Benjamin Wilbur, the biographer of Ira Allen (1928) made extensive but not exhaustive use of the documentary sources in a way that Henry Stevens had not been able to do. Prior to the time of Wilbur and Wardner, there had been nearly a century and a half of interpretation, attempting to exonerate the Allens from collusion with the British, not least by the editors of the VHS *Collections.* Faced with the sudden weight of evidence to the contrary, Wilbur remained cautiously agnostic about how serious the Allens were in forming a "separate government under the Crown," observing that Vermont, outside the United States, had every right to take whatever action that was needed to save the Republic; that Ira Allen's negotiations in 1781 enabled Washington to move his army south to defeat Cornwallis; and that the negotiations with the British were crucial in establishing the independence of Vermont.

For Ethan Allen's life to 1770, and for his retirement from politics, 1784 to his death in 1789, only secondary sources have been cited, of which the most useful were the works of Pell, Jellison and Bellesiles listed in the Bibliography.

INTRODUCTION

A Few Lawless Vagabonds is a study of the three-way relationship between Ethan Allen, the Republic of Vermont (1777–1791) and the British province of Quebec, also known as Canada. On these three interconnected tracks, the story is taken from the early days of the New Hampshire Grants (later Vermont) in the 1750s; the career of Ethan Allen starting with his political involvement over the legitimacy of New Hampshire's land grants in 1770; and the role of the British in Quebec and New York from the outbreak of the Revolutionary War in 1775 to its conclusion in 1783. The high point of this three-way relationship consisted of a sincere attempt (it is argued) on the part of Ethan Allen and his family to bring the Republic of Vermont back into the British Empire as a "separate Government under the Crown" through the Haldimand Negotiations of 1780–1783. This attempt has not been exhaustively studied, either from the point of view of the Allen family or of the British in London, New York and Quebec.

After a biographical sketch of Ethan Allen's early life, the book launches into the controversy over the New Hampshire Grants, which led to the establishment of the Republic and which, through Vermont's relations with the British, as well as the province of New York, lasted until after the conclusion of the Revolutionary War. This controversy had two related aspects: whether it was New York or New Hampshire that had political jurisdiction over the Grants and whether the land titles granted by New Hampshire were still valid in view of the land patents later issued by New York. The key issue was whether the King's Order in Council of 1764, awarding jurisdiction to New York in preference to New Hampshire, was by implication backdated so as invalidate the New Hampshire titles. The struggles of the Green Mountain Boys, led by Ethan Allen, on behalf of settlers under New Hampshire titles resulted in Vermont's Declaration of Independence—from New York—early in 1777 and thence to the establishment of the Republic later in the same year.

The controversy over the Grants and the royal Order of 1764 were of a constant and important condition of the survival of the Vermont Republic against the territorial claims of revolutionary New York and New Hampshire, the hostility of the Continental Congress towards Vermont, and the response of the British towards the conditions required by the Allens for Vermont's rejoining the British Empire. This author argues strenuously, against the stance of most previous scholars, that the royal Order *created* New York's jurisdiction rather than reconfirmed it, so Ethan Allen was correct in contending that the New Hampshire titles issued prior to 1764 had an enduring validity.

Ethan Allen took part in the Revolutionary War from May, 1775, when the Green Mountain Boys took Ticonderoga, until September 25, when he was captured by the British outside Montreal and spent nearly three years as a prisoner of war. The Ticonderoga and Montreal episodes are covered in detail, followed by an evaluation of Ethan Allen's motives, concluding that he was not a revolutionary by conviction and that he was not a great military commander of the American Revolution.

While Ethan was a captive, Vermont became independent, which was one of several options for the state that Vermonters had proposed in the previous decade. The task was then to defend the Republic: against the territorial claims of revolutionary New Hampshire and New York; against the attacks of the British; and despite the hostility of the Continental Congress. In doing so, there is an examination of how the Vermont Council, with Ethan back from captivity, lost control of the political agenda, allowing New Hampshire at one point to claim all of Vermont as its own.

The narrative and the analysis of the Haldimand Negotiations show, as far as the evidence permits, that the Allens were utterly serious about rejoining the British Empire, a project that came close to realization in October 1781. That the Allens were serious was suggested by Vermont historians in the 1920s but then went into abeyance, to be vehemently denied by Ethan Allen's biographers at the turn of this century. The thesis of this book is thus a radical proposition, showing that the Allens, in the course of the secret negotiations, actually took Vermont out of the Revolutionary War.

A discussion of the political philosophy of Ethan Allen, rarely attempted to date, shows that Ethan was not a revolutionary, not a great republican, not an egalitarian democrat, but an oligarch. He was, however, a Vermont nationalist who led the struggle to maintain Vermont's independence against all comers and thus deserves his reputation as the principal founder of the state of Vermont. But paradoxically so, since he worked for Vermont as a separate government under the Crown, a rare combination of patriot and betrayer of the public trust.

Each of the poles of the three-way relationship between the Allens, the Republic and the British have been well studied in their own right, though even here, there have been omissions and distortions. Historians have not generally given enough credit to General Sir Guy Carleton's expedition up Lake Champlain in 1776 and most have underestimated the sheer folly of General Burgoyne's foray into New York and Vermont in 1777, for which he and his superiors were all culpable.

The chief distortion that scholars have indulged, concerns Ethan Allen himself. Ethan was, of course, a giant of a personality: charismatic, energetic and successful. With such historical figures, there is always a temptation to clothe them in some radical ideology, then assume that their motives were ideological. From this perspective, Ethan was a warrior hero of the American Revolution, a libertarian democrat, republican in sentiment and thus a natural emblem of the Republic of Vermont. Such a view of Ethan has receded and advanced over the years, but in the last two decades it has returned to the fore, in the work of Michael A. Bellesiles and Willard Sterne Randall. For these authors, Ethan's capture of the fortress of Ticonderoga in 1775 was the revolutionary act of a military leader bent on the overthrow of royal authority, and that the one thing that he did not pursue in the Haldimand Negotiations was a rapprochement with the British. This author will show, on the other hand, that such a view of Ethan can only be maintained by distorting the factual record, by assuming motive instead of arguing it and by omitting those parts of the record that depict an entirely contrary perspective on the man and his milieu. It is of interest that the Ethan who remains is still an historical figure of great stature, more impressive than his biographers have ever depicted.

The outlook of most British and Canadian historians towards Vermont is disappointing, for instance, the works cited in the Bibliography by Fryer, Harvey, Reuter and Watt. These historians generally depict the Americans merely as outlaw rebels against the royal authority, which would be one among many legitimate perspectives, were it not for the denigration of all things American, and Vermonters in particular. Thus for Robert Harvey,

Ethan Allen was merely a hillbilly or "hillbillyish," and his attack on Ticonderoga was a case of aggression, a "bizarre act of belligerence," since the fortress was of minimal strategic importance.[1] Ill-advised remarks such as these, from a well-known historian, have to be taken seriously: it needs to be argued that Ticonderoga was indeed of great strategic importance, being a bastion on "The Great Warpath" from Montreal to Albany; and (an easier task) that Ethan Allen was more than just a wild mountain man.

The hostility of Mary Beacock Fryer to Vermonters knows no bounds. She claims Vermont's phasing out of slavery in its Constitution was an insignificant move, a matter of "Green Mountain bluff," thus vindicating the lawful retention by emigrant Loyalists of their slaves.[2] She prefers to forget that when slavery was (with great reservations) phased out in Upper Canada in 1793, the original model was the first clause of the Vermont Constitution of 1777. Fryer states, contrary to all the evidence, that in the Battle of Hubbardton in 1777, the Green Mountain Boys "ran away" and that the subsequent Battle of Bennington was won by the "cunning" of General Stark and not by his generalship.[3] Why? Because Stark hanged a few Loyalists, which is evidently a reason why he could not be a successful general. These distortions are based perhaps on a reluctance to admit that Vermont produced a political culture just as vital and viable as anything founded by the Loyalists in Upper Canada.

The contentions of Harvey and Fryer are obtuse; but they are minor compared with Claus Reuter's statement that 500 Brunswick soldiers at Bennington (1777) were attacked by over 4,000 Americans.[4] In fact, Stark had only half that number at Bennington, of whom around 1,350 were committed to the battle. Instead of scholarly enquiry aimed at an understanding of the conflict, with an underlying sympathy for the Loyalist cause, these historians fight the battles of the eighteenth century all over again, but only from the Loyalist point of view.

The great exception to such historical bias is Hazel Mathews in her book *Frontier Spies* (1971). For Mathews, the conflict in Vermont between Loyalists and Patriots, and the shifting patterns of alliance and rivalry, were not due primarily to a grand matter of principle, liberty versus royal oppression. They were due, rather, to local religious, social, family and economic factors, making it impossible to pontificate in a grand verdict on who was right and who was wrong. Among the exceptions, who acted out of high principle, were Justus Sherwood and Seth Warner, both Green Mountain Boys, who ended up on opposing sides; they were equally honorable and equally successful.

Seen in this light, the Republic could have gone a number of ways: it could have remained independent for some time; it could have been annexed by New Hampshire or New York; it could have affiliated to the Continental Congress; or it could have become part of the British Empire in North America.

Mathews aside, the chief fault of the Loyalist historians is to see the Patriots merely as an unorganized bunch of rebels. By contrast, some American historians have a tendency to systematize the Patriot cause too much. Take this assessment of the Allen family by the distinguished American historian Chilton Williamson:

> From 1775 to 1780 the Allens fought a war and made a revolution. The purpose of the war was the overthrow of British control of the St. Lawrence; the purpose of the revolution was the establishment of an independent state. If both had been successful, the Allens would have solved, at least in part, their political and economic problems.[5]

Now, it is certainly true that the remaining Allen brothers, Ira and Levi, worked for free trade between Vermont and Canada in the 1790s, but their political attitude towards Canada changed with the times. On occasion, they wanted Vermont (by then a state of the American Union) to be neutral in the event of any war between the US and Canada; they sometimes went further in contemplating (with relish) the separation once again of Vermont from the United States, and at other times they envisaged an invasion of Canada which would indeed, if successful, have overthrown "British control of the St. Lawrence." But this was in the 1790s, long after the Revolutionary War and the death of Ethan in 1789 (he had effectively retired from politics several years earlier).

So did the Allens really fight a war in 1775–80? Ethan certainly made war on the British until he was captured near Montreal on September 25, 1775. Levi had been with him at Ticonderoga in May, and young Ira was elected Lieutenant in the Regiment of Green Mountain Rangers the following July. But the only actions after the failed invasion of Canada in 1775–76 were actually defensive, against British raids and expeditions (and for almost three years 1775–78, Ethan was a captive of the British). There was also one confrontation with the New York militia in 1781. To talk of the Allens' purpose in the war years 1775–80 has no bearing on the actual course of military events. Their real purpose was the survival of the New Hampshire Grants, as Vermont after 1777, against the British, the Continental Congress and New York (royal New York until 1777, when it declared itself an independent province of the Continental Congress).

On the establishment of an independent state, Chilton Williamson is quite correct, but this was not a singular aim in 1775, when the other options for the Grants were re-annexation to New Hampshire, or even, merely, the direct confirmation of the New Hampshire titles by the British Crown—in the event, which most people predicted, that relations with Britain would be restored to their "former harmony."

What Williamson put forward was a version of what Ethan's modern biographers have done: to impose a pattern on events and actions instead of detecting one. Williamson is like Bellesiles and Randall in seeing Ethan as a professional revolutionary from the start. This is what Williamson suggests when he talks of the Allens' purpose in fighting the war between 1775 and 1780. But, as will be seen, there is little evidence of a political program behind Ethan's campaign of 1775. The other possibilities, such as an indirect way of attacking royal New York, are far more plausible than a political aim like free trade with a Canada annexed to the United Colonies.

The name of Ethan Allen (1738–1789) in the title of this book requires explanation, for the narrative and analysis concern Ethan's family as much as himself. In the period 1770–1783, the most important members of the Allen family, led by Ethan, were his brothers Heman (1740–1778) and Ira (1751–1814); but the other brothers played a role, Heber (1743–1782), Levi (1746–1801) and Zimri (1748–1776). While Ethan was in British captivity from September 1775 to May 1778, Heman played a vital part in the establishment of the Republic. Some commentators use the term "the Allens" to designate not only Ethan's family but a wider group of his associates, including Thomas Chittenden, the first Governor of Vermont, and Ethan's friends, the brothers Jonas and Joseph Fay. That convention will be followed in this book, unless the context makes clear that "the Allens" designate only Ethan's immediate family.

There is a further complication in that the Allens were only part of a yet wider influential, unofficial group known as the Arlington Junto.[6] But the conspiratorial group who were privy to the Haldimand Negotiations[7] comprised members who were outside the Allen family and the Arlington Junto. It was all very confusing. It was meant to be.

CHAPTER I

The "Fronter"

JOSEPH ALLEN, A PROSPEROUS farmer of Litchfield, Connecticut, married Mary Baker of Roxbury in 1736; their first child, Ethan, was born on January 21, 1738. Joseph sold the Litchfield farm in 1740 and, like many other residents, moved to a new site in nearby Cornwall. One factor was religious: Joseph was repelled by the burning ardor and self-righteous exclusivity of the Litchfield New Light Congregationalists, which consigned some people to hellfire and bloody damnation. He became instead an Arminian Anglican, rejecting predestination.[1] The frontier settlement of Cornwall is a key to understanding Ethan: it was a wild, inhospitable place, infested by black bear, wolves and rattlesnakes and subjected to the fear of the rare but sudden and frightening Indian raids. Ethan first learned of the ways of the wild in Cornwall, and a prime concern of his brief career as a revolutionary in 1775 was to bring the Indians of Caughnawaga and St Francis in Canada over to the American side.

Joseph prospered in Cornwall, becoming a relatively large farmer and selectman, a pillar of the community, independent in thought and action, industrious and outspoken in his sunny belief that all men and women could be redeemed and find their salvation. When Joseph died in 1755, Ethan was devastated; much of his outlook on life, work and religion he had derived from his father. He could not believe that his father would burn in hell as the fire and brimstone pastors of the Great Awakening predicted; this became a foundation of Ethan's later Deist views, with a benevolent Creator, however heretical in Christian terms.

About nine months before his father died, Ethan had been sent to nearby Salisbury to study under the Congregational minister, the Reverend Jonathan

Lee, to prepare him for Yale College. At the beginning, Ethan could read and, no doubt, write with difficulty, having a good knowledge only of the Bible and Plutarch's *Lives*; by the end of his education he was an avid reader and a competent writer, with an intellectual curiosity enriched by both disputation and contemplation. He sometimes signed his letters, "The Philosopher." But now the prospects of learning and advancement were dead; as the eldest son, Ethan returned to the family farm in Cornwall. There he remained until 1763, improving the farm and buying up wild land in the Cornwall area. In January 1762 he became part-owner of an iron works in Salisbury, about twelve miles away in the very northwest corner of Connecticut, which he built up to include water rights and the timber needed for smelting. On June 23 of that year, he married Mary Brownson, a union said to be unhappy (it was certainly distant), but one which lasted until Mary's death in 1783, she having five times given birth, of whom two children survived to adulthood. In the summer of 1763, Ethan left the farm in Cornwall in the hands of his brothers and two sisters, moving to a large house and a small farm by the ironworks. This was a productive enterprise but, apparently due to a lack of success in land speculation, Ethan was obliged to sell half his share of the ironworks and farm in mid-1764 to his brother Heman, who was to make Salisbury the base for his activities in the Grants for the rest of his life.

The months between the beginning of 1763 and the fall of 1764 were among the most important in Ethan's life, for it was in this period that he associated with Dr. Thomas Young of nearby Amenia, New York, whom he had first met two years earlier. Young was apparently not much of a physician but he was well read and learned; he also became an early revolutionary, taking part in the Boston Tea Party of 1773. From mid-1763 to Young's departure for Albany in the fall of the following year, the two men spent much time together, discussing philosophy, cosmology, political theory, theology, the relationship between God and the natural world—just about everything under the sun. Eventually they decided to write a book together, a tract in Deism, the "natural religion" shorn of revelation, the supernatural and a survey of nearly all of Christian doctrine.[2] Whether Ethan was the leading author of *Reason, the Only Oracle of Man*, which finally appeared in print in 1784, is not of great importance, for Ethan's intellectual achievements were not in original thinking. Nor were the *Oracle*, or his other longer work, the *Brief Narrative* of 1774[3] well organized, as they lacked any natural flow. Rather, Ethan developed a talent for grasping polemical arguments and their consequences for political action as well as critical analysis and appraisal, for which his later writing provides ample evidence. Ethan retrieved the incomplete manuscript from Young's widow almost twenty years later.

Ethan's career as a troublemaker began at about the same time as Young's departure for Albany. A huge man whose size and voice created terror enough in themselves, he was variously accused of the unlawful confinement of neighbors' hogs, assault, drunken brawls and blasphemy. He also, again unlawfully, had himself inoculated by Young against smallpox in 1764 which, in view of the epidemic that raged during the invasion of Canada in 1775–76, quite possibly saved his life. He agreed to leave Salisbury in return for the withdrawal of charges for assault, this in the context of his reputation for blasphemy; he and Heman sold their interests in the ironworks in October 1765.[4] By the spring of the following year, Ethan's family was in Northampton Massachusetts, where Ethan became the part-owner and overseer of a lead mine. In July of the following year, he and his family were ordered to leave town, again probably because of Ethan's blasphemy and disruptive conduct.[5] Later in the year, he and his brother Zimri settled on a farm in Sheffield, Mass., close to Salisbury, and this became his base, if not his home, for the next decade.

From 1767 until Ethan took up the cause of the Connecticut proprietors of the New Hampshire Grants in 1770, he was a frequent visitor to the Grants, sometimes with Levi, often enough hunting deer for pelts to be sold in Heman's store in Salisbury and, we can assume, with an eye to the sort of property that his friends and family had already acquired. This again was a formative experience. Ethan was alone in the wilds, in all weathers, for weeks on end, befriending Indians and other lone hunters. As hardy and accomplished as any fur trapper in the District of Maine or the Canadian northwest, he was an exotic combination of intellectual and "fronter."

The lines of Ethan's character were firmly drawn by the time he was taken on to represent the proprietors of the Grants in January 1770—except for one thing: there was no indication up to that point that Ethan had the makings of a great political leader. He was a domineering personality, certainly, but the main objects of his domination were his own family. His whole career to date had been turbulent and erratic. He had a passion for learning, and even more for disputation and dissent, always ready to debunk authority, whether academic, political or religious. He was a dual personality, intellectual on one side and a lover of nature and the wild on the other, yet neither were evident in the way he conducted his working life. From the time he left the family farm in Cornwall he was constantly on the move, variously as investor, speculator, industrial supervisor and hunter; successful as a minor industrialist at the iron mine, a failure with the lead mine, and all the while a drunken brawler and loud blasphemer as well as a serious student of philosophy, natural and moral.

His one constant occupation was speculation in land and property, what Michael A. Bellesiles has described as his "entrepreneurial ambition."[6] His failures may have been due to bad judgment, possibly lubricated by the "flowing bowl," but equally they may have been due to a characteristic impulsiveness, which became evident in later life. For instance, the iron mine was already struggling with cashflow when he and Heman bought the large house and farm near the mine in Salisbury, and he seems to have bought the lead mine in Northampton on an impulse, without consideration of a century of its mediocre success and general failure. By 1770, Ethan's resume was spotty at best, and his own future uncertain. It was, after all, as early as 1763 that his cousin Remember Baker settled as a farmer at Arlington in the Grants, doing what hundreds of others from Connecticut did: seeking good land to the north when local opportunity was exhausted. Ethan did not follow suit, not because he did not like hard work but because the conventional life of the settler held no charm for this restless, mercurial man of action.

CHAPTER 2

Controversy: The New Hampshire Grants

THE STORY OF THE New Hampshire Grants in what is now Vermont began in 1741, when Benning Wentworth, an Anglican merchant, returned from England with a commission as the first Royal Governor of the Province of New Hampshire. Before that, a charter had been granted in 1635 to Captain John Mason as Lieutenant-Governor of a district that stretched sixty miles north from the ocean and sixty miles west, to what was known as the Mason Line. Wentworth's demesne was greater. To the south of the region between the Connecticut and Hudson rivers lay the provinces of Massachusetts Bay and Connecticut. Before Wentworth took up his appointment on December 13, 1741, a royal Order in Council had fixed the boundary between Massachusetts and New Hampshire and determined that the latter would extend westwards "till it meets with our other Governments." For Connecticut and Massachusetts (though the latter was disputed), the western boundary with New York was twenty miles east of the Hudson River. Accordingly, Wentworth claimed the same for the western extension of his province, to the north of Massachusetts.

In November 1749, just after Wentworth had made the first of his land grants west of the Connecticut River, he wrote to the Governor of New York, describing his own commission and asking him how far north and east the government of New York extended. The Governor replied, contending that New York's title was based on the letters patent issued by King Charles II to his brother James, Duke of York. There were several charters and confirmations, starting in 1664, of which the key was one granted to James on June 29, 1674, following the end of Dutch rule over New York. James was granted "all

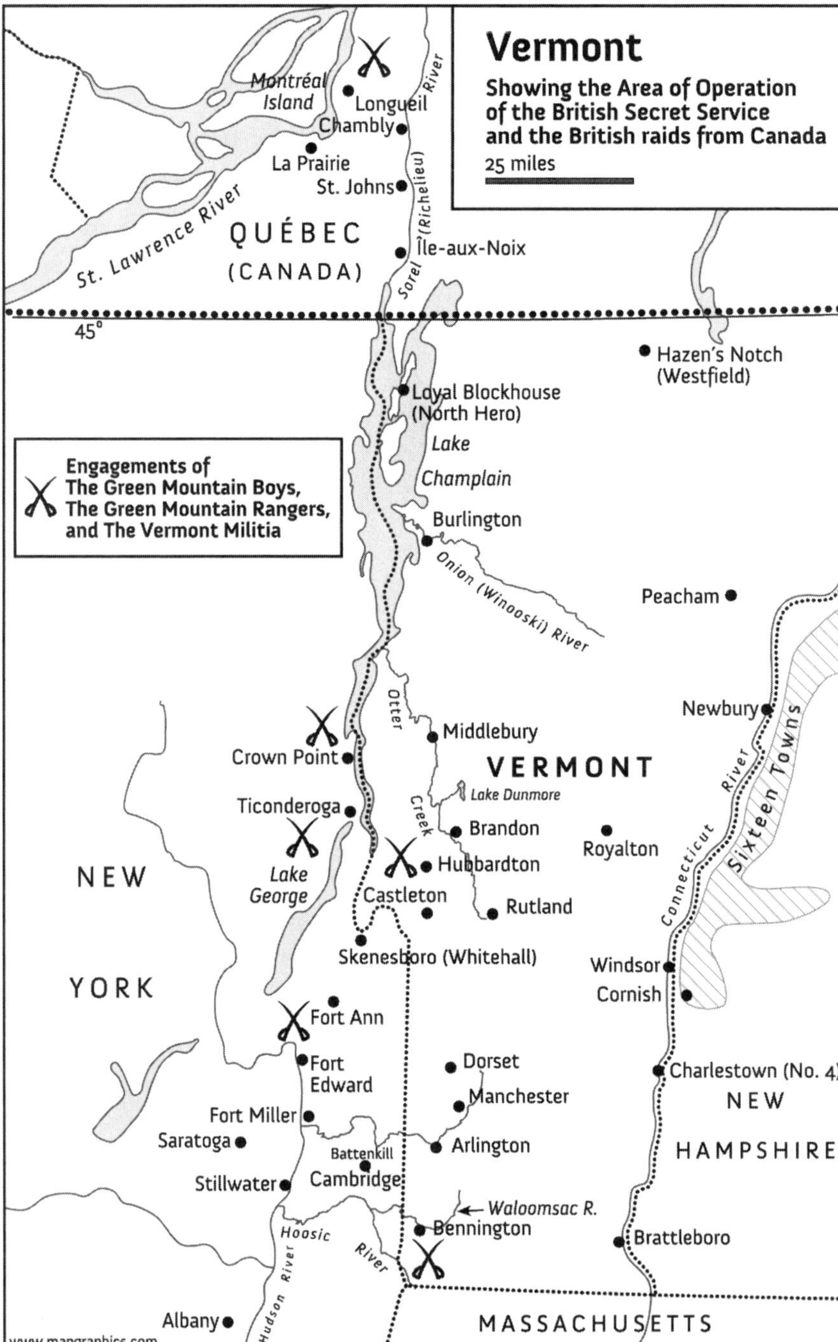
Vermont
Showing the Area of Operation of the British Secret Service and the British raids from Canada
25 miles
Engagements of The Green Mountain Boys, The Green Mountain Rangers, and The Vermont Militia
Montréal Island
Longueil
Chambly
La Prairie
St. Johns
Sorel (Richelieu) River
St. Lawrence River
QUÉBEC
(CANADA)
Île-aux-Noix
45°
Hazen's Notch
(Westfield)
Loyal Blockhouse
(North Hero)
Lake Champlain
Burlington
Onion (Winooski) River
Peacham
Newbury
Sixteen Towns
Otter Creek
Middlebury
Crown Point
VERMONT
Lake Dunmore
Ticonderoga
Brandon
Royalton
Connecticut River
Hubbardton
NEW YORK
Lake George
Castleton
Rutland
Skenesboro (Whitehall)
Windsor
Cornish
Fort Ann
Fort Edward
Dorset
Charlestown (No. 4)
Manchester
NEW HAMPSHIRE
Fort Miller
Saratoga
Arlington
Battenkill
Stillwater
Cambridge
Waloomsac R.
Bennington
Brattleboro
Hoosic River
Hudson River
Albany
MASSACHUSETTS
www.mapgraphics.com

the Land[s] from the West Side of *Conecticutt River*, to the East Side of Delaware Bay." This meant that New York claimed all of Vermont and the regions of Massachusetts west of the Connecticut River. As to Connecticut, there had been a settlement between that province and New York in 1683, confirmed by King William III, that the boundary was twenty miles east from the Hudson.[1] Such arrangements did not prevent Ethan Allen from contending that the Yorkers would claim title wherever they could get away with it, such as a grant to a part of Salisbury, Connecticut.[2] (This was possibly because Salisbury was adjacent to the Massachusetts lands covered in New York's Walloomsac Patent of 1739.) The fact remains that the Grants controversy involved New York's relations with Massachusetts as well as New Hampshire.

There was another wrinkle. Massachusetts had mistakenly granted a charter to Roxbury, Conn. and agreed to subject "Equivalent Lands" to the jurisdiction of Connecticut. These were three towns north of the survey line of 1741, on which the boundary between Massachusetts and New Hampshire rested, thus favoring New Hampshire and bringing the towns into that province. Wentworth confirmed the charters of Brattleborough, Fulham (now Dummerston) and Putney in 1753, plus one for Westminster in 1752, also due to jurisdictional change. These became one of the bases of Massachusetts' later claim to Vermont.

The issue between New Hampshire and New York over the grants first arose in 1750. When Lieutenant-Governor Cadwallader Colden of New York claimed the Connecticut River as the eastern boundary of New York, Wentworth replied on April 25 that, until the dispute was settled, "I shall desist from Making any further Grants on the Western Frontier of my Government, that may have the least probability of Interfering with your Government." This undertaking he promptly broke by granting Halifax on May 11, 1750, the first of sixteen made by the outbreak of war with France in 1754. There followed an exchange of letters, with protests and petitions to the Crown on the part of both New Hampshire and New York, accompanied by a great deal of political maneuvering. This lasted until the "Royal Determination" of 1764 awarding jurisdiction over the Grants to New York, and even that did not end the feud between the two provinces.

The king forbade any further disputes until he had made a decision, and in 1753 deliberation was postponed, mainly on account of the French and Indian War, the American theater of the Seven Years War. Wentworth had begun his program west of the Connecticut River by granting Colonel William Williams and fifty-nine associates the town of Bennington on January 3, 1749. According to the royal instructions to colonial governors, towns were to be six miles square. A grant conferred a title. The grantees held title to one or more "rights" or shares of about three hundred sixty acres each. One of these rights was reserved as a glebe for the Church of England, one for the first settled minister, one for a school, one for the Society for the Propagation of the Gospel in Foreign Parts, one for a Town of an acre in the centre of the grant, and two, contrary to royal instructions, for the Governor. (Wentworth also got a fee of twenty pounds or more for each grant.) The rest were granted to businessmen and speculators, often political cronies of Wentworth, who, in turn, peddled lots to would-be pioneers. Later, a big distinction would be made between the "right of soil," the right to settled land, and the title for wild lands, which Ethan Allen referred to as His Majesty's Wilderness Land.[3]

According to the royal instructions, title should be given to fifty or more families, putative settlers, but Wentworth soon began to grant title to any group, however small, that could meet his price. Most of Wentworth's grants were in flagrant violation of the royal instructions of 1741.[4] After ten years, each grantee or his "Heirs or Assigns" would have to pay "Proclamation Money" of a shilling (there were twenty to the pound) for every hundred acres that he owned, possessed or settled, paid at the Council Chamber in Portsmouth, N.H. Thus, New Hampshire alone of the New England colonies charged quit-rents (on paper), which were entirely foreign to the settlers in the Grants, the majority of whom emigrated to the Grants from Connecticut. New York came to levy quit-rents, two and a half times as great as those of New Hampshire. Grantees were also obliged to plant five acres of every fifty within five years in his or her "share or Portion of land in the said Township" and continual improvement on pain of forfeiture and regranting. There was a problem with this provision, which Wentworth evaded in the granting of titles. Most of the titles granted were in areas subject to French and Indian raids. Settlement was difficult or impossible, an open invitation to speculation, especially by members of the Governor's family as well as his political and business associates.

This pattern of titles without settlement continued until the fall of the fortress of Quebec in 1759 and the end of the threat of French and Indian raids. Wentworth resumed making grants, held in abeyance since 1754. In 1761, there were sixty-one town grants, ten in 1762, thirty-five in 1763 and five in the first half of 1764, ending with Hubbardton in June. By 1764, Wentworth had issued grants for 126 towns of nearly three million acres, 65,000 of which Wentworth had taken for himself.[5]

New York woke up to the fact that, in the past four years, New Hampshire had surreptitiously made grants totaling 112, on lands claimed by New York. On September 26, 1763, Cadwallader Colden, Lieutenant-Governor and Commander-in-Chief of the Province of New York, wrote to the Lords of Trade and Plantations, contending that the boundary of Massachusetts did not extend as far west as that of Connecticut and, in the absence of any other ruling, the same should apply to New Hampshire in respect of the Grants. His argument was a feeble one: that when the charter of William III referred to Connecticut, what was really meant was Connecticut River, thus ending Massachusetts on that river. He would confirm the rights of the settlers on payment of New York quit-rents. He added acidly that the governments of New England were founded on "republican principles," contrary to the spirit of the British Constitution.[6]

Early in 1764, Colden issued a proclamation asserting that the charters of Charles II gave New York title to all lands west of the Connecticut River. (He had already threatened legal ejection of the Grantees in a proclamation of December 28, 1763.[7]) Not so fast, said Wentworth in his own proclamation of March 13, 1764.[8] He cited His Majesty's Determination of 1739, setting the western boundary of Massachusetts-Bay twenty miles east of the Hudson and stated it was evident (self-evident) that New Hampshire could do the same. Wentworth said that if His Majesty altered jurisdiction, he did not doubt that all Grants made by New Hampshire "that are fulfilled by the Grantees" will be confirmed by the Crown. He challenged New York's "pretended Right of Jurisdiction" and enjoined the officers of New Hampshire to "deal with" anyone who interfered with "the Inhabitants or Settlers on said Lands."

On July 10, 1764, the British Board of Trade made a representation to the King concerning the boundary between New Hampshire and New York.[9] This document stated that the western limits had never been settled, because of the disruptions of the Seven Years War. There were two distinct issues: the question of provincial boundaries and jurisdiction and, secondly, the status of grants in the region made by both New York and New Hampshire. On the "first Object of Consideration," the Board unhesitatingly proposed that the boundary "should be declared to be" the western banks of the Connecticut River from the northern boundary of Massachusetts Bay to the 45th degree of northern latitude. The Board stated that this would prevent New Hampshire from making further grants but it pointed out that a boundary decision would not remove the difficulties arising from Grants "which have already been made westward of the Connecticut River." On this, the Board made no recommendation. It only concluded with a scathing attack on Wentworth, criticizing both the propriety of the grants and the way in which they were carried out. Wentworth had broken all of the royal instructions, and his grants "seem to have been made with a view more to private interest than public advantage," casting doubt on whether this Gentleman was "a proper person to be entrusted with Your Majesty's Interests in this important Station." The King immediately issued an Order in Council on July 20, 1764 (which the Grantees came to call the Royal Determination or Adjudication), deciding the boundary issue in favor of New York. The King in Council

> doth hereby order and declare the western banks of the river Connecticut from where it enters the province of Massachusetts Bay, as far north as the 45th degree of north latitude *to be* the boundary line between the two provinces of New Hampshire and New York.[10]

Much turned on the phrase "to be." First, it meant that New York could no longer base its claims on the royal charters of the seventeenth century, since "to be" meant "from now on" (For an alternative interpretation, see the *Critique of the Dispute Between New Hampshire and New York Over the Grants*, below). This implied, secondly, that no decision had been made concerning the grants made prior to mid-1764. On April 10, 1765, the Governor of New York issued a proclamation, making public the Order in Council of 1764 and stating that the county sheriffs of New York would exercise jurisdiction. Wentworth in turn directed that the Grantees manifest "a spirit of due obedience to the authorities and laws of the colony of New York," but he clearly assumed that the New Hampshire titles would be respected: naturally, since he, his family and his cronies had so much invested in the disputed lands. Neither were the settlers in the Grants too worried either—at first. Ethan Allen and three of his associates wrote to Governor Tryon of New York on June 5, 1774, reiterating the view that

> The Alteration of Jurisdiction in 1764 could not effect private Property: Surely his Majesty by this Alteration, did not purpose to take away the personal Property of a large number of his loyal Subjects; and transfer it to other Subjects; the English Constitution will be no Means admit of this . . .[11]

Ira Allen expressed a similar view in 1793: the settlers acquiesced in the change of jurisdiction, "never entertaining an idea that the title of their lands would be called in question, when both were royal governments .... The change of jurisdiction could not alter the state of private property."[12]

But the settlers were vulnerable. There was one question of whether New York would recognize their titles. Another was the jurisdiction of New York, with its quit-rents and a form of government different from the direct local democracy of the townships. Land tenure in New England, based generally on fee simple (freehold title) was different from New York, which had, predominantly, a manorial system with tenants within its bounds. Governor Tryon thoroughly approved of the system, because it "creates subordination and counterpoises, in some measure, the general leveling spirit."[13] Many of the Yorkers in the Grants were in fact very recent immigrant tenants from the Province of New York, particularly the Argyle Patent, and owed their livelihoods to the big absentee landlords such as James Duane and John Tabor Kempe, the Attorney-General.

New York was also governed by appointed officials in county governments, and this system too was exported to the Grants, coming to a head over the role in the Grants of the Yorker Justices of the Peace. The judicial system of New York was seen by the Grantees as the arm of an aristocratic elite. The settlers were to find that the courts, both the judges and the lawyers representing the plaintiffs, were themselves major holders of New York patents in the Grants. Even before the Royal Determination of 1764, New York had started to make military grants on the east side of Lake Champlain, grants that veterans of the French and Indian War took up in lieu of a pension.

By mid-1765, there were about two hundred families in the southwestern corner of the Grants. In the summer of 1765, Yorker surveyors with their transfers and chains began to appear around Bennington and Shaftesbury, encroaching on the settled lands of the Wentworth proprietors; New York began to issue patents in the region, some overlapping the New Hampshire Grants.[14]

At that time, Colden announced that all Wentworth titles would have to be confirmed, with a fee paid to the Province. Many of the settlers would have been hard pressed to pay these fees and they rightly objected to the principle of having to pay twice for the same land. When only twenty-nine (20%) of the Wentworth Grantees had applied for confirmation by November 1765, New York overplayed its hand and, in June 1766, ordered all holders of unconfirmed Wentworth titles to arrange, in person, for the payment of the fees. For those actually settled on New York patents, the situation was worse: they would be evicted, with the assurance that they would be compensated by generous grants of wild lands. Worse was to follow. On February 12, 1767, a decree of the New York Council required the presence of a Grantee in person or by attorney of the principal proprietors before any action towards a confirmation of title. This provoked a reaction from the New Hampshire Grantees.

At the time, actual settlers were in a small minority. There were over six thousand named Wentworth proprietors. In 1769, "only fifty-one of the 128 townships granted had any inhabitants whatever, and many of these had but a handful of settlers" on 40–50,000 acres in the Grants. Other estimates come close to these figures.[15] One of the settlers (he was also a speculator), Captain Samuel Robinson, was sent to London carrying petitions with about 650 signatures, of whom roughly 175 were actually the heads of settler families. The petitions were amalgamated into one[16] where it was claimed, falsely, to represent over a thousand Grantees on the western side of the Connecticut River.[17] With exorbitant fees being charged by New York for confirmation of the Grants, it seemed to the petitioners that the Grantees would forfeit those lands "granted away," i.e. those which overlapped New York patents, and pay exorbitant fees for those not granted away (half a crown as opposed, on paper, to the New Hampshire quit rents of a shilling "Proclamation Money" or nine pence sterling). The petitioners wanted royal confirmation or ratification of the grants and further relief as required. Contradicting the Royal Determination of 1764, the petitioners asked for either a separate Government/Colony for the Grants or that the Grants be annexed to New Hampshire. The King was asked to "dispose of our distressed state as he thinks fit."[18]

Robinson was an Anglican and got the support of the Society for the Propagation of the Gospel in Foreign Parts (SPG), which was concerned to shore up the position of Anglicanism in New England against the nonconformist churches and sects. In its petition,[19] the Society pointed out that the New Hampshire Grants had lands reserved for public and religious purposes. The language of the petition is not always clear but the gist of it is that New York made no such reservation in its own patents (this was largely incorrect), failed to protect existing settlements with their public and religious provisions, and is charging exorbitant fees for the confirmation of unsettled lands. But the object of the petition is clear: that New Hampshire Grants with their reservations for "pious uses" should be "ratified and confirmed" by the King. The Society made no distinction between settled and unsettled lands.

Though Samuel Robinson had a few friends in high places, the Committee for Plantation Affairs referred only to the SPG petition in its deliberations, recorded on May 19, 1767.[20] The Board then reiterated its severe criticism of Wentworth in making the grants but stated that the only way to secure the religious provisions was to confirm the grants themselves. So if the Honourable Lords considered that it would not be advisable, for the present, "to come to any direct decision upon that Question"

> . . . we think it will be highly necessary and expedient, that the most positive orders should be immediately sent to His Majesty's Governor of New York, to desist from making any grant whatever of any part of those Lands, until His Majesty's further Pleasure shall be known.

The message was clear: the New Hampshire titles should in time be confirmed; the Society merely provided a handle. But the King in Council did only the minimum; it directed "that the Governor or Commander in Chief of His Majesty's Province of New-York, for the Time being, do not upon Pain of his Majesty's highest Displeasure, presume to make any Grant whatsoever, of any Part of the Report [by the Lords of Trade and Plantation Affairs], until his Majesty's further Pleasure shall be known concerning the same." Further, New York was not to "molest any person in the quiet possession of his grant who can produce good and valid deeds for such grant under the seal of New Hampshire until you receive further orders reflecting them."[21]

The result of this decree was to increase the confidence of the Wentworth proprietors; speculation in titles and rights expanded, so did settlements. For more than two years New York awaited His Majesty's further pleasure, but late in 1769 it decided to wait no longer. A Board of Trade Report of July 6, 1770 noted a petition from the soldiers and merchants of New York to permit the Earl of Dunmore, now the Governor of New York, to grant lands already surveyed and to confirm to others "the grants that have already been made."[22] Dunmore received no permit but in the thirteen months to December 1770, the charters of fifteen towns were confirmed, with caveats and reservations over existing military grants, and New York issued patents to about 600,000 acres in the Grants. (One hundred and seven new grants were made between 1764 and 1775, amounting to two million acres or more, a quarter of which overlapped Wentworth titles, settled and wild.) The harassment of proprietors overlapping the new patents resumed with an incident sparking a new turn in the controversy. A small team of New York surveyors and commissioners with a writ of ejectment showed up on October 19, 1769 at the farm of James Breakenridge, on the western edge of Bennington, which overlapped a New York grant under the early Patent of Wolloomsac (1739).[23] Breakenridge and over sixty of the local farmers drove out the surveyors in what the New York governor later described as a "disorderly riot." Yorker Justice John Munro, reporting on the "rebellious activities" of the Grants settlers, read the riot act to no avail, saying that he had not enough men to do any more than arrest Silas [Samuel] Robinson.[24] By the time of the first foray on October 19, 1769, suits of ejectment had been brought against New Hampshire settlers in the New York patents, as well as Breakenridge. Settlers in the Grants petitioned John Wentworth, the Governor of New Hampshire, to take measures that "we may have Quick Relief in our Difficult Condition." The settlers even offered to pay quit-rents at the Council Chamber if it were "greatly to our advantage"![25] That winter and the following spring, a group of proprietors residing in the northwest of Connecticut started a defense fund and extended their organization into the Grants. There were, for example, meetings in Sharon, Connecticut on January 23, 1770; and at Canaan on March 3, March 19, May 19 and June 4, 1770. Enter Ethan Allen.

In 1770, Ethan was not gainfully employed, neither was he rich or of independent means. The Connecticut proprietors were clearly impressed by Ethan's presence, energy and ability, for he had neither the qualifications nor the experience for taking on the legal challenge from New York. Nor is there indication at all that Ethan had any long-term plans for the Grants, with the legal route as a first stage in securing the New Hampshire titles through the defense of settlers' rights. Ethan became a political animal by accident, through a circumstance which he exploited for want of any better prospect.

In May, Ethan Allen started to organize the legal defense of the Grantees and obtained the documents he needed from the office of Governor John Wentworth, Benning's nephew and successor. Wentworth had quietly discouraged the New Hampshire grantees from applying for New York confirmations. Even more privately, he believed in the restoration of New Hampshire jurisdiction over the Grants, which he did not publicize, lest he incur the displeasure of His Majesty and of New York. Thus he did not give open support to Ethan's party. Accompanied by an accomplished lawyer, Jared Ingersoll, Ethan proceeded to Albany late in June, for the Ejectment Trials.

There were nine suits altogether. The first of these, against, Breakenridge, was heard but suspended (a subsequent trial found against him). The second was *Small and Carpenter*. Isaiah Carpenter had purchased a right and settled in Shaftesbury in 1765. In 1769, Lieutenant-Governor Colden granted 3,000 acres to a retired British veteran, Major John Small, which overlapped Carpenter's holding. What started as a test case of proprietary rights turned into a decision over authority and jurisdiction. Judge Robert R. Livingston, with George D. Ludlow, had no difficulty in accepting the motion of James Duane, counsel for the plaintiff, that the Wentworth titles were inadmissible, saying that New Hampshire had no authority to grant them. Thus, the court simply declared for New York, putting New Hampshire entirely out of the picture. A question of the defense of settlement had been trumped by the assertion of jurisdiction. The court adjourned; the other cases were not heard or they were not adjudicated and the writs of ejectment stood.

Though there was an attempt to bribe Ethan into acquiescence, he was outraged and insinuated that ejectments would be met by force. His outrage had two grounds: the composition of the court and the legalities that lay behind the ejectments. The two counsels for the plaintiffs, New York Attorney-General John Tabor Kempe and James Duane, were themselves major holders of New York patents, a "junto of land thieves" as Ethan put it. (The Judge held patents in lands claimed by Massachusetts Bay.) By the time he had finished, Kempe held nearly 50,000 acres in the Grants. Duane, with Kempe and Major Walter Rutherford, were awarded in 1765 the patent of Princetown with 26,000 acres, parts of which overlapped the New Hampshire Grants of Arlington, Sunderland, Dorset and Manchester. Duane and his associates acquired title to 48,000 acres from Lord Dunmore in 1770, as Socialborough, covering parts of Rutland, Pittsford and Clarendon. After the Ejectment Trials, he continued to build up his holdings in the Grants, said to number a hundred and ten square miles or 100,000 acres, in which he had "unhappily involved almost all his Property."[26]

Like Wentworth earlier, the Yorkers flouted the royal instructions for grants, which limited individuals to a thousand acres. But the Yorkers were actually worse, since they had defied the royal orders to cease making grants and confirmations. In view of the vast holdings of a few wealthy men, it was no wonder the Yorkers continued to assert jurisdiction over the Grants, until they conceded defeat in 1791, with Vermont's admission to the union, albeit with an indemnity to New York of 30,000 Spanish dollars. The boundary between New York and Vermont was near enough where Benning Wentworth had drawn the line between the New Hampshire Grants and the Province of New York.

Speculators such as Duane and Kempe were little different, morally, from those holding New Hampshire titles. Ethan's objection was that they had no right to New York patents; they were merely land thieves. The other reason for Ethan's outrage was that New York had openly defied the King's authority. The Royal Determination of 1764 had made no ruling on the status of the Wentworth grants; New York had issued patents contrary to the decree of 1767 and then unlawfully tried to enforce them. "[They] do not make the least Hesitation, to act in direct Opposition to the Authority of the Crown. . . ."[27] They presume "to regrant our lands, from under our feet, in open defiance to the regal authority of Great-Britain."[28] Whatever the overall balance of right over the years between New Hampshire and New York, the recent Yorker moves were blatantly corrupt and unlawful. That Ethan resorted to force was understandable.

Ethan took on his assignment as an agent of the Connecticut holders of New Hampshire titles as proprietors, not settlers. They hoped to defend the settlers from ejectment but the only legal argument they had was that the New Hampshire titles were valid. If the court had decided to defend the settlers against ejectment, this would still not have resolved all of the proprietors' concerns, which were to defend title and thus the power to sell rights to wild lands to future settlers. It was also a long shot to suppose that questions of settlers' rights of possession would be settled without any reference to title. Ethan took the legal route to justice seriously; but there is no evidence either way as to his expectation of the results, nor is it at all plausible to suppose that he had a long-term plan for the Grants, of which the legal response to the writs of ejectment were the first stage.

Not long after the Ejectment Trials, several farmers met in Bennington, affirmed the legitimacy of the Wentworth titles, and resolved to uphold their rights by force if necessary. When Lieutenant-Governor Colden heard the news, he is reputed to have threatened to drive the rebellious mob back into the Green Mountains, so the group named itself The Green Mountain Boys. Ethan was named Colonel Commandant, while the Boys were organized into local companies in the Bennington area, with Seth Warner, Robert Cochran, Peleg Sunderland, Ebenezer Marvin and Gideon Warren as lieutenants, all this by the fall of 1770. A further three companies were organized by the early part of 1775, under Ebenezer Allen, Remember Baker and Micah Vail. "Company" is a loose term, since some units comprised a handful of activists while others could draw on volunteers who were not regular members of any company. When Ethan summoned the Green Mountain Boys for the assault on Ticonderoga in May 1775, some of these came from areas to the north of the localities in which the Green Mountain Boys were organized. The Boys came under Committees of Safety, which successively forbade the inhabitants of the Grants from holding any Yorker office; forbade Yorker officials from deporting individuals out of the Grants; and prohibited settlers from taking grants or confirmations from the Governor of New York.

At the same time, the Grantees sent a series of five petitions to London, some repeating the request to confirm the Wentworth titles, others asking for the reannexation of the Grants to New Hampshire. The only movement on the part of the British government was a repeat in 1772 of the edict of 1767 against New York issuing patents, and a series of recommendations in a report of the Lords of Trade to the Privy Council of December 3rd, 1772.[29] The government in London otherwise took no action. Ethan and his associates had two aims: to stop encroachments on the Grants by driving away Yorker officials, surveyors and settlers; and by dissuading the existing settlers from applying for or accepting confirmations from New York. While there was inaction from London, the Yorker government bungled the issue. To have confirmed settlers' rights at the payment of a token registration fee, without validating New Hampshire titles, would have neutralized the Green Mountain Boys. Instead, New York started charging substantial fees for confirmation and took an inordinate amount of time in confirming titles. One way of looking at this is greed: the Yorkers wanted all of the New Hampshire lands, including those settled. Another perspective is that the Yorkers thought they would win, that they could overcome all opposition in the Grants.

Ethan made it clear to the Green Mountain Boys that there was to be no killing or maiming, just humiliation, harassment, destruction of property and physical abuse. He did this because of the comparison with the Anti-Rent War in Massachusetts in the previous decade: British regulars had been deployed in 1766 only in a case of extreme disorder and the violent resistance to Yorker authority.[30] Ethan had close experience of the Anti-Rent War, since some of the disturbances took place adjacent to his base across the border in Salisbury, Connecticut. He knew that British regulars would not be deployed against a mere riotous mob, provided there were no killings.

There were few cases in which the families of Yorkers were evicted without ensuring that they could reach New York without freezing or starving. There was one case, that of Reverend Benjamin Hough, a Yorker Justice of the Peace, in which the treatment was particularly severe. Hough had tried to dissuade settlers from "joining the Mob"; he was cruelly beaten, separated from his family, then expelled in the middle of winter. The treatment of Dr Samuel Adams of Arlington was less harsh. He had repeatedly urged his neighbors to seek Yorker confirmation of their rights and title, and armed himself to defend his own conduct. He was captured and abducted to Bennington, where he was tried by the Committee of Safety. Adams was sentenced to hang in an armchair, beside the stuffed catamount, twenty feet in the air for two hours on a pole outside Stephen Fay's tavern. He mended his ways; but it is hardly surprising that he became a Loyalist. Sometimes depicted as a tame country doctor, he was a hardened soldier who commanded his own company of Loyalists, Adams' Rangers, and he settled after the war in what became Upper Canada. For all that, Ira Allen observed that many of the Yorkers "had been whipped almost to death."[31] Most of the harassment of Yorkers was carried out against unarmed civilians: the Green Mountain Boys were vigilantes rather than a para-military organization of irregular troops.

From mid-1771, there were a series of incidents which led to the outlawry of Ethan and eight of his associates. These included the expulsion of the Yorker surveyor William Cockburn and a major incident of July 18, in which a posse comitatus advanced (once again) to "assist the sheriff in taking possession of the House of James Breakenridge." The Sheriff desisted at an "armed confrontation." Duane passed a report on the episode to Attorney-General Kempe.[32] Late in October 1771, the Green Mountain Boys expelled about a dozen Scottish families from Rupert, where Robert Cochran had holdings under a Wentworth title The Yorker Justice of the Peace, John Munro, held a New York patent to 4,000 acres of land in Shaftesbury and Arlington. When he expressed doubts about arresting the "abominable wretches, rioters and traitors" responsible, Tryon declared Ethan and eight others outlaws, including Baker, Breakenridge and Cochran, on November 27, 1771, with a price of twenty pounds on their heads.

Ethan and his men responded defiantly to the outlawry, offering fifteen pounds for Duane and ten for Kempe, on bringing them to Fay's tavern in Burlington. Justice of the Peace John Munro in Shaftesbury got no practical help from Tryon; but he did attempt to enforce the declaration of the previous November. One night late in March 1772 he and a posse of Yorkers surprised Remember Baker at his home in Arlington, cut off his thumb in a struggle and abducted him, intending to take him to Albany. But several of the Boys responded and overtook the captors about halfway to Albany, released Baker and took Munro and two others prisoner to Bennington. Munro was soon released, concluding that the rebels could only be overcome and brought into obedience by main force from New York.[33] Seth Warner went to Munro's place to recover Baker's rifle, knocked the good Justice to the ground with the flat of his sword, and got himself added to the list of outlaws for his pains.[34]

One of those not outlawed but later listed among the fourteen who had unlawfully rescued Remember Baker was Justus Sherwood, who had property in New Haven, adjacent to Rupert.[35] Sherwood would go on to play a prominent part in this story, becoming an accomplished Loyalist officer, heading the Northern Department of His Britannic Majesty's Secret Service and operating out of the province of Quebec. He was put in charge of the negotiations to bring Vermont back into the British Empire; but (despite his private contempt for Ethan) he and the senior Allen remained good friends—too close, according to one interpretation, for Vermont's own good. There was another twist to the story: despite turning Loyalist, Sherwood remained an enemy of Munro, who also became a Loyalist military officer during the Revolution.

What followed was an armed standoff with Yorker settlers, sympathizers and justices on one side, and the Green Mountain Boys and their supporters on the other. Tyron made noises of conciliation, while reasserting New York's authority on May 19, 1772.[36] Ethan replied stoutly on June 5, reiterating the Grantees' right of soil but not denying the authority of New York. It was "our Misfortune of being annexed to the Province of New-York."[37] There is a curious parallel. The New York elite was to put forward a similar argument three years later: that the quarrel was not with the royal authority; it was only with a "Despotick Ministry." When this was purged, harmony between the American provinces and the Crown would be restored. Ethan, who in time also used the language of the despotic ministry, wrote that the real problem was with avaricious "intreaguers."

The attempt at compromise was the result of the letter from Lord Hillsborough to Tryon of April 18, 1772, ordering him not to deviate in any way from royal instructions. The New York Council advised him against "severe measures" and to offer a compromise, with "proper relief" to the Grantees. Stephen and Jonas Fay were sent to negotiate with the Governor and Council in New York. One proposal was the possibility of the "new Proprietors" of lands overlapping the Grants buying out the old proprietors; but this was inconclusive.[38] There was an agreement that the Grants would be quiet if New York ceased suits for ejectment and criminal prosecutions until His Majesty's pleasure be known. Tryon offered to suspend the declaration of outlawry. Even before the Fays arrived back in Bennington on July 8, the truce was broken when a party of Green Mountain Boys drove out several families of Yorker settlers, tenants of Col. John Reid, from a New York patent on the lower Otter Creek.

An angry Tryon demanded that the tenants be repossessed as a condition of furthering the settlement of the dispute,[39] but Ethan persuaded a meeting of the Committees of Safety in Manchester to respond in such a manner that amounted to an explicit rejection of the offer. This he did on August 27.[40] He asserted that the only objectives of the Green Mountain Boys were "Firstly; The Protection and maintaining our Property. And, Secondly; to use the greatest Care and Prudence, not to break the Articles of Publick Faith, or insult Governmental Authority." Ethan added a further condition to the agreement: that Tryon and the Council "make no further settlements or Locations on our Lands" (i.e. New Hampshire titles), until the King had ruled on the validity of the Wentworth grants. He also refused to repossess Colonel Reed (Reid) of his property. Tryon and the Council came to the conclusion that the Grantees were impossible to deal with and ended all negotiations on September 8, 1772, then terminated the truce in the following month.

On October 21, the Manchester Convention (Committee of Safety) sent James Breakenridge and Jehiel Hawley to lay the Grantees' case before the Board of Trade in England. They were obliged to do this in spite of the reiteration earlier in 1772 of the royal order to New York of 1767, prohibiting grants and confirmations. The Report of the Lords of Trade to the Privy Council on December 3, 1772[41] was surprisingly favorable to the Grantees, though it reflected previous sympathy for the Wentworth settlers. It recommended that holders of New York patents in Massachusetts be compensated by an equal acreage in other parts of the Grants. (The Massachusetts-New York border was reconfirmed in 1773, which implied that the New York patents in western Massachusetts had been unlawful.) Where lands had actually been settled or improved, the figure was fifty acres of "waste Land" for every three acres possessed. Secondly, in cases where settled lands in the Grants patented by New York overlap with New Hampshire grants, the proprietors of the latter should be protected. Thirdly, title to all other granted lands should be confirmed, without any other conditions such as quit-rents unless they were contained in the grant. This implied, though it did not state, that New Hampshire grants of wild lands were validated; the Report was silent over the status of the vast wild lands granted by both New York and New Hampshire.

Lord Dartmouth, Secretary of State for the Colonies, wrote to Tryon on April 10, 1773, informing him that the report of the Lords of Trade had been approved by the King in Council.[42] But Tryon objected on July 1, proposing (1) that all New York patents be validated; (2) all New Hampshire titles be declared void; (3) all New Hampshire settlers not covered by New York patents be confirmed under terms prescribed by the King; and (4) New Hampshire settlers in New York patents be compensated with waste lands without quit rents.[43] This in effect blocked the implementation of the British report since it ran counter to the pro-settler sympathies of the government in Whitehall. There was no response from the British and the Yorkers sought a solution with British regular troops.

In September 1773, the acting Commander-in-Chief, Sir Frederick Haldimand in New York, informed the Colonial Secretary, Lord Dartmouth, that military aid had been requested against rioters in Charlotte County and asked for instructions as to this and similar cases; but on October 6 he informed Dartmouth that the requisition for troops had been dropped. In October, Dartmouth told Haldimand that military aid was not to be given in cases of rioting unless the civil powers failed; the King had not approved the strengthening of the garrison at Ticonderoga. Again in December, he reiterated that military aid should not be granted unless absolutely necessary.[44]

The background to the exchange in October shows that Haldimand had already turned down Tryon's request for military aid, a course of action which Dartmouth endorsed in December. The New York Council had called for military force, because of the disorders in the Grants and a series of petitions, including another from Lieutenant-Colonel John Reid, late of the 42nd (Royal Highland) Regiment, whose tenants had been expelled. The Council asked that Governor Tryon request Haldimand to strengthen the garrison of Ticonderoga and Crown Point, so as to intervene in the Grants at the request of the civil magistrates. Haldimand responded on September 1, saying that the use of British regulars would only induce contempt for the civil magistrates: the idea that "a few lawless vagabonds" could prevail against New York would reflect a weakness leading to bad consequences. The New York Council then accepted that there would be no strengthening of the garrison at Ticonderoga on the grounds that New York would have to pay for the transport of the extra troops.[45]

In the three-way relationship between Tryon, Dartmouth and Haldimand, the latter faced a problem that was again to plague him when he dealt with Ethan Allen in the Haldimand Negotiations: he had to make decisions with some immediacy but he also had to get clearance from his superior, Dartmouth, in the case of the Bennington vagabonds and Sir Henry Clinton in the case of the Negotiations. In both cases he very properly sought advice from a higher authority but in both cases he felt prepared to jump the gun and make a decision before clearance arrived.

In the next year, with the British preoccupied with the situation in Boston, Haldimand did suggest moving two regiments from Canada to Crown Point. In August, Haldimand was recalled on the grounds that if a replacement for Thomas Gage, the commander-in-chief, were ever needed, the position would have to be filled by a "natural born subject," not someone of foreign origin, like the Swiss Haldimand. He was given his due when he replaced General Sir Guy Carleton as Governor and Captain General of Canada in mid-1778. Carleton, privately disgusted at his treatment by Dartmouth's successor, Lord George Germain, was granted relief in September 1777.[46]

Haldimand's responses were typical of the British government. The sympathies of the government lay with the New Hampshire settlers but its lack of appreciation of the seriousness of the situation led to paralysis and a failure to implement a definitive and equitable solution. For the Green Mountain Boys were not merely "a few lawless vagabonds"; they threatened the whole Yorker position and interests in the Grants. Thus On November 24, 1772, John Munro had resigned as Justice of the Peace in despair, saying that he was unable to enforce the law; that "the friends of Government are few" and only force could resolve the issue. (On August 22, 1773 he wrote further to Tryon, saying that "the mob has again broke loose," that his property had been further destroyed, and that he needed relief.)[47]

Dartmouth's letter of October 14 also gives us a clue as to the British attitude towards the New Hampshire Grants, for the Colonial Secretary intimated that it would be highly improper to support possessions granted after the royal order to New York of 1767, which may be of "very doubtful title." This was one of the very few occasions when the British government hinted that grants in defiance of royal instructions were invalid: the corrupt land grants of Governor Wentworth were never used as the occasion for the denial of New Hampshire titles. In the following September, General Gage in Boston wrote to Lieutenant Governor Colden (Tryon being in England), telling him that a final decision on the New Hampshire lands was expected; until then, in accordance with the previous decision of Haldimand, no military force was to be used.

The Grantees expected a favorable decision from the King in Council, but there were no rulings from London until events were overtaken by Lexington-Concord in April 1775.

Even in September 1774, Ethan could, referring to implementation, write optimistically about the "Royal Confirmation we daily expect."[48] The expulsions continued: in November, Ethan led the Green Mountain Boys in an attack on the person and the farm of Benjamin Spencer, a Yorker Justice of the Peace in Clarendon. Spencer was forced to resign his Yorker office. There were dozens of incidents of this sort[49] in the Grants prior to May 1775, when the attack on Ticonderoga took place and Yorker authority was in practice suspended.

Outraged by the assaults on Spencer and the Reverend Benjamin Hough, New York passed a law on March 9, 1774, increasing the rewards on the outlaws: Ethan, Warner, Baker, Cochran, Sunderland, Breakenridge, Silvanus Brown and John Smith. The law published a series of truly draconian measures, including the death penalty for harassing Yorker officials and amnesty for those who killed while enforcing the law. The Preamble of the law declared that

> *... many Acts of Outrage and Cruelty have been perpetrated by a Number of turbulent Men, who, assembling from Time to Time in Arms, have seized, insulted and menaced several Magistrates, and other Civil Officers, so that they dare not execute their Functions—rescued Prisoners for Debt—assumed to themselves military Commands, and judicial Powers—burned and demolished the Houses and Property, and beat and abused the Persons of many of His Majesty's Subjects—expelled others from their Possessions—and finally, have put a Period to the Administration of Justice within, and spread Terror and Destruction throughout that Part of the Country which is exposed to their Oppression ...*[50]

At a further meeting in Manchester, Ethan persuaded the Committees of Safety to meet force with force. This was not only a rejection of the "Bloody Law" but the Committee went further than in the past by explicitly challenging the authority of New York.

The final chapter in the history of the Grants before Lexington-Concord arose out of an incident that had little to do with the New York patents and which Ethan exploited to advantage. New York had created the new county of Cumberland in the southeast quadrant of the Grants in July 1768; Gloucester to the north was created in March 1770 and, on the west side, Charlotte, to the north of Albany County, in 1772. County government east of the Green Mountains was fairly well established by 1775, with a court system and delegates from Cumberland County to the New York Assembly from 1772. There was no contentious issue of land titles in Cumberland County and, on the matter of the Grants, the proprietors and settlers generally favored confirmation by New York. There was a rash of confirmations of townships and farms in 1774–75 at a low rate, owing to the financial deflation of the time.[51] Nor was there much opposition to Yorker jurisdiction over criminal cases.

There was, however, a rash of grievances: the cost of court action; the great increase in the number of lawsuits brought for the recovery of debts; the cost and inconvenience of serving on juries, and the excessive fees charged by attorneys at law. Of these, the main issue was the recovery of debts owed by impoverished farmers and imprisonment for the same. An anti-court riot (not the first of its kind) took place at Westminster on March 13, 1775 over some impending foreclosures of farms and property. The Yorker sheriff and his deputies shot two rioters to death, which came to be known as the Westminster Massacre. The Green Mountain Boys arrived at Westminster in force and, in a complete reversal of previous loyalties, were welcomed by the eastsiders. This was what Cadwallader Colden, acting as Governor in Tryon's absence, had predicted: the Westminster faction would be joined by the "Bennington Rioters" even though there was no "common cause" between them.[52] The Yorker case was not helped by the fact that the two conservative representatives of Cumberland County in the New York Assembly, Crean Brush and Samuel Wells, secured a thousand pounds to shore up the court system and prevent further attacks on Yorker authority.

Led by Ethan, a convention at Westminster with delegates from both Gloucester and Cumberland counties sent a remonstrance to the king. It asked him to remove the Grants from the authority of New York and to annex them to some other government "or erected and incorporated into a new one."[53] In this way, what had been a minor theme since 1767 came to the fore. The proposal of a "distinct Government or Colony" had been raised by Samuel Robinson in his petition of 1767 and Ethan had mentioned the possibility of a new "Political System" for the Grants settlers in his letter to

Oliver Wolcott on March 1, 1775.[54] Ethan's response to the Bloody Law had challenged Yorker jurisdiction and authority; but this was now publicly eclipsed by a greater demand and it was supported on both sides of the Green Mountain divide. From it can be traced the idea of an independent Vermont. Not that the earlier recognition of Yorker authority was the same as deference to the king: Cumberland County set up a Committee of Correspondence in 1774. Leonard Spaulding, later a delegate at the Vermont Constitutional Convention in 1777, was imprisoned for insulting George III in a protest against the Quebec Act.

From the time of the Westminster Massacre until after the end of the Revolutionary War in 1783, Cumberland County was in a state of turmoil, so much so that events on the east side threatened the stability, possibly the existence, of the Vermont Republic of 1777. After the American Revolution, New York attempted to continue the government of the Grants, principally by raising militia. The reasons why some of those on the east side of the Green Mountains supported the cause of Vermont independence were manifold. In the beginning, New York was wary of inciting the eastern counties to revolutionary insurrection since it feared that this sentiment would be turned against the New York authorities. Nor did the (tepidly) revolutionary New York Provincial Congress provide any help in redressing the grievances of the eastern Grantees. In any case, Cumberland County was too remote from the centers of New York power for its government to be effective. This did not mean that the Grantees would turn automatically to the alternative of independence, since there was a bewildering and changing flux of loyalties and sentiments. There were conservatives and whigs; pro- and anti-Allens; Loyalist Yorkers and pro-rebel Yorkers; pro- and anti-New Hampshire annexationists; pro-and anti-Vermont *independentists;* religious theocrats and above all, those who held tenets which were incompatible with those of otherwise like-minded citizens.

There was one factor above all that swung the east-siders towards independence. This was the adoption of the Constitution of revolutionary New York on April 20, 1777 after nine months of consultations and without public endorsement. Already, on August 7, 1776, the New York Provincial Congress had voted that quit rents due to the King were now to be transferred to any government that the state might establish. The Constitution now legitimized New York patents, including those in the Grants (Art. XXXVI) and it made suffrage contingent on the actual payment of taxes to the state by renters of property.

The Governor could control legislation through the provisions for proroguing the legislature and by the power of an unelected Council to modify legislation (Art. III). Judges were appointed until age sixty, something not lost on the Grantees who had experience of New York justice in the Ejectment Trials and whose judges were still there in the guise of revolutionaries (Attorney General Kempe excepted; he had been attainted). For the Grants, the provisions governing suffrage were even worse. Freeholders to the value of twenty pounds and the holders of property paying forty shillings rent a year could vote (Art. VII). This would exclude the majority of the residents of the Grants, where representation in the Senate and Assembly was in any case skewed against those living in Charlotte, Gloucester and Cumberland counties.

New York continued to make civil appointments and to assert jurisdiction over Charlotte, Gloucester and Cumberland Counties; of these, Cumberland County sent delegates to the New York Assembly until 1784. But there was really no New York government in Vermont after 1777: the Arlington Junto suppressed Yorker insurrections and attempts to mobilize the militia against Vermont, though the Yorker actions were more like riots than a popular uprising.[55] New York continued, however, to raise militia battalions from three of the four erstwhile Yorker counties of Vermont: Colonel Jacob Bayley's Cumberland and Gloucester militia brigade was present in the vicinity of Saratoga, at the surrender of General Burgoyne in October 1777. Until 1784, Vermont's authority in Cumberland County continued to be challenged by both Tories and Yorkers: the demise of Yorker authority did not mean the end of the Yorker threat to Vermont.

It was the hostility of the Grantees to the New York Constitution that swung Colonel Jacob Bayley, a major landholder in Gloucester County, reluctantly towards independence. This he now regarded as inevitable, since the people of Gloucester County were now violent "almost to a man for a separation from New York."[56] Bayley resented the power and the godlessness of the Allens, whose base was remote from Bayley's fief in the Coos (Cowass) Country of the northeast. The Allens were "avowed enemies to the cause of Christ, at least by practice."[57] Initially, Bayley favored reannexation of the Grants by New Hampshire. He seemed to turn his allegiance to New York when John Wentworth declined to confirm some of Bayley's titles, since the New Hampshire Governor had backed away from his surreptitious attempts at the reannexation of the Grants, contrary to the ruling of 1764. So Bayley turned to New York for confirmation of his New Hampshire titles: he applied for a confirmation of his own town of Newbury on February 5, 1772 under Tryon's half-fee plan and received it on March 19.[58] From then on, Bayley accepted the jurisdiction of New York, becoming Judge of the Inferior Court of Common Pleas for Gloucester County, 1772–77. On August 1, 1776 he was commissioned Brigadier-General of the Cumberland-Gloucester Brigade of Militia of revolutionary New York.[59]

Though he subsequently threw in his lot grudgingly with the Allens and the west-siders, he still accepted the authority of the New York Provincial Congress. This had been organized in New York City on May 23, 1775, after the capture of Ticonderoga by Ethan Allen and the raids on St. John's. Despite the Westminster Massacre and the petitions for independence or reannexation to New Hampshire, there was some support for the Provincial Congress. Charlotte County sent delegates to New York on the day after the inauguration of the Congress: Captain John Williams and Colonel William Marsh (Ethan's later nemesis in the controversy over the command of the Green Mountain Boys). Cumberland County sent three delegates in June, and on the 29th Bayley was elected delegate from Gloucester County. He did not attend the Congress because of the need to defend the northern frontier.[60]

Bayley's name first appears as a supporter of the independence movement in January 1777[61] but he was hesitant about petitioning the Continental Congress for recognition of independence until he became a delegate to the Vermont Constitutional Convention in July.[62] Despite his support for independence and his influential presence on the Vermont Council of Safety and in the Vermont Assembly after 1777 (an exercise in damage control if nothing else), Bayley remained loyal to the revolution and on good terms with Governor George Clinton of New York and with General Washington.[63] He was appointed Commissary-General of the Northern Department of the Continental Army before the Battle of Bennington in August 1777, after which he and his New York militia brigade took part in the Saratoga campaign.[64]

Bayley's career seemed to exhibit a series of shifts of loyalty, from New Hampshire to New York to Vermont, sometimes allying himself concurrently with rival factions in the three jurisdictions. For instance, he became Judge of the Vermont Probate Court of the Newbury District in 1778 and was a member of the anti-Yorker Court of Confiscation. Underlying this pattern are two tenets which Bayley held strongly and consistently. The first was to fight the British at every opportunity, defending the northern frontier and to invade Canada from the Coos Country. Bayley came to despise the Allens for their collusion with the British and the cessation of hostilities which they achieved. He wrote to President Weare of the New Hampshire Assembly on November 22, 1780, observing that the truce that Ethan Allen had made with the British until February 1781 was a case of "treasonous conduct." He urged an attack on Canada, which had been the subject of a petition from Cumberland County in March.[65] Two years later, he had no reason to change his views:

> ... Vermont will make a great noise by calling in their militia ... but you may depend on it will not be to oppose the Enemy but to deceive the population and prevent the militia from assisting you.[66]

Bayley's second consistent aspiration was, despite his shifts in loyalty, to work for the reannexation of Vermont to New Hampshire. In this, for a brief period, he came close to success.

All this was in the future. Despite the drama of the Westminster Massacre and the shift of the east-siders to independence, the Yorkers were winning the battle of the Grants. By the spring of 1775, Tryon or Colden (acting as Governor) had "issued patents to approximately 2,000,000 acres of Grants lands, or about one-third of the total area of present-day Vermont."[67] Hiland Hill's figures were 2,115,610 acres in 1765–76, with an additional 303,100 acres in military patents.[68] Most of these were for wild lands already granted by Wentworth and some overlapped settled lands. Further, ninety-two out of one hundred and thirty-six New Hampshire Grants had applied for Yorker confirmation under reduced fees, of which forty were in Allen country, on the west side of the Green Mountains. The rash of confirmation fees in 1774–75 was due to a rise in the value of money and a consequent drop in the price of confirmation fees.[69]

IN A DOCUMENT DATED September 23, 1774, Ethan set down his *Brief Narrative of the Proceedings of the Government of New York, Relative to Their Obtaining the Jurisdiction of That Large District of Land, to the Westward from Connecticut River.*[70] In what was a war of the pamphleteers, the *Brief Narrative* was a response to two pamphlets by James Duane in the previous year, *A Narrative of the Proceedings Subsequent to the Royal Adjudication* and *State of the Evidence* and *Argument in Support of the Territorial Rights of New York*

Against the Government of New Hampshire and the Claimants Under It. The *Brief Narrative* was published in Hartford and distributed widely in the Grants and neighboring provinces early in 1775. The Narrative comprises the first third of the pamphlet, followed by nine sections of argument refuting the Yorker case and concluding with an appendix, a transcription of the proceedings of the Assembly of New York in 1773. It is a curious document. The Narrative part begins with the events of 1764 and concludes in August 1774. It is interspersed with copies of letters, documents and lengthy observations: the *Brief Narrative* is not a smooth account of the evolving dispute. Several important events are omitted, such as the first edict of outlawry in 1771.

The Arguments are to "demonstrate that the Property of the District of LAND aforesaid, was conveyed from the Crown, to the NEW-HAMPSHIRE GRANTEES, by Virtue of their respective CHARTERS."[71] Sections I and II of the Arguments contend that the charters of Charles II are invalid and cannot support the claims either of New York or New Hampshire. In view of the fact that New York's jurisdiction now rested on the Royal Determination of 1764, this argument would seem to be otiose, but for the fact that Duane dwelt on the charters and New York had continued to assert jurisdiction, based on the edicts of Charles II. For instance, Tryon in a proclamation of December 11, 1771 asserted that ". . . it is the ancient and incontestable right of this Colony to extend to the Connecticut River, as its Eastern Boundary."[72] (He issued the proclamation because of a well-founded suspicion that Governor Wentworth wanted to restore the jurisdiction of New Hampshire over the Grants.) The New York Assembly made the same claim in 1773.[73]

The crux of the argument is in Section III. It first follows Benning Wentworth in arguing that New Hampshire extends westwards to a line twenty miles from the Hudson. Ethan Allen then acknowledged the change in jurisdiction of 1764 but "upon such Alterations of Jurisdiction, private Property is never changed or subverted."[74] So the New Hampshire titles remained intact. For this reason, the Yorkers relied on the seventeenth-century charters to corroborate their case. This author contends below that Ethan was correct in his argument: the Royal Determination did no more than inaugurate New York's jurisdiction in 1764. Section IV opens by stating that the preceding arguments are "full and conclusive" but, for greater certainty, elaborates a further argument over the validity of the charters of Charles II. Ethan points out that the claim to land from the west side of the Connecticut River to the east side of the Delaware Bay is utterly incoherent: "the best

Mathematician on Earth cannot ascertain these Limits, except upon arbitrary Principles." So it is impossible for New York to rely on the charters for their "ancient" jurisdiction.[75] Section V notes that if the charters are valid, both Connecticut and Massachusetts would be invaded by New York, clearly not the intention of the Crown in the charters of the late 1600s. There follows a series of arguments about what was intended, including New York's relations with the former Dutch possessions; but these (as Ethan had previously stated) were not essential to the Grantees' case.

Sections VI–VIII reassert the arguments over the twenty-mile limit, with examples. Section IX is a compendium of documents relating to the preceding arguments: Benning Wentworth's Proclamation of March 13, 1764; the royal order of July 4, 1767 telling New York to stop making grants and confirmations; and the conclusions in the Report of Lords of Trade of December 3, 1772; with a final commentary. All told, Ethan's arguments, while somewhat haphazard and repetitive, with no great claim to originality, are forceful and persuasive.

Critique of the Dispute Between New Hampshire and New York Over the Grants.

In April, 2012, Professor T.H. Breen wrote that Governor Benning Wentworth of New Hampshire had no authority to issue any land titles in the Grants, and that New Hampshire "had never owned a single acre of Vermont." Wentworth had engaged in a "spectacular fraud."[76] How an accomplished scholar of the period could make such an absurdly one-sided statement is quite baffling. The fact was that the Grants were disputed territory over which both sides had arguments; both tried to use the power hierarchy to achieve what they thought were their political rights. It is quite true that Wentworth's grants were corrupt and contrary to the royal instructions (so were those of New York), but in British eyes, this had no bearing on the legal status of the New Hampshire land grants.

In 1939, Matt B. Jones published *Vermont in the Making 1750–1777,* a work based on exhaustive scholarship and interpretation. His views on the legal status of the Grants have resulted in a wide following, for instance in the work of such scholars as Chilton Williamson, Charles Jellison, Michael A. Bellesiles and Willard Sterne Randall. Jones made two contentions over the status of the Grants:

1. The leaders of the "New Hampshire group" argued that jurisdiction over

the Grants had been vested in New Hampshire prior to the Order in Council of July 20, 1764, so the New Hampshire Grants were based on an ancient and indefeasible "right of soil"; but this supposition is false.[77]

2. In 1932, the US Supreme Court, in an "authoritative interpretation," decided that the Order in Council of 1764 confirmed but did not change the eastern boundary of New York as made by Charles II in his grant of that province to James, Duke of York in 1664, which would "seem to be conclusive" in refuting the first contention above. The legal theory of the Grantees "was demolished."[78]

Jones set down the language of the Order in Council of 1764, using this phrase: "the western banks of the Connecticut River from where it enters the province of Massachusetts bay, as far north as the forty-fifth degree of northern latitude [were] to be the boundary line between the two provinces of New Hampshire and New York."[79] But there is no argument for interpolating and inserting "were" instead of "is" before "to be," especially as the Crown did not set down a Preamble, referring to the charters of Charles II. Nor did the Yorkers ever hold up the Order in Council as evidence of their triumph: perhaps they were less confident than Jones that the order *merely* confirmed the ancient jurisdiction of New York.[80] Jones on the Ejectment Trials argued that the law and the facts were on the Yorker side when the court ruled that Wentworth never had any authority to grant title. But since this rests on the bald assertion that the Order of 1764 merely confirmed the jurisdiction of New York, this argument is invalid. All the defendants wanted to do was to have the writs of ejectment cancelled, irrespective of jurisdiction. Whether they ever thought they could evade the issue of jurisdiction and title is another matter.

Nor did Jones examine Ethan Allen's arguments for contending that the Order of 1764 created jurisdiction, namely that the charters of Charles II were incoherent, invalid and, if New York began along the whole length of the Connecticut River to the west, that province would have invaded Connecticut and Massachusetts. Allen did not rely solely on these contentions, since he also argued from natural justice that the Crown did not wish to invalidate title to property west of the Connecticut River. The British government came close to this position when it contemplated the unqualified protection of possession, while evading the question of legitimate title by saying only that grants should be confirmed irrespective of jurisdiction. At one point, revolutionary New York seemed to accept that the Order of 1764 created jurisdiction, when in a Proclamation of February 23, 1778, it referred to grants made "antecedent to the late establishment of the eastern boundary of this state"; but this was at a time when New York was prepared to validate and confirm the New Hampshire grants. The term "establishment" was indeed used by Lieutenant Governor Colden in his Proclamation of 1765, when he said that the Order of 1764 *established* the boundary between New York and New Hampshire, which implied that, beforehand, the boundary had been an open question. This suggests that the Order of 1764 did indeed create something new.[81] But the drift of Yorker thinking was to deny that the Order created jurisdiction because that would imply the legitimacy of New Hampshire government prior to 1764.

The reliance on a Supreme Court verdict is equally weak. Legal experts frequently challenge the correctness of court decisions, on grounds of both fact and law. Later court decisions can overturn previous ones. Nor does the historical reasoning of the court have any special status; otherwise historians would always have to defer to the courts whenever historical reasoning conflicted with the findings and interpretations of the courts. The case in question was actually decided in 1933.[82] All the decision did was to validate the Order in Council of 1764 and go on to state that the boundary decision of 1764 was confirmed in subsequent American law: the case said nothing about the applicability of the Order in Council in the years prior to 1764. The decision does not affect Jones' unsubstantiated assertions over the status of the Order in Council.

There is one further piece of evidence, albeit circumstantial and tangential: that the British did not wish to invalidate New Hampshire titles in the ruling of 1764. They never held up Benning Wentworth's corrupt practices as a reason for invalidating the New Hampshire titles; Michael A. Bellesiles' contention that they did deny the validity of these titles is not correct.[83] With regard to actual settlers under New Hampshire grants, the consistent outlook of His Majesty's Government, 1764–75, was to protect the "improved possessions" of the settlers but to make no ruling over their titles to the land. The British government could not protect actual possession if they had invalidated New Hampshire titles in 1764 by awarding past jurisdiction to New York; the best they could have done for the New Hampshire settlers in any denial of title was to evict them and fob them off with extensive waste lands as they proposed to do with those settlers in western Massachusetts under illegitimate New York patents.

The issue was not one of "a few lawless vagabonds." After all, if the British had met the demands of the Wentworth settlers, there would have been no Green Mountain Boys to take Ticonderoga. All along, the British had the right policy; they only failed to implement it. So what could they have done? The use of force was not really an option for the British. Haldimand had quite enough problems on his plate when he was asked to supply British regulars to suppress the Green Mountain Boys. He would have had to detach a regiment from New York or Canada to push into the Grants and hope that all of the Green Mountain Boys would be foolish enough to draw up against the British muskets and bayonets, then annihilated in a decisive defeat. If not, the regulars could have laid waste to eastern Albany County (there was little to burn), taking care not to destroy the Yorker settlements, only to have to return to do the same in a couple of years. When Haldimand suggested instead that Tryon use his militia, he did not appreciate that the Royal Governor had tried to use his militia to enforce the ejectments, only to find to his dismay that his militiamen, having grievances similar to the Grantees, simply turned around and went home.

The British in Whitehall asked Tryon to compromise by meeting the demands of the New Hampshire settlers, while retaining all his other lands in the Grants and his power to issue patents in the future. But when Tryon objected, the British neither enforced the terms of the settlement nor granted him the services of British regular troops. With Dunmore and Tryon, the British were clearly having as much trouble in North America with their friends as with their enemies, illustrating the oft-made point that the colonies had achieved such a state of de facto independence that it was impossible to reassert imperial authority by any means, least of all by military force.

Tryon and his surrogates, principally Cadwallader Colden, repeatedly ignored royal instructions and orders. Thus the only way to resolve the issue would have been to recall Tryon and replace him with a loyal placeman, with strict instructions to implement what the British government had always recommended. But Tryon was a good soldier and a strong governor with powerful family and friends in London. Even if the British were willing and able to remove him they would have wielded a sledgehammer to crack a nut, however much the British had underestimated the strength and size of the nut.

Settlement of the northern frontier could not be directed from Whitehall. In New York and New England, the availability of investment monies and credit outstripped the pace of settlement with the result that the British policy of "improvement" would invariably give way to the speculative sale of vast tracts of land. Abuse and corruption were thus, as it were, built into the system which the British government was powerless to correct.

CHAPTER 3

Ethan Allen and the Assault on Ticonderoga, May 10, 1775

FROM THE POINT OF view of the New Englanders, Ticonderoga was of crucial importance. In violation of the Treaty of Utrecht (1713), the French built a wooden fort on the eastern bank of Lake Champlain at Chimney Point, then in the 1730s a new stone fort with a redoubt at Crown Point, named Fort St Frederic. From there the French, with Canadian militia and their Indian allies, launched raids throughout the 1740s into Massachusetts, the British settlements in New York, and what became the province of New Hampshire. They began seigneurial settlements in the vicinity of both Chimney Point and Fort St Frederic, partly to establish a French presence in the area and partly to supply the French garrisons. To counter the British Fort William Henry, later known as Fort George, at the southern end of that lake, the French built the great Fort Carillon (Ticonderoga) between 1755 and 1758. Situated on the western side of Lake Champlain where it was only a mile wide, it could interdict marine traffic on the Lake. To protect themselves against the threat of the French and Indians, the Connecticut River settlers erected forts: No. 1 (now Taunton); No. 2 (Rockingham); No. 3 (Walpole); and No. 4, the northernmost in 1747 (Charlestown), later the terminus of the Crown Point Military Road.

At the outbreak of the Seven Years War in 1756, the settlements near Crown Point and at Chimney Point were abandoned, but the war raged, with the loss to the English of Fort William Henry and with major British attacks on Ticonderoga. The French evacuated Ticonderoga and Crown Point in 1759 and, with the conclusion of peace in 1763, the French threat to British North America receded; the Lake Champlain forts lost their strategic importance and became run down. Correspondingly, Fort Dummer on the Connecticut River was abandoned. However, the past role of the Champlain forts as well as their future value to the British was not lost on the New England colonists once the Revolution came. The British controlled Lake Champlain and could seal off New England from the other centers of revolt. From Ticonderoga and Crown Point, they could launch raids from Canada into New England, like the French before them. As the British commander in New York put it in a letter to Lord Dartmouth on May 15, 1774: the drawing of two regiments from Canada to Crown Point "under the pretense of rebuilding that fort which from its situation not only secures the communication with Canada but also opens easy access to the back settlements of the Northern colonies and may keep them in awe."[1] With Ticonderoga, Crown Point and Skenesborough in Patriot hands, the rebels could remove the immediate threat to New England and the settlements in northern New York, while severing the link between the British garrisons in Canada and those in Yorktown (New York City), a link which the British failed disastrously to restore in 1777. The common cause that the Green Mountain Boys had with the colonists of Connecticut and Massachusetts was the British threat to the Grants, particularly those settlements adjacent to the Lake Champlain forts. In particular, the Allen family saw the great danger to the Onion River Company, whose tract, Ethan claimed, was about 45,000 acres and increasing, as well as a blockhouse and a road between Otter Creek and the mouth of the Onion (Winooski) River.

The three-way relationship between the Grantees, the Yorkers and the British had, by the outbreak of the Revolution, taken a peculiar turn. Major Philip Skene had acquired nearly 34,000 acres as a military grant just south of Lake Champlain and centered on Skenesborough (now Whitehall, New York). He had settled twenty-nine tenant families and built up a whole complex of rural industries, including sawmills, gristmills, a foundry and even a small shipyard on the Lake. His ambition was to create a province that would straddle New York and Vermont, bounded, at its most grandiose, by the Connecticut River, the Mohawk River, Lake Ontario and the 45th parallel. Meanwhile, he had become a Yorker Justice of the Peace in the new county of Charlotte (1772). This was carved out of Albany County, which straddled New York and the Grants. Charlotte included the lands of the Grants north of the Batten Kill.

Ethan Allen had become friends with Skene, discussed his offices and aspirations and, no doubt, thought that Skene would be less sympathetic to the New York patents in the Grants. Earlier, Skene had circulated a petition to Governor Tryon, asking that Skenesborough be the county seat of Charlotte.[2] Ethan responded that the Grantees could not sign it because "we Imagine it would Counteract our Petition Now Lying before his Majesty and Council for our Annexment to the province of Newhampshire."[3] Ethan encouraged Skene in his proposal to go to London late in 1774 to have his aspirations recognized. Skene succeeded in getting himself appointed Governor of Crown Point and Ticonderoga, displacing the role of Carleton in Quebec.[4] He had also agitated in London to get recognition as Lieutenant-Governor of Skenesborough, which would not thus become an autonomous province but would have placed the district under the higher authority of the Province of New York. Skene made a start in that he was to get a vote of approval from the settlers. The whole proposal came to naught when Skene hastened back across the Atlantic. On the voyage, he learnt from a ship off Newfoundland of Lexington-Concord, so he avoided his manor, but was arrested by the Patriots on arrival at Philadelphia. "Governor Skene," as the Americans called him, was a big catch. But friendship with Allen did not save his son from imprisonment at Hartford when Herrick captured Skenesborough after the fall of Ticonderoga and Crown Point. There is really no indication that Skene's attitude towards the New York patents would have been any different from that of Tryon, though Ira Allen thought that the New Hampshire Grantees "would have been relieved from the oppressive conduct of the Governor and Council of the colony of New York."[5] The issue was never put to the test. Skene was exchanged in November 1776 and took part in the Saratoga campaign of 1777, in which his over-optimistic estimate of Loyalist sentiment in Vermont was one factor in the British defeat in the Battle of Bennington.

ON MAY 15, 1775, SIR Guy Carleton in Quebec wrote to Lord Dartmouth, Secretary of State for the Colonies and President of the Board of Trade, with intelligence from Montreal that Massachusetts was trying to make use of the "turbulent spirits of Montreal" or to intimidate the Canadians "and even tamper with the Indians."[6] One of the turbulent spirits was Thomas Walker, "a great Republican," as Carleton observed dryly. This was at a time when Carleton was convinced there were several Yankee "emissaries" at work in Quebec, subverting the *habitants* and slipping tracts that intimated rebellion under their doors.[7] In a letter dated April 6, Carleton wrote:

> . . . the day before yesterday most of the Merchants as well as most of the English, Scotch and Irish of their town assembled at the Coffee House here [Montreal] and were harangued by the New Englander [John Brown], I am told their Assembly was to choose two deputies to be sent to the Congress to be held in Philadelphia on the 10th of next May.[8]

The election of delegates to the Continental Congress, with a subsequent admission of Canada to the United Colonies, became and remained the official line of the rebels. But there were also threats: in a letter on the following day,[9] Carleton reported that, if the Canadians took up arms on the side of the king, 30,000 troops will march into Canada and lay waste the whole country.

Carleton thought there were three agents from New England present,[10] likely John Brown of Pittsfield, Mass. and the two Green Mountain Boys he had picked up en route to Montreal. There were also three more agents at LaPrairie who had met with merchants for a "suspicious purpose." At the Coffee House, "one Brown" of New England read a letter signed by (Samuel) Adams, Mackay and Warren. He and Walker harangued the meeting but were unsuccessful in getting a committee elected to correspond with the Committee in Boston. (In fact, there was already "a Committee of Correspondence at Montreal" but it declined to give any tangible help to its New England counterparts.[11])

Carleton surmised that Thomas Walker, James Blake, William Heywood, and George Measam, along with James Price (who later bankrolled Montgomery's expedition to Quebec), intended to answer the letter from Boston. In fact the four who replied were Thomas Walker, James Price, William Heywood and John Welles, the last replacing Isaac Todd, who backed away. Brown then threatened fire and sword if the Canadians took up arms against the Bostonians. So Carleton reported in his letter of May 15 that Brown's project had failed; there were only promises of a few individuals to render the Bostonians all services in their power. This was essentially correct, though Brown was more optimistic that, in the event of hostilities, the Caughnawaga Indians would come down "on the side of their brethren the English in New England."[12] The leaders of Anglo-Canadian society subsequently supplied a few military officers and substantial financial and material help to the American invaders, but there was nothing like a revolutionary movement as in the other colonies; the merchants of Montreal and Quebec were more interested in trade than revolution. Among those whom Carleton named, several were later listed as having deserted to the enemy, including Walker, Blake, Heywood, Price and Welles.

How did the project to capture Ticonderoga arise? The Massachusetts Provincial Congress considered that a rupture with Great Britain was inevitable and, in that event, the mother country would use Quebec as a base from which to devastate the colonies with regular troops, local militias and their dreaded Indian allies. On February 15, 1775, the Congress asked the Boston (Massachusetts) Committee of Correspondence to establish relations with Quebec and to invite the residents to set up similar committees in the province. The Committee, headed by Samuel Adams, accepted a volunteer, John Brown of Pittsfield, Massachusetts, a "tall and powerful" Yale-educated attorney and a major of militia, to travel to Canada to ascertain whether the citizens would take the rebel side in the event of an open conflict; also to deliver a letter, dated February 21, to the friends in Montreal and Quebec from the Boston Committee. The letter was addressed to Walker, Todd, Blake, Price, William Heywood and his brother, and others in Montreal, as well as Zachary Macaulay, John Aikin, John Patterson, John Lee, John Wells (Welles) and Ronald Monteith in Quebec. Brown, who well knew the situation in the Grants, passed through the heart of Allen country, asking for help and guides in his passage through the settlements on the south side of the St. Lawrence to Montreal. He met with Ethan Allen and was assigned two Green Mountain Boys, Peleg Sunderland and Winthrop Hoit. A main purpose in their recruitment was to sound out the Indians as to their support for any future move by the Yankee rebels. Sunderland, who later took part in the capture of Ticonderoga, knew the Indians of St. Francis (Odanak) and could speak the Abenaki language. Winthrop Hoit was, like Brown, one of the outstanding revolutionaries in the Northern Department. Captured in the French and Indian War, Hoit was taken to the Caughnawaga village outside Montreal, where he spent four years as a willing captive (not unusual) of the Caughnawagas and spoke their Mohawk. He was valued as an Indian interpreter. Until he was captured in a British raid in November 1778 he was occupied in subverting the Indian tribes in Canada. So valuable was he to the American cause that the British authorities in 1782 forbade his exchange for nearly a year. He ended his days in Swanton, Vermont, where he survived until at least 1813.

Brown later wrote to Adams from Montreal urging that, in the event of hostilities, Ticonderoga must be seized:

> I have established a channel of correspondence through N Hampshire Grants, which may be depended on.... One thing I must mention to be kept as a Profound Secret—the fort of Tyconderoga must be seized as soon as possible should hostilities be committed by the King's troops, the people of N Hampshire Grants have engaged to do this business and in my opinion they are the most proper persons for this job, this will effectually curb this Province and all the troops that may be sent here.[13]

It is therefore certain that he discussed Ticonderoga with Ethan Allen.

A second route whereby Ethan became the leading figure in the capture of Ticonderoga and Crown Point was the immediate result of Lexington-Concord. He was attending the convention of Grantees in Westminster on the eastern side of the Green Mountains, called for April 11, when word came of Lexington-Concord, which took place on April 19. Ethan returned to Bennington straight away. There some of the Green Mountain Boys and other leading residents had "attempted to explore futurity, but it was found to be unfathomable."[14] But Lexington-Concord seemed to be the outbreak of open war and the consensus became that the capture of Ticonderoga was the next move, to be executed by the Green Mountain Boys, led by Ethan. This could not have occurred if an attack on Ticonderoga had not already been in the wind, not least from Ethan's meeting with Brown in the first half of March.

A third route also emanated from the Boston Committee of Correspondence in Cambridge, Mass. In the wake of Lexington-Concord, Colonel Samuel H. Parsons was returning from Cambridge to Hartford, Conn., when he encountered Captain Benedict Arnold with about forty Connecticut Foot Guards. Parsons contended that there was a need for artillery in the forthcoming siege of Boston and Arnold observed that there was a large stock of cannon at Ticonderoga.[15] Arnold continued to Cambridge, while Parsons arrived at Hartford on April 27 and immediately broached the issue of a venture to capture Ticonderoga. There he met a rebel group which included Captain Edward Mott, a recently appointed company commander in Parsons' militia regiment. Mott, it seems, had just returned from the rebel camp outside Boston, where Ticonderoga had been discussed, as it certainly had been before Brown met with Ethan Allen.[16]

Events moved rapidly. Five or six well-connected citizens decided on a surprise attack, not by a sizeable militia force which Connecticut was capable of providing, but by a small, secret group, with the help of the Green Mountain Boys. The main motive was to capture artillery and supplies for Boston. The group raised £300 on April 28 from the Connecticut Treasury and entrusted the money to Noah Phelps and Bernard Romans, who set off for the Grants the same day. From the beginning, the rebel group presumed that Captain Edward Mott would lead the expedition; he left to join Phelps and Romans the next day with five men. By the evening of the 30th, when the expedition reached Salisbury, it had grown to sixteen Connecticut men, including Levi Allen.[17] The group, though not an official body of the Colony of Connecticut, was at least "quasi-legal"[18] and became known as the Committee of War.

On the night of May 1, the expedition reached Pittsfield, Mass., where the group recruited the militia colonel, James Easton, and his major, John Brown. They soon gathered at least thirty-nine men of Easton's regiment, then set out for Bennington, where they arrived the next day.[19] Mott proposed to raise two hundred men, of which Ethan Allen undertook to raise a hundred.[20] Since food was scarce, two men were sent to Albany for provisions.

Ethan had been forewarned of the project. He had sent Heman Allen to Hartford, the nearest hotbed of dissent; his brother was present at the meeting on April 27 and was able to convey the plan to Ethan before the expedition arrived in Bennington on May 2. The Committee of War undertook to pay the expenses of everyone involved in "the secret expedition against Ticonderoga" whether or not they had any direct connection to the Colony of Connecticut. As well as a guinea for "sundries," Heman was paid two pounds and sixteen shillings for "going express after Ethan Allen, 120 miles." Monies were also paid to the three other Allen brothers, to John Brown, Dr Jonas Fay and the wives of Ethan Allen and Seth Warner.[21]

The militia officers of Connecticut and Massachusetts organized the expedition with great enterprise: they sent out pickets under Ethan Allen's direction to block the roads to Skenesborough, Fort Edward, Lake George, Ticonderoga and Crown Point, so that their garrisons would not learn of the coming assault. On May 3, Noah Phelps and Ezra Hecock were sent from Bennington on a spy mission to Ticonderoga. Phelps entered the fort on the pretext of needing a shave and engaged in several conversations, not least with the fortress commander, Captain William Delaplace. He saw that Ticonderoga had not been greatly reinforced (only in fact by Lt. Jocelyn Feltman and ten men); that there were breaches in the fortifications; that some of the powder in the fort was damp and that, most significantly, the garrison had not yet gotten word of Lexington-Concord. Though Phelps aroused some suspicion, he did not alert the garrison and rowed back to his rendezvous at Castleton on May 9, mission accomplished.

The leading members of the group reached Castleton in the Grants on May 7. In Bennington, Colonel Easton had chaired an informal meeting and now there was a more formal meeting of the Committee of War on May 8, comprising Noah Phelps, James Easton, Epaphras Bull and Elisha Phelps, with Mott as Chairman. The aim was to debate strategy and assign commands. Ethan was to lead the field, with Easton second in command and Seth Warner third. A party of thirty, under the command of Captain Samuel Herrick, was to be dispatched the next day to occupy Skenesborough. The remaining men, about a hundred and forty, were to be sent down the Lake via Shoreham to a point across from Ticonderoga under Ethan Allen's command, in light of the promise that the men should be commanded by their own officers. Essential to the project were boats to get across the Lake: to this end, Herrick was to row and sail Skene's boats down the lake to Hand's Cove on the east bank opposite Ticonderoga. On the night of the 9th Captain Asa Douglas of Jericho was sent north to Crown Point to try "to hire the king's boats, on some stratagem."

On the evening of May 9th, Benedict Arnold, appointed Colonel by the Massachusetts Committee of Safety, arrived with a commission to raise up to 400 men to "reduce" Ticonderoga. Like the Connecticut contingent, one of his main aims was to secure the cannon for use at Boston. Arnold repeatedly demanded to take charge of the expedition and was rebuffed: Mott's men had been promised their own officers, all to be paid and maintained by the Colony of Connecticut; they would serve no others and Arnold had no troops of his own under command. For greater certainty, Mott wrote out a commission to Ethan on May 10, confirming that he had been given the command of the party to take possession of Ticonderoga; and that he should keep the command of the garrison until he got further orders from the Colony of Connecticut or the Continental Congress.[22] On the 22nd, Arnold, having requested the relinquishment of his command, was told by the Massachusetts Congress that the Ticonderoga affair had been formally handed over to the Colony of Connecticut.[23] When Ethan wrote to the Massachusetts Congress earlier, on May 11, he made no mention of Benedict Arnold. Ethan agreed to have Arnold accompany him in the assault on Ticonderoga, but on his left, so that Arnold would not have the place of honor at the right of the line.

By the evening of the 9th, the rebels, now turning into Patriots, were at Hand's Cove, unobserved by the garrison of Ticonderoga. Ethan figured much later that he had two hundred and forty Green Mountain Boys under command, while Easton estimated a total of all fighters again at about two hundred and forty.[24] John Brown estimated that there were at the cove upwards of a hundred Green Mountain Boys and about fifty militia from Connecticut and Massachusetts, while Mott estimated the combined force at about a hundred and forty. This was in fact Ethan's own estimate at the time.[25] Some of Ethan's force were recruited from areas north of the centers where the Green Mountain Boys were organized: Major Samuel Beach "went on foot to Rutland, Pittsford, Brandon, Middlebury, Whiting and Shoreham, making a circuit of sixty miles in twenty-four hours," with a total of 170 gathered at Castleton on May 8.[26]

But as the night wore on, there was no sign of the boats. The day was saved by Asa Douglas who, by a ruse, had commandeered a bateau. A second boat also arrived from the north: a scow or flat-bottomed rowboat, owned, as it happened, by Major Skene. Allen made one trip across the Lake in the bateau, which could hold forty men. A second run before dawn comprised the bateau and the scow. That Ethan had a total of 83 or 85 men assembled, with two bateau-loads and one with the scow, is a plausible count.[27] He surprised the garrison almost without a fight, capturing sixty-eight prisoners, of whom twenty-four were women and children. The next day, Seth Warner (apparently at his own insistence) was sent with a hundred men fifteen miles north to Crown Point, which was also taken by surprise, in a joint operation with Remember Baker. The Green Mountain Boys captured the garrison of nine (eight privates and a sergeant) plus ten women and children; fifty cannon and a huge supply of powder and stores. Ethan also got word that Herrick had captured Skenesborough, with more supplies, several bateaux and smaller boats—and Major Skene's schooner. This had been used as an iron ore and timber carrier in the run to St. John's.

Arnold then took the initiative. An experienced sailor, he assumed command of Major Skene's schooner, capable of mounting six or more cannon, with the aim of capturing the British sloop-of-war (a vessel of over seventy tons) at St. John's, before the news of Ticonderoga and Crown Point had reached the British garrison. By this time, he had thirty-five to fifty of his own men under command.[28] Allen, Warner and the Green Mountain Boys were to follow in four bateaux from Ticonderoga; but Arnold on May 18 captured the sloop armed with sixteen guns and the garrison of St. John's (a sergeant and twelve men) before the mountaineers arrived. Full of resentment and frustration (no doubt), Ethan decided to occupy St. John's, against the advice of Arnold, who considered it "a wild, impracticable scheme," contending that it could not be held against British regulars. Ethan with between a hundred and a hundred and fifty Green Mountain Boys, with fourteen *habitants* in the party, were promptly driven out on May 20, with three killed or captured, something that severely dented Ethan's military reputation.[29] Later in the month, a council of war decided to fortify Point au Fer on the west bank of the Lake, where there was a friendly *seigneur*, rather than the Ile-aux-Noix.

During the expedition to St. John's, Ethan had written on May 18 to James Morrison, a member of the Montreal Committee of Correspondence, but addressed to "Mr. James Morrison and the Marchants that are friendly to the Cause of Liberty in Montreal." He told Morrison that "I expect the English Merchants as well as all Virtuous Disposed Gentlemen will be in the Interest of the Colonies"; with their assistance, Canada would soon succumb. He asked to buy supplies to the value of five hundred pounds and said that he had directions to come in friendship with the Canadians and the Indians.[30] This was the first indication that Ethan's sights were set on Montreal, despite the British garrisons in St. John's and at Chambly. Following Ethan's letter to Morrison, Arnold contacted Thomas Walker in Montreal on May 20, advising him that the rebels were sending an embassy to the Caughnawagas and requesting his advice and assistance. Four days later, Ethan wrote to "the Councillors at Konawago," saying that an embassy would arrive, consisting of Captain Nimham, a Stockbridge Mahican, and (again) Winthrop Hoit. The letter was addressed to four tribes, the Konawagas (Caughanawagas), the Swagatchies (the Cayugas and Onondagas of Oswegatchie, up the St. Lawrence River); the Canesagangas (Khanesatagas at Oka or the Lake of the Two Mountains) and the St Francawas (the Abenaki of St Francis or Odanak).[31]

Ethan wrote that "King George has made war on us Americans." We determined "to fight the King's Troops in Canada but not to fight with our Brothers the Indians or our Brothers the Canadians." He appealed for active support but, at least "we hope you will not fight for King George against us as we have done you no wrong."[32] In the letter, Ethan tried to depict the Grantees and the Indians as sharing a common culture. He said that he hunted and fought like an Indian and that, together, they could ambush the British troops in the Indian manner. There was little exaggeration in this.

Carleton intercepted both letters, the one to Morrison and the other to the Caughnawagas. Ethan sent a second letter addressed to "the French people of Canada" on June 4, through James Jeffrey, a member of the Montreal Committee "once of Boston," saying that there are no controversies "between us" and asking again for their neutrality.[33]

By May 19, Carleton had heard of Lexington-Concord, but with no details.[34] Though there were doubts about his loyalty (since he admitted to having spoken with Arnold), Captain Moses Hazen reported on the 20th that Arnold had captured the British sloop, bateaux, stores and provisions at St. Johns as well as Ticonderoga, Crown Point and the craft on the lake. Hazen also brought news of Ethan Allen's abortive attack on St. John's. Carleton acknowledged Ethan's role at Ticonderoga, but apparently knew little about him; he was "said to be an outlaw in the Province of New York." Carleton was clearly apprehensive about the Canadians and the Indians: "The gentry and clergy have been very useful, but both have lost much of their influence."[35]

The Continental Congress, recovering from the embarrassment of being the lords of Ticonderoga, directed that the cannon be taken to the south end of Lake George, to be returned to His Majesty when the "former harmony" between Great Britain and the Colonies was restored, consistent with the "overruling law of self-preservation."[36] This sentiment was far more common than the idea that there had been a decisive break with the old order, Brigadier-General Richard Montgomery, for instance, holding onto such a view even until his death at the end of the year. Ethan responded at length on May 29, saying that the removal of the guns would leave the western settlements open to attack and ruin. He proposed, instead, an expedition against Montreal in the expectation that the Canadians and Indians, overawed by the American force, would remain neutral. The Americans "would Easily make a Conquest of that Place" and "Set up the standard of American Liberty in the Extensive province of Quebec whose Limit was enlarged purely to Subvert the Liberties of America."[37] Ethan was not alone in these sentiments: Captain Elisha Phelps considered that an army of at least three thousand men should be sent immediately to occupy St. John's and the Canadian forts, even (remarkably) that a further small army should move on to take Detroit.[38]

For the Continental Congress, conciliation was the order of the day. On May 29, 1775, it sent a letter in French to the *habitans* [sic] of Quebec, taking the familiar line that our right to liberty, given to us by the Creator, was being taken away by an "*Administration despotique.*" The letter presented the recent

Quebec Act as tyrannical. (Though the legislation did indeed contain some reactionary provisions, it essentially emancipated the French Catholics.) Ticonderoga and Crown Point had been taken because of the great law of self-preservation (*par cette grande loi, notre conservation propre*) and we mean no harm, since the capture of the forts was in our mutual interest (*interet reciproque*). The last paragraph expresses the hope that the *habitants* will join us in the defense of our mutual liberty and that they will work with us in drawing the king's attention to the oppressions and injustices inflicted upon us both by a "licentious Ministry."[39] On June 1, the Congress resolved that no expedition or incursion against Canada should be undertaken by any colony or the forces at Ticonderoga.[40]

The Provincial Congress of New York sent an even more accommodating letter to the *habitants* of Canada on June 2. "Ministerial tyranny" has led some to take forts "in this colony, which are near to your frontier." We, the Americans, come in friendship: the attack on St. John's was "without our Council or participation," carried out only to "prevent any hostile invasion by the troops in your province."[41] The letter, signed by Philip Livingston, represented the predominant view among the New York elite: once the Despotic Ministry has been removed, peace and harmony with Great Britain would be restored.

For the invasion of Canada, Ethan did not envisage a small force such as had captured Ticonderoga. He spoke of an army of two or three thousand men. When he wrote to the New York Provincial Congress on June 2, he contended that he could take Montreal with fifteen hundred men and "a proper train of artillery."[42] He wrote to the Massachusetts Provincial Congress from Crown Point on the 9th, again contending that two or three thousand men with "Intripit Commanders" could neutralize Canada.[43] Allen knew his audience: when he wrote to the Continental Congress, he talked of regaining the vast western lands of Quebec for America; when he wrote to the Massachusetts Congress, he stressed the nullification of the Quebec Act.

The point to stress about all this is that Ethan thought that at least fifteen hundred men were needed to take Montreal. Even if the Green Mountain Boys were upgraded to a full regiment, they could still form no more than the nucleus of an invasion force (in fact, a regiment of up to 500 was authorized). The circumstances that Ethan faced outside Montreal late in September were, it appeared, very different from those of early June.

On June 19, 1775, the Continental Congress appointed Philip Schuyler Major-General and, on the 22nd, Richard Montgomery Brigadier-General. Schuyler was appointed to the command of the New York Department on

July 20. Congress debated the feasibility of an invasion of Canada and, later in the month, authorized Schuyler to occupy St. John's, Montreal and other parts of the country if he considered it practicable and "if it will not be disagreeable to the Canadians."[44] Montgomery's concern was that the British were building a fleet at St. John's to regain control of Lake Champlain. Canada was open to an American invasion. On June 23, Ethan Allen and Seth Warner appeared before the Continental Congress in Philadelphia, with a mandate from the leaders of the Green Mountain Boys. Their aim was to get Congress to authorize the invasion of Canada with the Green Mountain Boys as a regiment of the Continental Congress. The mission was successful. The Green Mountain Boys were awarded back pay for the Ticonderoga expedition and were to become a regiment of New York:

> *Resolved*, That it be recommended to the Convention of New-York, that they, consulting with General Schuyler, employ in the Army to be raised for the defence of America, those called Green Mountain Boys, under such officers as the said Green Mountain Boys shall choose.[45]

The resolutions were forwarded to the New York Provincial Congress, which debated the issue on July 4. Ethan was at the door, requesting admittance. Though the case was now altered, the issue of the Grants remained, with many of the members of the provincial congress holding New York patents. Ethan was admitted on a vote of 18-9, which doubtless underestimated the hostility to the New Hampshire claims. On July 20, he wrote to the New York Provincial Congress, stating that he hoped they were in a new era and "as soon as the opportunity may permit and the publick cause not suffer thereby, shall hold myself in readiness to settle all former disputes and grievances on honourable terms."[46]

Allen and Warner had got what they wanted: the Green Mountain Boys were to become a regiment of the Province of New York. Allen and Warner were invited at Schuyler's suggestion to name their proposed officers of the regiment. What Ethan thought of becoming an officer commissioned by the provincial congress in a regiment of Yorkers is not recorded: he had suggested to the Continental Congress a regiment of rangers, raised in the Grants, in his letter of June 2. Then an episode occurred, entirely unforeseen. On July 26, a convention of west-side towns met in Dorset to elect officers for the regiment. Warner was elected Lieutenant-Colonel by 45-5, a huge majority against Ethan. Samuel Safford, not then one of Ethan's associates, was chosen Major by 28-17. Who ran against Safford is not known, but Ethan and Warner had recommended Major William Williams of Massachusetts to Congress, if the opportunity should arise.[47] Altogether, twenty-three officers were elected. Of the names that Schuyler received, Baker, Cochran and Sunderland were rejected; Warner as Lieutenant Colonel, Heman as Captain, Ira and Ebenezer Allen as Lieutenants were elected, as well as four others of the sixteen Allen nominees of July 5.[48] Ethan was out. Had the vote been taken by the Boys, he would have coasted to victory.

There are only hints in the documented sources as to what had transpired. On July 13, 1775, Stephen Fay wrote to General Schuyler from Bennington, saying that only Ethan Allen and Seth Warner had been "universally approved" as Field Officers; they will nominate their officers "as they are the best judge of the merits of their Corps."[49]

The fact that the letter came from Fay shows that the Allens wanted to control everything relating to the Green Mountain Boys. But the plot leaked out; it is hard to believe that Warner was not the principal conduit. For on July 16, William Marsh, later a Loyalist, wrote to Schuyler from Manchester, saying that neither the settlers nor the Committee of the Towns on the New Hampshire Grants had been consulted on the important matter of the officers of the Green Mountain Boys; "some designing man or men is about to obtain the Command as well as the Distribution of the Commissions for Captain and Lieutenant." Marsh wrote as a Charlotte County delegate to the New York Provincial Congress and said there would be a general meeting to give a further response.[50] Schuyler, if he was not actually complicit in the attempt to dethrone Ethan, certainly welcomed the move, since he held Ethan responsible for the wrecking of Skene's estate; he had supported Ethan financially to the tune of two hundred pounds, when it seemed clear that Ethan would command the Boys. Yet he proved to be utterly loyal to Warner, despite the fact that Warner had been indicted along with Ethan and the other leading Green Mountain Boys.

The decisions are shrouded in obscurity.[51] There was no love lost between Ethan and Warner and it was the latter who benefited the most, since he achieved sole command of the Green Mountain Boys. That there was a feud between the two was confirmed by Schuyler, who wrote to Washington in August, saying that it was so bitter that it was affecting recruitment. Like others, Warner objected to Ethan's leadership, asserted forcefully and contemptuous of disagreement or timidity. Warner too was a devout Congregationalist who disliked Ethan's religious profanity and godlessness. In fact, the whole Allen clan was regarded as blasphemers and deniers of the Trinity, who publicly insulted both Christ and the clergy.[52] Warner was less of an adventurer than Ethan, though he later got the reputation for querying his superiors' orders. But at least he would not engage in hare-brained schemes like Ethan's foray to St. Johns or his later attack on Montreal. However, the answer may be simpler: the time for irregular, vigilante action, of the intimidation and violence against civilians was over. The Boys were now regulars and subject to the discipline of the New York commanders and the authority of the Continental Congress. Ethan was no longer the man for the job. The deepest reason behind the rejection may well have been the predomination of pro-Yorker sentiment, even on the west side, Ethan's own fief. The delegates could have seen the expedition against Ticonderoga as an attack on New York (Ethan considered that it was), which was willing to compromise over the Grants, a needless disturbance of the peace. They were "the old farmers on the New-Hampshire Grants, who do not incline to go to war."[53] In strictly military terms, Ethan's reputation had suffered because of the fiasco of the attack on St. John's and this alone could account for his rejection.

Ethan Allen's Motives in the Assault on Ticonderoga

Understandably, there is a tradition that Ethan was a rebel and revolutionary from the start. He opens the *Narrative of Ethan Allen's Captivity* with this bold passage:

> Ever since I arrived to a state of manhood, and acquainted myself with the general history of mankind, I have felt a sincere passion for liberty. The history of nations doomed to perpetual slavery, in consequence of yielding up to tyrants their natural born liberties, I read with a sort of philosophical horror; so that the first systematical and bloody attempt at Lexington, to enslave America, thoroughly electrified my mind, and fully determined me to take part with my country. . . .[54]

Allen had indeed written on March 1, 1775 to Oliver Wolcott, soon to become a Connecticut delegate to the Second Continental Congress on May 10 in Philadelphia:

> Provided the Controversy between Great Britain and the Colonies

> Should Terminate in a War the Regiment of Green Mountain Boys Will I Dare Ingage to Assist their American Brethren in the Capacity of Rangers.[55]

This letter was written before Allen met with Brown, when the issue of Ticonderoga was first raised. There was no doubt that, in the event of war, the Green Mountain Boys would be on the side of the Patriots.

From the opening of his *Narrative,* Allen goes on to say:

> And while I was wishing for an opportunity to signalize myself in its behalf, directions were privately sent to me from the then colony (now state) of Connecticut, to raise the Green Mountain Boys; (and if possible) with them to surprise and take the fortress of Ticonderoga. This enterprise I cheerfully undertook. . . .[56]

The impression that Allen wants to give is that he was thoroughly committed to active rebellion long before the Ticonderoga expedition arrived in Bennington. The trouble is that while "wishing for an opportunity," he had not engaged in any subversive activity other than his feud with the Yorkers—the Committees of Safety in Ethan's fief on the west side of the Green Mountains were directed against New York, not the Crown, nor was Ethan a member of a Committee of Correspondence, much less the Sons of Liberty. Maybe the Grants on the west side of the Green Mountains were too remote from the centers of resistance; the fact remains that Ethan showed no sign of revolutionary activity or a "passion for liberty" until he undertook the assault on Ticonderoga.

Ethan said that he got secret instructions from Connecticut to take Ticonderoga, even telling the Boys on the morning of the attack that he had been ordered to do so by the "general assembly of Connecticut,"[57] which is not correct. The Assembly was not aware of the expedition until after it had departed from Hartford. What had happened was that the Connecticut party had hoped and expected to enlist the support of the Green Mountain Boys and, in view of their numbers and the promise to have them led by their own officers, Ethan was readily appointed commander of the attempt on Ticonderoga. Allen had got no private directions, either from Mott or indirectly through Heman a few days before.

None of Ethan's previous actions had constituted any direct attack on the Royal authority, or any challenge to the King's decision-making power.

On the contrary, he had supported all the moves to get the King to revert to his position in the period 1749–64, when the New Hampshire Grants had been made under royal authority. He also supported the mission of Breakenridge and Hawley to England in the previous year and the current petition to reannex the Grants to New Hampshire. Ethan's quarrel was with rival expressions of royal authority, not with royalty as such.

There are several possibilities as to Ethan's motive in attacking Ticonderoga.[58] But when we look at the situation in the Grants on the eve of the attack, some plausible interpretations can be made. As we have seen, Ethan was losing the battle against the Yorker confirmations. When we add to this the possibility that London would confirm the Yorker claims over both wild and settled lands at the expense of the New Hampshire proprietors, the attack on the royal authority at Ticonderoga made sense. The old quarrel with the government of New York would be "swallowed up" by the general conflict for liberty, the Yorker government being "detested more than that of the British."[59] A Yankee rebellion was also a defense of the New Hampshire Grants. Naturally, Ethan did not realize that any revolutionary government in New York would be just as hostile to the Grants as the king's men, more so as it transpired, and that the Continental Congress would favor New York at the expense of Vermont.

When Allen demanded the surrender of Ticonderoga, he was asked by what authority he made the demand, and he says that he answered, famously, "In the name of the great Jehovah, and the Continental Congress."[60] It is quite possible that he used these actual words[61] but, as Ethan wrote at the time, the authority of the Congress was then very little known. It was in fact as little known to Allen as it was to the British officers at Ticonderoga. At the First Continental Congress of 5–26 October 1774, the delegates ordered a number of acts of disobedience but there was no program of forceful resistance. After the capture of Ticonderoga and Crown Point, the Congress asserted, specifically, that the King's property at Fort Ticonderoga should be respected, predicting that the captured cannon would be returned, once the "former harmony" with the Crown had been restored. The Grants had, of course, no delegates at the Continental Congress, while one delegate from New York was Allen's implacable enemy, James Duane, who had represented the plaintiffs in the Ejectment Trials of 1770. In attacking Ticonderoga, Allen was either defying the Continental Congress or he was unaware of their deliberations in the previous year. He was more likely to have taken Ticonderoga in the name of the Colony of Connecticut. The Congress was "entirely ignorant of the enterprise."[62] The name, the decisions and the authority of the Continental Congress came later. It was only on May 16 that the Massachusetts Provincial Congress wrote to the Continental Congress, indicating its willingness to "submit to such a general plan as you may direct for the Colonies" and recommended the Congress take over the direction of the Army that was being assembled.[63] After his captivity, Ethan observed in passing that the party set to capture Ticonderoga and Crown Point could not determine for certain "whether such a measure would be agreeable to congress or not."[64]

When Ticonderoga had been taken, John Brown was sent immediately to the Second Continental Congress in Philadelphia, along with the British colors captured with the fortress. Benedict Arnold continued to dispute Ethan's leadership, forcing Edward Mott to issue his commission to the Grantsman. This confirmed the order to Allen to take Ticonderoga "and its dependencies" and to keep command of the garrison "till you have further orders from the Colony of Connecticut or from the Continental Congress," a recognition of the authority of the Continental Congress after the event. Ethan, however, made no such deference at the time. He had Brown, en route to Philadelphia, drop off a letter to the Albany Committee of Correspondence, which was known to have been supportive of the expedition to capture Ticonderoga. In requesting immediate reinforcement, he said that his actions were "pursuant to my directions from sundry leading Gentlemen in the Colonies of Massachusetts Bay and Connecticut," a reasonable way of saying that he had come voluntarily under the direction of the Committee of War and a more modest statement than the claims made in the *Narrative.*[65]

By the time that Allen wrote his *Narrative* from memory in 1778–79, much had happened. Burgoyne had been defeated at Saratoga, the Regiment of Green Mountain Rangers had distinguished itself at Hubbardton and Bennington, and Vermont had declared independence. Yet the enemy was still New York, but now as a state rather than a colony or province, refusing to admit Vermont to the Continental Congress or to recognize its independence. At the same time, Allen had to demonstrate his loyalty to the Confederation, which he did with visceral attacks on the British, the Hessians and the Tories, whom he held responsible for the deaths of two thousand Patriot prisoners in New York. In view of his treatment during his transportation across the Atlantic and back, his anti-British sentiment is well founded, though he was always quick to point out the occasions when he was treated with humanity and respect. What cannot be done is to see his anti-British and anti-Tory sentiments as an underlying hostility to the Crown and as evidence that he was a revolutionary from the start. The capture of Ticonderoga prevented the exercise of Yorker authority in the Grants, backed as it was by the Crown. This was the limit of Ethan's anti-royalist sentiment.

The latest attempt to see Ethan Allen as an anti-royalist revolutionary from the start is to be found in Willard Sterne Randall's *Ethan Allen: His Life and Times* (2011). Randall's basic premise is that all of Ethan Allen's anti-Yorker activity was really an attack on the Crown's royal authority. He thus becomes an early revolutionary, in the vanguard of all the revolts in New England against royal government and the British armed forces. The trouble is that right up to the outbreak of the revolution, Ethan was hoping that a royal decision would either confirm the New Hampshire titles or at least the rights of settlers under New Hampshire grants. Randall's account also ignores the Allens' later attempts to have Vermont become a "separate government under the Crown" and the fact (to be argued below) that Ethan in the 1780s saw the future of Vermont as lying exclusively with the British Empire. In view of Ethan's repeated assurances to Sir Frederick Haldimand that Vermonters were not Republicans by inclination, it is hard to make out a case for saying that the Allens were committed exclusively to the idea of republicanism.

Randall's view also involves serious distortions. The Westminster Massacre of March, 1775 is seen as "a harbinger of the American Revolution" and a revolutionary act:

> The Revolutionary War and the movement for independence from British colonial government, and therefore from the British Empire, had already begun in the events on the Vermont frontier. The events of March 1775 have been glossed over. . . .[66]

In reality, the Westminster Massacre had little to do with Ethan's opposition to Yorker activity in the Grants and it was typical of the riotous opposition to the New York landed establishment all along the Hudson Valley to the west.

When it comes to the Ticonderoga expedition, Randall asserts that Ethan was both the originator and the planner of the attack on Ticonderoga. Upon getting word of Lexington-Concord late in April 1775, the "strategically inclined" Ethan "set to work formulating a strategy." This was to seize control of the Lake Champlain forts and "forward hundreds of cannon to the primitively armed Patriots investing Boston."[67] Randall's account ignores John Brown's letter of March 29 in which Brown said that he had recruited the Green Mountain Boys for an attack on Ticonderoga. Ethan had "set to work" long before he got word of Lexington-Concord. And far from wanting the cannon for Boston, Ethan actually deplored the removal of the cannon to the south end of Lake George, since, this would "ruin the Frontier Settlements."[68] The cannon from Ticonderoga and Crown Point did indeed reach Boston by the March of the following year, after a spectacular winter march. They were instrumental in forcing the naval evacuation of the garrison under Sir William Howe.

CHAPTER 4

The Capture of Ethan Allen at Montreal, September 25, 1775

FOR A TIME, IT looked as though the decision to exclude Ethan from command would not stick, as the Boys hesitated to move without him in charge. The situation was serious: Schuyler reported to Washington in August that "the controversy between Allen and Warner is carried to such length" that it will affect recruitment."[1] Ethan continued to hold out the hope of "an Honourable Preferment in the Army," stating that commissions will come from the Continental Congress, which was not the case with the Green Mountain Boys to date. Schulyer at Ticonderoga tried to mollify Allen and promised to take him along in the expedition to Canada as a civilian scout, even without a commission. Mindful of the fact that he actually led a military expedition to Montreal in September, Allen later wrote "... I had no commission from Congress, yet [Schuyler and Montgomery] engaged me, that I should be considered as an officer the same as though I had a commission; and should, as occasion might require, command certain detachments of the army. This I considered as an honourable offer and did not hesitate to comply with it ..."[2] There is no evidence at all that this was Schuyler's stance. On the contrary, he wrote to Hancock, the President of the Congress on October 5, observing that:

> I am very apprehensive of disagreeable consequences arising from Mr Allen's imprudence. I always dreaded his impatience of subordination; and it was not until after a solemn promise, made me in the presence of several officers, that he would demean himself properly,

> that I would permit him to attend the army; nor would I have consented then, had not his solicitations been backed by several officers.[3]

Now-Major John Brown, meanwhile, had been active. On July 24th, he was sent on what was his second expedition to Canada after the outbreak of war. Carleton intercepted a letter from Brown to Thomas Walker, James Price and "to others they may communicate with," dated Chambly, August 1, 1775. They asked for an early meeting; the Caughnawagas were invited too, according to the terms of a letter from Schuyler, sent "with discretion."[4] The British were most anxious to apprehend Brown.[5]

Brown wrote on August 10, 1775 that the British were weak but the Canadians would only support the Americans if no reinforcements arrived. So an offensive against Canada was a matter of urgency. On the same day, Remember Baker reported to Schulyer on the state of the garrison and defenses of St. John's which he had, on a scouting expedition, gleaned from "sundry Indians and Canadians."[6] James Livingston reported to Schuyler on British preparations and that a 300-acre bounty offer had not persuaded many Canadians to join Carleton. He suspected that some of the few regulars would desert.

Remember Baker was killed in a further scouting expedition on August 22, 1775; an indignant Schuyler wrote to Washington, stating that Baker's action was unauthorized and contrary to orders.[7] Baker's skirmish wounded several Indians, making it necessary for Schuyler to assure the Caughnawagas that Baker's action was unauthorized. This was an aspect of Schuyler's Proclamation in French of September 5, 1775, made at Ile-aux-Noix.[8] The "Grand Congress" had sent an army to expel the British troops who were acting under the orders of a Despotic Ministry. The war was not against Great Britain but only those corrupt Ministers who had subverted and deceived Parliament. They would enslave their countrymen—the American army would secure the rights of all Canadians regardless of religion and protect their property. Early in September, after Ethan had moved with the army to the Ile-aux-Noix, he and Brown went on an expedition to Canada, carrying Schuyler's Proclamation to James Livingston for distribution among the Canadians.[9] On September 8, Livingston wrote to Schuyler; he promised to raise a sizeable group of inhabitants if the army appears—a positive response to Schuyler's Proclamation.[10] Livingston recommended cutting the roads from St. John's to Chambly and Montreal. At Livingston's camp at St. Mathieu, south of Montreal, they got the impression that Carleton was preparing to evacuate

Montreal. (In fact, he was prepared to do so only at the appearance of a major American force.) Then the *habitants,* awaiting in Ethan's neat phrase, "the scale of power," would join the invaders.[11] Ethan returned to the Ile-aux-Noix on September 14.[12]

Throughout September, Livingston was active in the cause. He wrote a circular letter in French with Jeremiah (or Jeremy) Duggan on September 16 (the day that the sick Schuyler handed over command to Montgomery), then another on September 18, both a summons to arms of the *habitants* at La Pointe Olivier. They said they were carrying out orders on behalf of the "General of the Bostonais" and in accordance with Schuyler's Proclamation. Lieutenant Governor Cramahé, in a letter to Lord Dartmouth of September 24,[13] said that "Major Duggan, formerly a barber, now a broken wheat merchant, and who has resided for some years upon that River [Sorel], can add no weight to their cause." He did not dismiss Livingston so lightly: "This gentleman is from the Province of New York, was licensed as an Attorney, but has not practiced for some years, turned wheat merchant, and has lived upon the Sorell these five or six years." Livingston, related to the great clan of New York (he was the cousin of Montgomery's wife, Janet) was to play a prominent part in the revolutionary movement, particularly in leading the 1st Canadian Regiment in the American Continental Army.

After Ethan arrived back at the American camp outside St. John's on September 14, he was assigned a further and more dangerous mission by Montgomery. Ethan wrote later that the purpose of the "second tour into Canada" was "nearly the same design as before."[14] Yet the aim was not merely reconnaissance and propaganda; it was actually to recruit *habitants* "in a regiment of Canadians," the "scale of power" now being enough to convince them to volunteer. Montgomery on September 19 wrote to Schuyler, saying, "I have sent Col. Allen to Chambly, in order to raise a corps."[15] Ethan left St. John's with "Captain John Dugan" (Jeremiah Duggan), his interpreter, and six or seven Canadians on September 17. The American militiamen on the expedition, it will be argued, also left St. John's with Ethan at the same time. Of the twenty Americans captured with Ethan, one was Irish, another Swiss; one gave his "place of abode" as Sheffield, Mass. (and quite possibly a neighbor of Ethan), one was from the Grants, while the rest were from Connecticut. It is therefore likely that they were all volunteers from Montgomery's Connecticut regiments, on the expedition to protect Ethan, his "guard,"[16] and to impress the *habitants* with a show of American force. (The British Army Return of August 1776, lists twenty-three rather than twenty-one American troops captured, quite possibly because two Americans were wounded and not put aboard the *Adamant.*)[17]

The first of many controversies over this expedition concerns Ethan's terms of service. John Brown too was on a scouting expedition. On July 22, 1776, in support of moves to recover Ethan from his captivity in New York, he signed a Certificate Respecting Colonel Allen:

> This certifies, that at the Isle-aux-Noix, at the time when Colonel Allen was sent on an enterprise in which he was taken prisoner, Generals Schuyler and Montgomery promised and engaged that in case Col Allen should have the misfortune to be taken prisoner, that every proper method should be taken for his redemption and exchange consistent with the rules of war in such cases.[18]

That Ethan's mission was not a mere scouting expedition is further confirmed by Levi Allen. He wrote to the Continental Congress on the same day asking that he be sent "under Flag" to the British fleet in New York to "recover Ethan Allen, together with the prisoners taken with him." Like Brown, Levi stated that there had been an understanding that Ethan would be exchanged if captured in "the hazardous enterprise in which he was taken." The curious thing is that, according to Levi, the understanding covered Brown as well as Allen (Levi is not the most reliable of sources). Though such things cannot be proved, it confirms the statement of Montgomery that the "hazardous enterprise" was not an attack on Montreal but an attempt to recruit Canadians in hostile territory. As a civilian leading uniformed troops, Ethan would not be protected by the rules of war and would have to be accorded priority in the urgent matter of a prisoner exchange.

Despite the fact that Allen had no command or mandate to lead troops in action, he was actually sent by Livingston on military operations:

> Yesterday morning I sent a party each side the river, Col. *Allen* at their head, to take the vessels at *Sorel,* if possible, by surprise. Numbers of people flock to them, and make no doubt they will carry their point. I have cut off the communication from *Montreal* to *Chambly*. We have nothing to fear here at present, but a few Seigneurs in the country, endeavouring to raise forces. I hope Col. *Allen's* presence will put a stop to it.[19]

The only American troops north of St. John's were a detachment of Green Mountain Boys, with troops from other regiments, stationed around La Prairie, on the south bank of the St. Lawrence. Warner had arrived at the Ile-aux-Noix on September 16 with 170 Green Mountain Boys; the troop had left Ticonderoga with fifty more, but these mutinied and remained at Crown Point, while Captain Ebenezer Allen's company, "every man of which was raised in Connecticut," arrived at Ticonderoga on the 19th.[20]

At La Prairie, the St. Lawrence had not yet narrowed to a quarter of a mile, about ten miles downstream at Longueuil. It is probable that some of Warner's regiment were at Longueuil, since Chaplain Benjamin Trumbull recorded in his journal that Warner was sent off to both centers; John Fasset recorded that the biggest part of the regiment left the American encampment for La Prairie on September 22.[21] If some were at Longueuil, they were likely a minority of the total force: Governor Carleton easily drove off the enemy and burnt the makeshift fort at Longueuil when he crossed the river soon after Ethan's capture. Major Brown probably took a route parallel to that of Ethan, down the west bank of the Sorel (now the Richelieu), as Livingston's letter to Montgomery indicated. Whether he had any men from Col. Easton's regiment with him is not recorded, but it is unlikely: two hundred of these were sent north in bateaux from Ticonderoga, starting with a group of sixty only on September 19.[22] In a letter written by Quebec Lieutenant Governor Cramahé on September 24, he said that Brown with two hundred men on the 18th had been defeated by a detachment of half that number, "comprised of some troops and Canadian gentlemen."[23] In fact, only a hundred of Brown's troops were on their feet and fit for duty. It is unlikely that Brown on his scouting expedition had any New England troops or militia with him, unless the "party" sent with Ethan was shared with Brown. Most or all of his men, said by Ethan again to number nearly two hundred,[24] were Canadian, no more reliable than those of Ethan's proved to be.

Ethan sent a letter to Montgomery on the 20th, from St. Ours on the Sorel, saying that he had 250 Canadians under arms and implied that they were with him on the march. He was optimistic that he could double that number: "as I march, they gather fast." Allen made it clear that he would return to St. John's in three days, with five hundred or more Canadians.[25] Ethan moved from Chambly towards Sorel, where the river joins the St. Lawrence, according to the task he had received from Livingston.[26] Brown and Warner were at La Prairie, up river from Longueuil. Montgomery at

St. John's had learned that all three had a project of making an attack on Montreal. Montgomery forwarded the news to Schuyler:

> Allen, Warner and Brown are at LaPrairie and Longeuil, with a party of our troops, and some Canadians; how many I cannot tell. They speak well of the good disposition of the Canadians. They have a project of making an attempt on Montreal. I fear the troops are not fit for it. Mr Carleton has certainly left that Town, and it is in a very defenseless situation.[27]

When and from whom Montgomery got this information, and how reliable it was, is not known. Possibly he got a message, directly or indirectly, from Ethan. Whether there was to be a joint expedition with Brown and Warner has yet to be examined.

Allen too, no doubt, had got the false news of Carleton's departure and a report that ships at the port of Montreal were loaded with munitions and supplies for evacuation to Quebec. His letter to Montgomery of September 20 shows that he thought that Carleton himself was aboard the vessels at Sorel. But in that letter, he said that "these objects I pass by," to return and "assist the Army besieging St. Johns." This was contrary to the instructions he had received from Livingston. So, instead of returning directly to St. John's, along the Sorel River, he headed up the St. Lawrence, towards Longueuil and La Prairie. This took him four days instead of the three days or thereabouts promised for St. John's. Ethan wrote in his *Narrative* that, after he had reached La Prairie, he planned to return to Montgomery's camp outside St. John's.[28] Unless he had already planned an assault on Montreal, the detour along the St. Lawrence is hard to explain. In the *Extract of a Letter From a Gentleman in Quebeck to His Father in Ayrshire, Scotland, dated September 30, 1775*[29] the author wrote: "Some of the rebel prisoners, who are *Canadians*, inform us that *Allen* hired them at the rate of fifteen pence per day, and moreover promised them their share of the plunder of *Quebeck* and *Montreal.*" The phraseology used in this letter suggests (no more) that the assault on Montreal was not planned on the spur of the moment, the day before the event took place.

On the 24th, Ethan and about eighty men set out from Longueuil for La Prairie. There is something curious about this number. James Livingston claimed to have three hundred men at his camp at St. Mathieu and he sent "a party" with Ethan on the mission to Sorel, how strong is not certain. There were also the six or seven Canadians who had left St. John's with Ethan. Livingston said that Canadians were "flocking" to Ethan and Brown, so the balance were those that Ethan had picked up en route. Livingston had no idea that Allen intended to attack Montreal, for which he would have needed far more men, which is possibly the reason why Allen later claimed that the attack had only been planned on the afternoon of the 24th, after he had left Livingston's camp. There is also the suspicion that when Allen said he had 250 Canadians under arms he was including at least some of Livingston's 300, since there is no evidence that Ethan had recruited any more than his eighty, minus those he had started with at St. John's and the "party" supplied to him by Livingston.

About two miles out of Longueuil, the party encountered Brown. According to Ethan's account, it was Brown who put forward the plan to attack Montreal.[30] Ethan claimed that he had been reluctant to go on this second foray, preferring to take part in the siege of St. John's. Respect for General Montgomery persuaded him to go. A more likely explanation is that he wanted to restore his military reputation in order to regain command of the Green Mountain Boys or to become a Continental colonel. He was en route, "preaching politics" from Longueuil to La Prairie, back to Montgomery's camp, when he met with Major Brown, who proposed the plan to cross to the island of Montreal the same night in two places, Longueuil for Allen and La Prairie for Brown. They would then surprise the city from two vantage points.

Allen returned to Longueuil, added about thirty "English Americans" to his party, and crossed to the island on the night of the 24th in three trips by canoe. He expected Brown's party to appear "on the other side of the town," each party to give three cheers to confirm that they had landed. When Brown failed to appear, Allen found himself "in a premunire" and sent messengers back to Brown at La Prairie and to Thomas Walker at l'Assomption, requesting "speedy assistance." An escaped prisoner told Carleton of the small size of Allen's force, which caused the former to change his plan to flee by boat to Quebec. Carleton advanced with thirty-four regular troops, thirty English merchants, about three hundred Canadians of all social classes, with a number of Onondaga and Mohawk Indians, greatly outnumbering Allen's force. In the fight that followed, Ethan sent Duggan with about fifty Canadians to the right as a flank guard and Richard Young with nine men to his left. All deserted (or simply escaped). Allen was down to forty-five in the center, some wounded. His flanks turned, Allen retreated, hotly pursued by the men "of the country" (not the British regulars) and their Indians. He was unable to cross to the mainland since the canoes had already left with those of the escapees they could hold. He surrendered with thirty-one men and seven wounded.[31] The British account lists twenty American troops captured, and eleven Canadians, which reflects Allen's tally exactly. The wounded were taken to hospital, the Canadians and the Americans transported to England. A Recapitulation of rebel prisoners taken to August 10, 1776, gives one officer (Allen) and thirty-five men taken at Long Point on September 25.[32] The *List of Rebel Prisoners Put Aboard the Adamant* of November 9, 1775, shows that the British were well aware of Allen's true status: "Ethen Allen, stiling himself Colonel but without a command."[33]

The figures, however, do not quite add up, since not all of the twenty American prisoners listed were captured with Ethan. Two of the American prisoners were "taken" elsewhere than Montreal Island. Perhaps these are the two recorded as captured at Sorel in the Recapitulation of August 10, 1776, in addition to one officer (Allen) and thirty-five men taken at Long Point.[34] One American, William Stewart, was wounded and not listed as confined on the *Adamant*; there was possibly one other. The list of eleven Canadians matches Ethan's number, with the addition of one more "taken carrying Letters and Messages" and not captured at Long Point. The thirty "English Americans" that Ethan added to his force are something of a mystery: the best explanation is that they were all American troops, twenty-one of whom were captured with Ethan, including at least one wounded. The rest would have escaped by boat or they were among the stragglers "not yet in" that Duggan reported to Warner on the 27th; understandably, because there were too many escapees for the canoes to carry. The remainder had to make their own way off the Island and to safety.

On August 12, 1776 Ethan Allen wrote to the Connecticut Assembly from Halifax jail in Nova Scotia.[35] He set down a list of nineteen prisoners "taken with me" and stated that thirteen Canadians were captured with him, of whom one had died. Ethan's list was reproduced exactly in the documents of the Connecticut State Archives.[36] The list matches nineteen of the twenty on the British roster. One name, John Venamy, is omitted from the Connecticut list; this is either a mistake on Allen's part or it is because Venamy was "taken by Col. Maclean" of the Royal Highland Emigrants and thus not on Montreal Island.

"English Americans" is also a curious expression, since most of the Americans on Montgomery's expedition were of English or British origin. Some could of course have been His Majesty's "Old Subjects," the Protestant merchants and artisans of the Montreal area, who were American or British. But this would have left little room for the American troops in the tally of a hundred and ten men, some of whom were, without doubt, captured by the British. Possibly, Ethan had something to hide or at least not make generally known, namely that he had, contrary to orders, assumed an active military command. Here he trod a delicate line, because he wanted to present the assault on Montreal as a bold and audacious move comparable to the capture of Ticonderoga, yet he could not present his leadership as the illegitimate assumption of command that it was.

Historians have accepted Ethan's account, blaming Brown for his capture and probably the failure to take Montreal.[37] Zadock Thompson in the mid-nineteenth century accused Brown of cowardice and, recently, Willard Sterne Randall has contended that Brown lost his nerve.[38] These allegations about Brown are quite implausible: DePuy in 1859 blamed Brown only for failing to notify Ethan of a change of plan, which was echoed by Walter Crockett in 1921.[39] Until he was killed in the Mohawk Valley in October 1780,[40] he distinguished himself in every action: at the capture of Chambly (October 1775); at the surrender of the British fleet on the St. Lawrence (November 1775); at the siege of Quebec (December 1775) and the assault on Burgoyne's Ticonderoga positions (September 1777). In short, he was a hero of the American Revolution.

Ethan's account in the *Narrative* is dubious at several points. First, Ethan gives the impression that he was on his way back to St. John's when Brown made the proposal to attack Montreal. But Montgomery had already been informed of a plan by Allen, Brown and Warner to assault Montreal. Allen could indeed have sent a runner to Montgomery on the 24th, informing him of the plan, but he had no contact with Warner, whom Montgomery had been informed was a party to the project. Further, Brown was a good soldier from Easton's regiment, unlikely to disobey instructions. He was on a scouting mission and had no mandate to attack Montreal. Second, the plan paints a picture of a small walled town. Two parties of Americans would pop up like a jack-in-the-box on opposite sides of the town, give three cheers to each other to confirm their mutual presence and take the residents by surprise. The reality was different. Montreal was a city of nearly nine thousand; unless the residents were widely sympathetic, it could not be held by a few hundred *habitants,* nor taken if the majority of the citizens were unsympathetic and it were garrisoned at even minimal strength.

Ethan's idea that Brown would land "on the other side of the town" is preposterous: the two parties were to be at least two miles from the suburbs.[41] Carleton's estimate was three miles. The three huzzas would have been pointless since the two parties would have been several miles apart and both on the southeastern side of the city, not on opposite sides. They would have needed runners to make contact with each other. As for the desertion of the English Americans and the *habitants,* it is clear that they never expected to have to fight. They were only there for the loot and, it is said, feared capture and hanging for treason. The most damning consideration of all is that Brown knew Montreal and its environs from his subversive expedition to the city earlier in March, and is extremely unlikely to have endorsed the plan of attack, based as it was on a total ignorance of the location of Montreal and its place on the Island.

Sending messages to Brown and Thomas Walker (who was soon to be arrested by Carleton) was a futile act of desperation: Brown could not supply significant reinforcements, at least right away, and Walker was too far away on the north side of the St. Lawrence to provide any assistance at all. The most logical thing would have been to appeal to Livingston, but he would have been exasperated to learn that Ethan was on the Island and attacking Montreal. What, if anything, Brown had proposed, is unclear. The most plausible speculation is that Carleton was believed have left Quebec as part of a military evacuation. A show of force outside Montreal would induce a delegation of "virtuous disposed gentlemen" to meet Allen, in order to surrender the city, as happened on November 12, with Montgomery on its outskirts. Carleton in his report surmised that Allen "expected to march in without opposition" with "all in the suburbs, some in the town and many from the neighbouring parishes" joining the invaders.[42] Allen did not expect to have to attack the city, nor did his *habitants.* In all, it was a case of what Schuyler feared: Ethan's "impatience of subordination."

Apart from Warner, who made no written comment, the condemnation of Ethan was universal. Montgomery wrote to Schuyler on September 28:

> I have to lament Mr Allen's imprudence and ambition, which urged him to this affair *single handed,* when he might have had considerable reinforcement.[43]

Montgomery enclosed a letter from James Livingston, written the previous day:

> Mr Allen should never have attempted to attack the Town without my knowledge, or acquainting me with his design, as I had it in my power to furnish him with a number of men.[44]

Major Timothy Bedel, whose New Hampshire regiment was with Montgomery outside St. John's (and from whose camp Ethan had departed) wrote, "I am sorry things were not done more prudently, Sir."[45]

Ethan's account is really an attempt to explain away the fiasco of his capture, with the implication that Brown was to blame. Seth Warner plays no part in Ethan's account. How many men he had with him at La Prairie is uncertain. Schuyler on September 20 had reported to Washington that there were 170 Green Mountain Boys at Ile-aux-Noix, to be joined by about seventy men from Captain Ebenezer Allen's company; these were added to the 1,394 American troops already at Ile-aux-Noix.[46] Montgomery in his return of men sent northward from Ile-aux-Noix stated that Colonel Warner had 132 men with his Regiment.[47] So it is likely that Warner had about this number around La Prairie, supplemented by two companies of the 2nd New York Regiment. Chaplain Benjamin Trumbull's journal stated that "On the 21st, Colonel Warner was sent off from Colonel Beadle's encampment with a Detachment of 200 men to LaPrairie and Longueuil."[48] Warner had no orders to advance on Montreal, and Ethan had lost his command over the Boys. The fact remains that Warner's force was the only one that had even the beginnings of credibility for an attack on Montreal. For this, the great majority of his troops would have had to be at Longueuil with sufficient boats to cross the river. Neither of these was the case. Warner informed Montgomery of Ethan's capture on September 27 while Cramahé reported the same to Lord Dartmouth on September 30.

Ira Allen's short account,[49] written long after Brown, Warner and Allen were dead, differs from Ethan's. According to this account, which Ira got, no doubt, from the horse's mouth, Warner as well as Brown was at the meeting with Ethan. If there were any Green Mountain Rangers at Longueuil, Ethan would have learned that the bulk of Warner's troops were at La Prairie. Warner and Brown were to cross to the island from La Prairie and Ethan from Longueuil. Since the two parties were nine miles distant from each other, they agreed "upon principles of honour" that if, for any reason, either party was unable to cross the river, "early notice should be given to the other." The night was windy and the pair at La Prairie judged it too dangerous to cross, without notifying Ethan. "The conduct of Brown and

Warner is hard to be accounted for, on any principles honourable to themselves." This is the earliest suggestion that Brown and Warner were responsible for Ethan's capture.

Ira's account too is suspect, because both Brown and Warner were experienced soldiers who probably would not have broken such a clear undertaking and left Ethan's group in the lurch. They would not have been deterred by a turbulent river, nor was Ethan. It was, however, far less practical to navigate the St. Lawrence from La Prairie than from Longueuil, the former requiring a two-mile crossing, all the more reason why Brown should not have given any commitment to Ethan. It is quite understandable that Ethan should have left the Green Mountain Boys out of his account, for he did not want to cast a slur on what was since 1776 a regiment of the Continental Congress. Nor would it have helped his leadership in Vermont to criticize his own kind. The whole episode is cloudy and all explanations are speculative. The most plausible speculation is that Ethan told the story to Ira but reversed the terms of the alleged agreement with Brown and Warner: they were actually to let Ethan know if they were indeed to attempt a crossing. But Ethan, impulsive and ambitious as always, crossed anyway. He appealed for help to Brown and Walker only when he was on the verge of defeat.

A further suggestion comes from Seth Warner's report to Montgomery.[50] No conclusions can be drawn from this letter, only impressions. The dominant impression is that Warner was surprised to hear on September 26 the news of Allen's defeat, but with no indication of his fate, as if he did not know that Allen had crossed the river to the Island. He had already written the letter when Captain Duggan arrived at La Prairie on the morning of the next day, confirming that Allen "is absolutely taken Captive." So he added this as a postscript to the letter. There is further evidence that Allen acted alone, in an unsigned letter, written in Philadelphia and possibly to the Continental Congress, on October 20, 1775:

> By accounts from Canada we learn that, on the 25th of September last, Colonel Ethan Allen, prompted by ambition, had imprudently, without orders, crossed over from Longeuil, with thirty of his own men and fifty Canadians, in order to get possession of Montreal.[51]

Washington echoed these sentiments when he wrote to Schuyler a few days later, condemning Allen as of a sort "too ambitious to outshine their general officers" with results "destructive to themselves."[52] The rest of the letter of October 20 underestimates the Patriot losses and overestimates those of the enemy, but the message is clear: Allen "without orders" had colluded with no one and was entirely responsible for his own defeat.

Here again, we have the thirty Americans, of whom at least twenty were from Connecticut regiments. Since Warner was said to have been sent to Longueuil as well as La Prairie, could they have been Green Mountain Boys? Zadock Thompson claimed that the troops at Long Point were a mixed force of Green Mountain Boys and Canadians.[53] One prisoner, William Stewart, whom Ethan later described as "one of the "Old Green Mountain Core," was wounded.[54] Ethan said that he recovered and was sent with the other prisoners to England[55] but his name does not appear on any of the lists of prisoners taken on September 25. It is possible that there was a second wounded prisoner, again not transported to England: Gideon Brownson, the cousin of Ethan's wife or Ethan's brother-in-law, Isaac Brownson. Neither of these was with Ethan in the assault on Ticonderoga; they may have been at Hand's Cove on the night of May 9. But the contention that they were wounded and captured on September 25 is made only in secondary sources.[56] Warner would have been outraged if Ethan had taken command of his men, especially Gideon, an officer of the Green Mountain Rangers, but when he wrote to Montgomery it is unlikely that he knew of anything that had transpired at Longueuil. He would have learned of the fate of his men only at the capture of Montreal or the British fleet, early in November. However, a second wounded prisoner was unlikely to have been Gideon Brownson since John Fasset recorded in his diary that he had seen him at Warner's camp on November 12. It is possible that some of the thirty were Green Mountain Boys, but the most likely origin of these troops was that they had been sent by Montgomery to accompany Allen when he left St. John's on September 17. In a letter of July 11, 1776, General Charles Lee referred to "the Connecticut privates who were taken prisoners with Allen."[57]

Ethan Allen as a Military Commander

Ethan's achievement in capturing Ticonderoga was both lesser and greater than the impression that was first created by his *Narrative*. With great efficiency and enterprise, it was the Committee of War which organized the expedition and, contrary to Ethan's claim, to have "cut off all intelligence between the garrison and the country," and it was the Committee, not Ethan, which arranged to block the approaches to Ticonderoga. Ethan was the overall field commander and to him goes the credit for Ticonderoga, though not the successes at Skenesborough and Crown Point. But the entire expedition could not have succeeded without Ethan's leadership of the Green Mountain Boys: what is striking is both the numbers involved and the speed by which the Boys were mobilized.

Ethan more than kept his promise to supply a hundred men. Most of the assault force was collected between the meeting at Castleton on the May 8th and the morning of the assault, with the actual crossing of the lake taking place before dawn on the 10th. This mobilization was extremely rapid. There are two possible factors which contributed to the achievement. The first was the decision at a convention at Manchester in January 1775 to properly arm the Green Mountain Boys for the defense of a provisional government in the Grants.[58] So it may have been that the Boys became more of an organized, standing regiment of irregular troops and less a band of vigilantes whose principal function was to harass and expel unarmed civilians, the Yorker tenant farmers, surveyors and officials. At the same time, the numbers involved suggest that some of those at Hand's Cove were not Green Mountain Boys but simply responded automatically to a call to arms. Some were recruited from areas to the north of the companies of Green Mountain Boys in Bennington, Rupert, Socialborough, Stillwater, Danby, Poultney and Arlington. The rapidity of the mobilization is all the more impressive because the majority of the Green Mountain Boys knew nothing of the project to capture Ticonderoga before recruiting began at Bennington on May 2. Take this observation from one of those on the expedition, who later became a Loyalist: "The party was mustered on the spur of the moment, scarcely anybody then having thought or heard enough.... To decide whether they would be liberty men or King's men."[59]

No one has ever questioned Ethan's charisma in getting the Boys to follow him, nor his personal bravery in the engagement outside Montreal. But the latter was really the only time that Ethan was ever in battle, since his retreat from St. John's was immediate and the enemy surrendered at Ticonderoga almost without a fight. Ethan in his *Narrative* tried to present the attack on Montreal as a bold and aggressive move, comparable to Ticonderoga, in accordance with Montgomery's aim of capturing the city, which the American commander did in November. Ethan implied that he failed because he had been let down by John Brown, which was specifically alleged by Ira. There was in fact a pattern to Ethan's failure: disobeying instructions and attacking "without orders" in the case of Montreal, and going against the advice of Benedict Arnold in the case of St. John's. Ethan omitted the St.

John's fiasco altogether from his *Narrative*, which was disingenuous to the point of dishonesty, since it was a principal reason why he lost the command of the Green Mountain Boys.

Supposing that Ethan had received a command, can we imagine him leading Allen's Rangers, in the manner of the British raids along the Mohawk Valley from Oswego? We could indeed: Ethan was a frontiersman who knew the ways of the Indians and could survive in the wild, in all weathers, for weeks on end. He was a natural leader of men. The trouble is that there is no reason at all to believe that he would have carried out his orders, then returned to base at the right time. Of those whom Benedict Arnold characterized as "wild men," Ethan was at their head. He was both magnificent and hopeless, and finally too willful and disobedient to have been a successful commander. His contribution to Vermont was still enormous, and one thing that made him so influential was the prestige he got from the capture of Ticonderoga. But a warrior hero of the American Republic? Never.

CHAPTER 5

Carleton's Campaign of 1775–1776

THE GOVERNOR OF QUEBEC in 1775 was an experienced soldier, Major-General Sir Guy Carleton. Critics at the time described him variously as cold, distant, reserved or morose; he was in fact an accomplished soldier and statesman, a Francophile at a time when the prime enemy was France. He was also a deeply humane man. In all of his actions, it is possible to see political considerations as having a primacy over humanitarian motives. For instance, he treated wounded American prisoners in 1776 with the utmost concern, in order to induce the rebels to compromise. While Commander-in-Chief in New York during the peace negotiations of 1782–83, he considered that the promises made to African-Americans who escaped to British lines were more important than honoring a solemn agreement with the enemy to return them to servitude. His main achievement to date was the Quebec Act of 1774, which accorded religious freedom to Catholics, some limited political privileges and the preservation or restoration of the French property rights and legal system. Carleton's thinking, which he shared with his predecessor, James Murray, was that Quebec should form the bastion of British power in North America, that it would be easier to win the loyalty of His Majesty's New Subjects, the French, than to rely on the Anglophones of the Thirteen Colonies. The Quebec Act represented a great feat of imagination. In securing the loyalty of the *noblesse* and the clergy, he was successful. He was afraid, certainly, that the Anglo-American merchants in the province might offer material help to the American rebels; but the capture of the lake forts and Benedict Arnold's successful foray against St. John's in May took him by surprise. The prime enemy was no longer the Most Christian King of France.

When Carleton returned from his sojourn in England in September 1774, he was optimistic to the point of euphoria.[1] His warm welcome induced him to believe that His Majesty's Canadian Subjects were so enamored of the Quebec Act that their enthusiastic loyalty to the Crown could be counted on, without reservation, so that he could raise a regiment (or more) for the King. The Commander-in-Chief, Thomas Gage, desperately needed troops to keep order in Massachusetts, so when he asked for the 10th and 52nd Regiments, Carleton willingly acceded, leaving him only with the understrength 7th and 26th Regiments, and some "Fusileers at Quebec." When Carleton marched to Montreal at the head of the 7th Regiment on May 23, 1775, Quebec was almost completely denuded of regular troops, "not one soldier in the town."

All told, Carleton had fewer than eight hundred regulars in the province, of whom "not six hundred are fit for duty."[2] Of the eight hundred, almost five hundred were with Major Charles Preston in St. John's (St Jean), nor was there a single warship, armed vessel, or "Place of Strength," "the ancient Provincial force enervated and broke to pieces." In addition to the regulars, he had the regiment of Royal Highland Emigrants, hardened Scottish veterans of the French and Indian War, under Colonel Allen MacLean, which became the 84th Regiment. In September 1775, there were eighty of these, plus twenty fusiliers and a militia company of French *habitants* to defend Montreal. When defeat was imminent in November, the Emigrants were disengaged and sent east for the defense of Quebec City, which Carleton knew was threatened by Arnold's force moving through Maine, along the Kennebec and Chaudiere rivers. The claim that the Emigrants were driven away by the rebels is not correct. By this time, MacLean's corps had increased to one hundred and twenty with sixty fusiliers, "but his militia have abandoned him."[3]

Carleton lost the opportunity to recruit Indians into his army. At least 1,600 Indians, mainly Iroquois (traditionally loyal), attended a meeting in Montreal, July 16–29, 1775 and, plied with gifts, pledged their loyalty to the Crown, though even then Carleton was skeptical about their reliability.[4] Apart from forty Abenaki sent to St. John's for deployment as scouts, Carleton did not recruit any Indians. He refused to allow them to be sent below the 45 degree latitude, the border of the province, despite urgings from Dartmouth and Gage. His reasons were partly humanitarian, caring for the safety of civilians in the Colonies against the ferocity of Indian invaders. But the predominant reason reflected the main strand of Carleton's policy: to do everything possible to return Americans to their loyalty. So most of the Indians in Montreal returned home, leaving a few to accompany Carleton in his defeat of Ethan Allen on September 25.

Carleton's attempts to mobilize the militia in 1775 were not successful. After an appeal for volunteers failed, he declared martial law and the mobilization of the militia on June 9, 1775. The senior clergy exhorted the *habitants* to obey the call but the response was poor. Three Rivers (Trois Rivières), Quebec City, and in a small way, Montreal, raised militia companies, but resistance elsewhere was strong. There was a surge in the recruitment of militia after the capture of Ethan Allen in September (about five hundred took part in the attempt to relieve St. John's the following month), but these mostly deserted and "numbers of them have taken arms against the Crown."[5] On the fall of St. John's, Carleton's remaining Indians deserted him too. Families of the *noblesse* volunteered in considerable numbers for the defense of Montreal and St. John's (thirty-six French officers were captured at St. John's, along with four officers of militia, of a total of seventy-nine Canadians).[6] A contingent of two hundred Canadians from Detroit did take part in the action at The Cedars in the following year, in line with a precedent: three hundred Canadians from Niagara had joined the campaign against Chief Pontiac in 1764. The Indian rebellion was just as much a threat to the French settlers as it was to the British garrisons. Ainslie claimed that there were 543 Canadian militia in the fortress of Quebec in November, after Carleton had expelled the unwilling.[7] In general, the predominant stance of the *habitants* was neutrality, with the activists supporting whichever side was in the ascendant at any one time, and reverting to neutrality when such advantage was lost. Carleton reported the fall of Chambly in a letter of October 25, 1775, remarking that both "the savages" and the Canadian peasantry "choose to be of the strongest side" and whenever there is a British setback, "they vanish."[8] The support that the Canadians gave to the Americans was mainly in the form of supplies and civilian labor, except those few hundred who joined the regiments of Livingston and Hazen in the American Continental Army.

Immediately after Carleton captured Ethan Allen, he sent a party over the river to Longueuil consisting of twelve regulars, officers and thirty militia. These drove off the enemy, a detachment of the Green Mountain Boys, and seized the stores that they had acquired in Canada. Montgomery, meanwhile, had on September 17 or 18 invested St. John's, which was garrisoned by five hundred and fifty regulars of the 7th and 26th Regiments, forty gunners and the French under Francois Marie de Belestre. A month later, on October 15, Montgomery sent Brown and Livingston, along with a hundred and fifty regulars, three hundred Canadians and two nine-pounder guns on the short but difficult route to Chambly. After a two-day siege, Major the Hon. Joseph Stopford surrendered ten officers, seventy-eight troops, thirty women and fifty-one children. Even worse, he failed to destroy or dump into the river a vast supply of food, ammunition, powder and guns.

The need to relieve St. John's became acute, so on October 30 Carleton led a force across the river, hoping to land at a point upriver from the Americans at Longueuil.

According to John Fasset, a Canadian prisoner revealed after the operation that the total force was 660, which included a hundred regulars, a few Indians and the remarkably high number of around five hundred Canadians. They were equipped with forty bateaux and smaller boats. But the place of the assault was mistaken and the first wave was fired on by a detachment of ten American troops. These were part of a total force of 170, mainly Green Mountain Boys under Warner, with elements of the 2nd New York Regiment. Carleton drew away from the shore and out of range. Warner left thirty of his troops in the fort and sent the rest with at least one four-pounder cannon to the shoreline, where they fought an extended engagement, as some of the assault force tried to wade onto the rocky south shore before Carleton withdrew.

A hearsay report is recorded in *A Journal Kept in Quebec in 1775* by Thomas Jeffrey.[9] Jeffrey had heard that Warner had suffered thirty or forty killed or wounded, but this is without foundation. Zadock Thompson (1842) wrote that Carleton's force was thrown into confusion and soon retreated with precipitation and disorder, while Daniel Chipman (1858) said the same thing in almost the same words.[10] The Americans claimed that Carleton suffered the loss of forty to fifty with a similar number of wounded.[11] The Americans also claimed a lower figure of between twenty and thirty killed, which accords with Fasset's estimate.[12] Carleton reported the loss of Chambly[13] and later, St. John's.[14] Surprisingly, neither Carleton nor his Lieutenant-Governor, Hector Theophilus de Cramahé, reported on the repulse at Longueuil, which they surely should have done, considering that the relief expedition was a major effort with significant casualties. In addition to the fatalities, the invaders lost three or four as prisoners, one of whom verified the failure of the expedition when taken to Preston at St. John's. Carleton was a courageous and enterprising soldier who invariably led from the front and who had been wounded four times in his long military career. But he failed to achieve a "lodgment" on the south shore, which was the essential preliminary to the relief of St. John's, so he suffered a resounding defeat.

St. John's was now exposed, short of food and ammunition. Montgomery turned the cannon and mortars from Chambly on the fort. He had bought off the Caughnawaga with four hundred pounds sterling and used civilian labor outside the fort, with the promise of plunder. On getting reliable information that the relief of his garrison had failed at Longueiul, Major Preston surrendered on November 2 with 536 officers and men, seventy-nine Canadians and eight English volunteers. Carleton's letter of November 5 gives the date of surrender as November 3; the Articles of Capitulation Proposed by Major Preston are dated November 2.[15] This, along with the rebuff at Longueuil, was the greatest setback in the campaign, drastically reducing confidence in the British cause. One result was the desertion of the remaining militia, a reversal of the trend following Ethan's capture. Another was Carleton's descent into extreme pessimism. The prospects for Montreal were, he considered, now poor and the inhabitants would surrender without reinforcements. He wrote on November 5 to Dartmouth that he would try to postpone "the evil hour" but "all my hopes of succour begin to vanish." The prospects for the fortress of Quebec were not much better. He had received word that Benedict Arnold was on the Chaudiere with 1,200–1,500 men, while he had "not one soldier in the town," and the Lower Town was no more loyal than the suburbs of Montreal. This resulted in the disengagement of the Highland Emigrants and their dispatch to Quebec.

As for a relief force, Carleton's fears were justified. On October 12, Sir William Howe, now the Commander-in-Chief in Boston, wrote to Carleton,[16] saying that it was impossible to meet Carleton's request for troops, received by Gage on October 10; it was "impracticable to send a battalion by water to Quebec." This was acknowledged by Lieutenant-Governor Cramahé on November 9. Meanwhile, Carleton had decided to evacuate Montreal. He loaded small, armed ships and eight small transports with all the guns, arms and supplies they could carry, destroying the rest. Carleton left Montreal on November 11 in the sloop *Gaspee.*

Montgomery, in the meantime, had sent a detachment under John Brown to Sorel, where he got guns across to a small island in the river, the Ile-du-Pas, interdicting the narrow channel through which Carleton's fleet would have to run to get to Quebec City. Adverse winds stalled the progress of the fleet. So Carleton left the ships and departed in a longboat by night, eventually arriving at Quebec on the 19th after a perilous journey. The American assumption that Carleton fled is not correct: he was anxious to get to Quebec to lead its defense. On the 17th, the winds changed in favor of the fleet but the officers declined to run the gauntlet of guns, partly due to a bluff on the part of Brown's force. (Brown indeed was a great bluffer, though a similar attempt to induce the surrender of Ticonderoga in September 1777 failed.) The guns and arms were dumped overboard and the fleet surrendered, along with its most senior officer, Brigadier-General Robert Prescott. Among the prisoners released were Thomas Walker and Moses Hazen, who had been arrested on suspicion of collusion with the enemy. Hazen went on to great things but Walker was given a laissez passer to Philadelphia and arrived in Albany with his family in a querulous sulk during the spring of the following year (he died in 1788).

Montreal had surrendered on November 13th. Article V of the generous Articles of Capitulation[17] declared that the citizens would not be compelled to fight against the mother country, nor to contribute to the war against her. Among those who signed as representatives of the city were John Blake of the Montreal Committee of Correspondence and two others, James Finlay and James McGill, who had signed petitions to the King—and would continue to do so in the future. Montgomery was well pleased with his victories but he was appalled by the British performance, especially the surrenders at Chambly and Sorel, saying that he feared for the British Army. He used the British fleet to transport his troops to join Benedict Arnold, whose army had arrived early in November, at the siege of Quebec.

On November 22, Carleton expelled from Quebec (both from the "Castle of St Louis" and the "District of Quebec") all those, with their families, who would not enroll or continue to serve in the militia.[18] He did this not only to defend the fortress against "certain rebellious Persons who have invaded this Province" but also "to rid the Town of all useless, disloyal and treacherous persons." From then on, he made no aggressive moves. The only expeditions outside the city were to gather firewood. Sporadic duels with the American artillery took place throughout the siege, at which the Americans were usually worsted. Montgomery was faced with the expiry of the terms of service of some of his troops on New Year's Day, 1776. Thus he and Arnold launched an assault on New Year's Eve (possibly early on the day before) with a diversion conducted by Livingston's Canadians and John Brown's Americans. In the assault by Arnold and Montgomery, the Americans lost thirty killed and 450 as prisoners, Arnold wounded and removed from the battle, while Montgomery was killed by a musket ball to the head. Carleton sallied out to destroy the American battery at Pointe La Roche, but otherwise took no offensive action. The Americans reinforced the besiegers with more troops and artillery; between the New Year and April, 1,200 men joined the besieging force.

On May 5, 1776, soon after the river was clear of ice, Carleton was reinforced by eighty sailors and a hundred men from a single regiment, the 29th. The same day, he led a charge of the new troops and the garrison against the Americans, who had already been ordered to retreat. They headed west in great disorder, abandoning their camps and what was left of their supplies and munitions. Still pursuing his policy of winning over the rebels, Carleton paused in his pursuit. On May 12, Carleton issued a Proclamation, requiring those who had been expelled from Quebec in November, as well as deserters, to obtain permission in writing to enter the "City of Quebec."[19] Two days earlier, he had issued another Proclamation which increased his reputation and prestige enormously. He ordered his militia officers to scour the adjacent woods and parishes for wounded rebels, convey them to the "General Hospital," and make it known to them that "as soon as their Health is restored, they shall have free Liberty to return to their expected Provinces."[20] The word of this spread among the retreating Americans and it had such an impact that Schuyler made attempts to segregate them from the troops in the State of New York, lest their morale plummet.

On June 1, Brigadier-Generals John Burgoyne and Baron Friedrich Adolph von Riedesel landed at Quebec with 8,000 British and German allied or mercenary troops in train, including the 24th Foot Regiment under Lieutenant-Colonel Simon Fraser, reported by Cramahé in a letter from Quebec to Germain of June 2, 1776.[21] Carleton was poised to destroy the remaining American troops after the victory at The Cedars (Les Cedres), west of Montreal, even though American reinforcements continued to arrive from the south.[22] But again he held back, allowing 7,000 American troops to escape: they evacuated in turn Montreal, Sorel and St. John's after an ill-fated offensive against the British positions in Three Rivers. Half of those who arrived at Ile-aux-Noix were chronically sick and on July 2, the American army retreated to Crown Point, which they then evacuated and destroyed, Arnold being the last American to leave Canada.[23]

The aim of the reinforcements from Britain was not merely to relieve Quebec and drive out the Americans, but to recapture Ticonderoga. However, few of the promised transports and shipbuilding materials had arrived from England, and the Americans had destroyed all remaining shipping in their retreat from St. John's. So Carleton had to embark on a major shipbuilding program at St. John's under the direction of General William Phillips. This caused a serious delay; in mid-July, when the campaign should have been well underway, Carleton wrote to Captain Forster at St. John's, promising the provisions that want of boats had prevented him from sending from Montreal.[24] When the ships were ready, Carleton sailed with the fleet and transports, decisively defeating Arnold's ships in October at the Battle of Valcour Island. The troops landed to find Crown Point deserted. Simon Fraser, now a Brigadier-General, was sent to reconnoiter Ticonderoga on October 27, and found it "crowded with troops." Despite the urgings of Burgoyne, Carleton decided against an attack on Ticonderoga or a feint, and early in November abandoned Crown Point and returned with his army to Canada.[25]

The whole of Carleton's campaign in 1776 has been criticized. Carleton knew well that he could not achieve much that year, owing to the need to build an invasion fleet and the consequent late start. Before that, he had done little more than send out patrols to the vicinity of Crown Point. He was further delayed for three weeks by Arnold's naval force and contrary winds. Carleton could not afford a long siege of Ticonderoga. To attack would have of course risked failure and a propaganda success for the Americans—the British forced to retreat back to Canada with their tails between their legs. Perhaps too he had in mind the experience of James Abercromby, whose 16,000 troops were repulsed in the "French Lines" outside Ticonderoga in 1758, with a loss of 15 percent of the attacking force. So there is a strong case for saying that Carleton made the correct decision. Even wiser was the decision to abandon Crown Point, where an exposed garrison would have been impossible to resupply or reinforce during the long winter and early spring. American historians contend that Arnold's naval engagement held up Carleton's force for three crucial weeks, resulting in the British failure. But over the whole year, three weeks was only a small part of the systematic delays in the British offensive and such delays were less important than the issue of what the British expected to achieve in the rclations between the forces in Quebec and those in New York.

Carleton assumed throughout the campaign of 1776 that Sir William Howe, the Commander-in-Chief of the British forces in North America, would not move north to meet his forces somewhere between New York and Ticonderoga. In September, he wrote:

> Unfortunately, the season is so far advanced that I dare not flatter myself I shall be able to do more, this campaign, than to draw off their attention, and keep back part of their force from General Howe, *who I doubt not is exerting himself to the southward*, though I have heard nothing from him since he left Halifax.[26]

The following month, he wrote from Crown Point:

> The season is so far advanced that I cannot yet pretend to inform your Lordship whether anything further can be done this year[27]

In November, back at Quebec, he wrote that he had contended in October that the army "must winter in Canada" and complained:

> I have heard nothing from General Howe, except by a letter containing a request to be supplied with Hay and Oats, and dated the day before an action is said to have happened upon Long Island. . . .[28]

All of Carleton's assumptions were correct and he was justified in returning his army to Canada. Lord Germain, the Secretary of State for the American Department since January 1776, following first Lord Hillsborough 1768, then Lord Dartmouth, took a different view. He wrote to Carleton on August 22, 1776 a letter which was not received until May 6 of the following year.[29] Carleton was to revert to civilian command and retain only those forces which were wanted for the protection of Canada. He was instructed to detach Burgoyne (or another suitable officer) with an expeditionary force to communicate with and put himself under the command of General Howe. In a further letter to Carleton of March 26, 1777, Germain said that in his letter of August 22, Carleton was supposed to return to Quebec with sufficient troops only to defend the province; the "principal object" of the continuing campaign in New York was to "effect a junction" with Sir William Howe. Burgoyne was to proceed "with all possible Expedition to join General Howe, and to put himself under his command." In order to quell the rebellion as soon as possible, "it is become highly necessary that the most speedy junction of the two armies should be effected." Germain even "had the mortification to learn" that Carleton's "repassing Lake Champlain" enabled "a considerable number of the insurgents" to march to New York and New Jersey, where they broke in "with some degree of success" to Howe's winter quarters. This was a reference to Washington's victory over the Hessians at Trenton in December 1776.[30]

It would be hard to find a more preposterous set of instructions and allegations. Though Howe commanded all the troops on the Atlantic seaboard, Carleton held an independent command and was not responsible to him, as he had been to Gage in Boston in 1775. In March 1776, Howe evacuated Boston and, in June, transported his troops from Halifax to Staten Island, New York. Germain wrote his letter on August 22, before Howe crossed to Long Island and defeated Washington on the 27th, that is, before he knew of Howe's movements and his impending success. Washington evacuated New York in September and Howe pursued him into New Jersey during the following two months. Howe had certainly not heard of any plans to link up with Carleton in the north. He assumed, quite wrongly, that a supply route to the north was open. All Carleton knew was that an action was said to have taken place on Long Island and that Howe had written to him on the day before. Carleton took it correctly that Howe was engaged in operations "to the southward," not to the north, where Carleton was stationed.

To write in August, even on the optimistic assumption that it would be received a couple of months later, that a major expedition should be undertaken, was far too late in the campaigning season to be anything more than a fantasy: it would have required a chain of supply back to Quebec and both logistical and tactical arrangements on Howe's part to effect the junction of the two armies. (Carleton in his letter to Germain of May 20, 1777 said that the letter of August 22 might at best have been received in "early November.") It is a mark of British strategic ineptitude that they made the same mistake in 1777, in a situation in which Burgoyne *knew* that he could expect no help from Howe until the end of the year at best. Carleton in 1776 was falsely accused of betraying what Germain had mistakenly alleged was the British strategy. For Germain to have blamed Carleton for the defeat at Trenton shows the utter venomousness of the man.

On May 20, 1777, Carleton responded to Germain's dispatch of August 22, 1776,[31] defending his conduct, disowning responsibility for Washington's success at Trenton, and alleging that the false accusation of poor performance was the "first reason" why the command had gone to Burgoyne. To this contention, Germain did not reply, only observing that the King had good reason to give the command, at the expense of Carleton, to Sir William Howe and his brother Richard, Admiral Lord Howe.[32]

Nor could Carleton have undertaken a land invasion down the west side of the lake. Not only was the terrain difficult but he was hampered by the lack of provisions. Burgoyne had suggested "to put myself at the head of only three British Battalions with a corps of artillery[,] some Canadians and a large body of Indians which we had at command, to [take] my route by Oswego and Fort Stanwix, and [establish] myself on the Mohawk River." Carleton strongly supported this idea, which was the prototype of the St. Leger raid in 1777, but abandoned it for lack of supplies. All told, it is hard to fault Carleton's performance before and during the expedition down the Lake. The one occasion in which his tactics can be faulted was in allowing the American forces to escape through St. John's to the Ile-aux-Noix. Not that the Americans gained much from the army that returned: Schuyler reported that most of those who returned to Ticonderoga were either sick or feigned sickness, anxious to go home. For all that, Carleton continued to believe in a compromise with the Americans even in August 1776, after the Declaration of Independence, and in contrast to Carleton's generosity in repatriating captured prisoners. There had been a cartel between Captain Forster and Arnold at The Cedars, allowing for an exchange of prisoners, but the Continental Congress repudiated this, because of the unpunished murder of two Americans by Indians.

Considering that his army was ill-fed, ill-paid, reluctant, unreliable, prone to disease and desertion, as well as being led by fractious, truculent, uncooperative officers, Montgomery's performance in 1775 was admirable. Brave and enterprising soldier as he was, his assault on the Lower Town of Quebec at the end of the year was the best of the alternatives open to him. The successive American commanders were faced with a similar choice in the first four months of 1776 but delayed their assault until their swollen army was laid low by disease and starvation, then driven away by Carleton, who did not wait for a single day to strike out with the meager reinforcements that he received on May 5.

Quebec Lieutenant Governor Cramahé despised "Mister" Montgomery, a former officer in the 7th Foot, "now styling himself Brigadier General" and refused to correspond with traitors. However, between Carleton and Montgomery, who had fought together at the siege of Havana in 1762, there was mutual respect. Montgomery addressed Carleton as "one of the most respectable servants of the Crown,"[33] and Carleton gave Montgomery a decent burial in Quebec. One dimension of the Revolutionary War is that it was led by two sets of British officers, previously colleagues with shared values but now on opposing sides. So it was with the two outstanding leaders, Carleton and Montgomery, the first American hero of the Revolutionary War.

Among the troops who returned to Quebec after Montgomery's failed assault were the Green Mountain Boys, more properly the Regiment of Green Mountain Rangers. During the retreat in the spring, they were among the American rearguards. Five days after the failure at Quebec, General David Wooster (an old enemy from the days of the feud with the Yorkers in the Grants) had written to Warner, urgently pleading for reinforcements. Both Washington and Schuyler were impressed with the alacrity of the response. Warner's "winter regiment," still under the auspices of the Provincial Congress of New York, arrived outside Quebec during February. By March 5, the regiment was 417 strong, fewer than the 736 men returned as "engaged" owing to the lure of the 40-shilling enlistment bounty that Schuyler had offered.

General Sullivan in a letter of January 18, 1776 wrote that the Green Mountain Boys had left the army "by being (as they thought) ill-used by General Montgomery."[34] It is possible that Warner had blamed Montgomery for an earlier situation in which the former considered that the Boys had been "ill-used." When St. John's surrendered, Warner was still at Longueuil; Montgomery ordered the Boys to prepare to pursue Carleton,[35] since their term of service expired only at the end of the year. But Montgomery had promised at St. John's to discharge the troops once Montreal was taken, so the Boys were in an ugly mood, and when Warner asked for volunteers, only a handful stepped forward. The officers then gave Warner a petition, contending that remaining with the army was "not proper as the circumstances were." Since the Boys were about to vote with their feet, Montgomery acquiesced, informing Schuyler in a letter of November 20, 1775 that "the rascally Green Mountain boys have left me in a breach after promising to go."[36] So the most likely explanation is that the Green Mountain Boys were no different from the rest of Montgomery's troops, many of them not anxious to serve in an extended Canadian campaign, as the mutiny of fifty of the Boys at Crown Point in the summer of 1775 indicated. For these men, the harvest was more important than the foray into Canada.

CHAPTER 6

The British Incursion into Vermont, 1777

WITH CARLETON'S BLESSING, Burgoyne left for England and arrived in mid-November 1776, taking with him the Governor's proposed plan for the campaign of 1777. The *Memoranda of General Carleton relative to the next Campaign communicated to Lt Gen'l Burgoyne to be laid before Government*[1] was really only the sketch of a campaign. Properly reinforced by troops from England, the main body would proceed by boat up the Lake, then down the Hudson to the Mohawk River. With enough troops, a "large Corps," commanded by Lieutenant-Colonel Barry St. Leger, could also be detached to proceed from Lake Ontario "to operate upon the Mohawk River." Further, "another Corps might possibly be employed to penetrate the Connecticut River." Carleton envisaged a detachment of the main body operating eastwards at the same time as the move south and not later, after a junction with Howe at Albany or at some point further south.

Burgoyne set down for Germain his observations on Carleton's proposed requisitions,[2] followed by his own *Thoughts on Conducting the War from the Side of Canada* on February 28, 1777.[3] The idea of sending the main body south was founded "upon the supposition that it be the sole Purposes of the Canada Army to effect a Junction with General Howe, or after cooperating in so far as to get possession of Albany, and open Communication to New York, to remain upon the Hudson's River, and thereby enable that General to act with his whole Force to the southward." This projection left it unclear as to what, if anything, Howe should do to "effect a junction": provided communication with New York were established, Howe would *then* be free to operate to the southward. If possible, a further force, commanded by St. Leger, would operate from Oswego along the Mohawk River. This reiterated Carleton's idea of a diversion from the American defense of Albany, where the two forces would later join up. If the enemy's forces were not too strong and if the British troops at Rhode Island were able to operate in the following spring, the most important purpose of the Canadian Army might be to "gain the Connecticut River." This proposal was again derived from Carleton; it would seem that it was contingent on the main force getting possession of Albany and dominating the Hudson. Should the route to the Connecticut River forts be protected by the Indian allies of the British and the forts themselves reinforced by further redoubts, it would be feasible to effect a junction with the Rhode Island forces so that "all the New England Provinces will be reduced by their Operations." Thus, for Burgoyne, the aim of the 1777 campaign was to enable Howe to operate "to the southward" and, in 1778, to cooperate with the British forces at Rhode Island to neutralize the New England provinces. How the British forces were to "effect a junction" was left unclear but there was some semblance at this time of a three-pronged offensive: Burgoyne, Howe and St. Leger. Thus Burgoyne would not be left stranded on the Lake or the Hudson, as Carleton had been in the previous year.

Burgoyne was quite open about his ambitions. He wrote to Germain on January 1, 1777, saying that he had lobbied the King for "active employment."[4] With the hint of an apology for going over his head, he hoped that Germain would support him in this endeavor. He also noted that he had a copy of Carleton's proposed plan for the 1777 campaign. At the same time, it is quite obvious that he intrigued with Germain to discredit Carleton. Germain alleged that Carleton had misused funds and supplies, while concealing his mistakes from the British in London.[5]

Howe had, late in 1776, envisaged an expedition north from New York to Albany. But by the end of December, he had, in view of the prospect of minimal reinforcements from England, changed his plan for a wide-ranging series of expeditions from New York. Before then, Philadelphia had been only one of several objectives; it was now to be the main focus of operations. This plan was known in London, even before Burgoyne had come out with his *Thoughts on Conducting the War from the Side of Canada* with Germain referring to Howe's "well digested plan for the operations of the next campaign."[6]

Germain approved the plan that Burgoyne had submitted in his *Thoughts*. But no orders were transmitted to Howe, only a copy of Germain's letter to Carleton of March 26, which Howe received on July 5.[7] In this letter, which contained no reference to the role of General Howe, Germain pointed out "that it is become highly necessary that the most speedy Junction of the two Armies should be effected." Carleton was to remain in Canada with a defense force of about 3,000 men while Burgoyne would "force his way to Albany" and St Leger would create a diversion on the Mohawk River. Carleton was superseded in command (as he had been since the dispatch of August 22, 1776) in that Burgoyne and St Leger were to put themselves under the command of Howe, once the "speedy junction" of the two armies had been effected.

Initially, Burgoyne had described "the sole purpose of the Canadian army" as "to effect a junction with General Howe" and this was endorsed on paper by Germain in his letter to Carleton of March 26. But how the junction was to take place was unclear. Far from indicating that Howe should play a positive part in the operation, the letter implied that the responsibility for the junction fell up upon Burgoyne and St Leger. Through Carleton, Germain instructed Burgoyne and St Leger to meet at Albany and take measures to secure the loyalty and obedience of the region's population. In doing so, they must never lose sight of their "principal object," a junction with Sir William Howe.

This drift of Germain's policy was actually confirmed by the response of Sir William Howe. As soon as he learned of the plans for the Northern Army but in the absence of clear instructions from Germain, Howe wrote a confidential letter to Carleton, on April 5, 1777. This letter set out his plans for the coming campaign. Carleton forwarded this letter to Germain on June 26.[8] Howe wrote that he was not strong enough to send a corps up the Hudson at the beginning of the campaign; Burgoyne's force, having taken Ticonderoga, could not rely on any assistance from here (New York), nor even communications from the Commander-in-Chief. He considered, however, that with Ticonderoga and Albany taken, the population, including the Indians, would prove to be so friendly to the King's cause that the rebellion could be suppressed without difficulty.

> In the mean while I shall endeavour to have a large Corps upon the lower part of Hudsons River sufficient to open Communications for Shipping thro' the Highlands, at present obstructed by several Forts erected by the Rebels for that Purpose, *which Corps may afterwards act in Favor of the Northern Army.*[9]

Instead of a speedy junction with Burgoyne, there was only a vague and tentative plan to "act in favor of the Northern Army" at some later date. Burgoyne's earlier tentative plan to have Howe operate "to the southward" *after* the junction of the two armies would not take place.

Burgoyne was acquainted in a general way with the plans for Howe through his contact with Germain in London. A little earlier, Howe had written to Germain on April 2, saying that the attack on Philadelphia would be late in the season and that the expedition would be sent by sea and river. This meant that he could not confine Washington between his own forces and those of Burgoyne. Howe delayed the dispatch of his letter and enclosed his letter to Carleton of April 5. Germain replied to Howe on May 18, saying that His Majesty had approved the change of plan (over the objective of Philadelphia), trusting that his operation will be executed "in time for you to co-operate with the army ordered to proceed from Canada and put itself under your Command."[10]

Howe did not receive Germain's letter of May 18 until August 16, when he was on the Chesapeake Bay. Howe replied on August 30, reiterating the stance he had taken in April, noting his Majesty's approval of the alteration of his plans (to advance on Philadelphia by water, later in the season), but saying that any move north was even less feasible, in view of the strength of the rebellion in his area of operations.[11] Burgoyne, by then well into his campaign, was isolated. All parties were gambling on the prospect that, if Burgoyne occupied Albany, the strength of Loyalism in the vicinity would ensure his safety until a possible "junction" at some unspecified time.

FROM DECEMBER 1776 HOWE had an evolving plan for his campaign of 1777. Overlaying Howe's project was Germain's plan for Burgoyne's expedition from Canada, which Howe was requested to assist. When Howe stated repeatedly that he was unable to do so in any timely fashion, there was no objection from Germain. Since the royal permission to forgo any advance north to Albany was quite definitive, Howe was the least to blame of the three principal players for the British defeat in the Saratoga Campaign. In the recriminations that followed Burgoyne's defeat, it was claimed that Germain made out orders for Howe in March to "join Burgoyne on the Hudson" but due to the Minister's inefficiency, these were never sent out. All that Germain promised in his March letters to Carleton was to inform Sir William Howe as soon as possible of the orders given to St Leger. In view of the fact that Germain's orders to Carleton and Burgoyne never even implied that Howe was to move north and Howe asserted, quite correctly, that his plans of April had been approved by the King, this apologia for Burgoyne's defeat lacks all credibility. Any such orders would only have contained the endorsement of Howe's plans that was issued on May 18. Even the copy of the letter that Germain wrote to Carleton on March 26, which Howe had not received when he wrote to Germain on April 2, contained no implication that Howe was to move north to Albany.

Burgoyne was told to "effect a junction" with Howe but there was never any guidance as to how this was to be done. Burgoyne undertook an expedition when there was every prospect that he would find himself in the predicament of Carleton in 1776; that is, with no indication that Howe would move north to effect a junction and, as it transpired, with Burgoyne not even in Albany. Germain, in trying to mount two major, interconnected, operations at the same time, had allowed the strategy for the northern force to slip away to its doom.

During June 1777, Burgoyne's fleet, with his army on board, moved down Lake Champlain to Ticonderoga. A return of the army on July 1 stated that Burgoyne had 5,724 British regulars, 3,016 German troops, 473 artillerymen, 250 Canadians and Tories and 400 Indians, a total of 7,863 fighting men. There were also 700 sailors. During June also, St Leger moved his force up the St. Lawrence to its starting point at Oswego, en route to Fort Stanwix on the Mohawk.[12] Burgoyne's force reached the abandoned Crown Point on June 30 and re-embarked for Ticonderoga on the following day. The great fort was not in a good state of defense, mainly because the Americans had thought that a British attack on the mainland would come by sea from Halifax and not up the Lake (a possibility that had indeed been envisaged by Burgoyne in his *Observations*). Schuyler had appointed a former British officer, Colonel Arthur St. Clair, as the fort's commandant and there he met with St. Clair and three brigadiers on June 19. The commanders agreed that both sides of the Lake should be defended, Ticonderoga on the west side and Mount Independence on the east. Should it be necessary to evacuate the positions, Ticonderoga should be the first to go. When the size of the invading British force became clear, the pressure to evacuate increased; but St Clair still thought the move was a mere feint. Apart from the garrison, Schuyler had only a further 700 men in the Northern Department, most stationed at Fort Edward.

To prevent the escape of the garrisons of Ticonderoga and Mount Independence, Burgoyne needed to block three exit routes: the waterway from Ticonderoga to Skenesborough; the creek connecting Lake Champlain to Lake George; and the wagon road leading from Mount Independence to Hubbardton and Castleton in the Grants. Burgoyne sent Fraser's brigade to seize Mount Hope at the outer limit of the Ticonderoga perimeter, which the Americans evacuated. This cut off the escape route to Lake George. In addition, he ordered von Riedesel's Germans on the east bank of the lake to circle around the isthmus, on the tip of which stood Mount Independence. Because of the marshes and the East Creek which protected the mountain from an easy attack, Riedesel was not able to complete the encirclement of the garrison before it retreated down the east side of the Lake. Thus the first British incursion into Vermont took place because of the British inability to encircle the garrison of Mount Independence or to channel the bulk of the American troops up the Lake to Skenesborough.

The British soon hit upon the great weakness of St Clair's defense. Mount Defiance, not garrisoned by the Americans for want of troops, overlooked both Ticonderoga and Mount Independence. The British noticed their tactical advantage on July 4. Their pioneers hacked a path up the mount and, the following day, hauled two guns onto the summit and opened fire on a vessel on the Lake. St Clair and his officers decided on an immediate evacuation, a move that was not challenged when St Clair was later court-martialed; though the evacuation cost Schuyler the command of the Northern Department. But Riedesel had still not cut the escape route from Mount Independence. At the most narrow channel of Lake Champlain, a heavy boom and bridge connected the two forts and provided a barrier, protecting the southern end of the lake from the progress of enemy shipping. The Americans loaded their bateaux with six hundred troops, the women of the garrison and as much of the stores as they could carry, protected by armed vessels. They rowed and sailed up to Skenesborough. The remaining troops, around 2,500, evacuated Mount Independence and escaped, with only a few shots aimed at the rearguard by Riedesel's forward contingent.

In a fast move, not anticipated by the Americans, the British smashed through the Lake barrier with naval guns and reached Skenesborough on their heels, destroying the boats anchored there and damaging Colonel Skene's estate. The Americans fought an engagement with the British at Fort Anne, then on July 9 retreated the thirty miles to join Schuyler at Fort Edward. By July 12, the whole of St Clair's army, debilitated but intact, had marched the 110 miles from Ticonderoga through Vermont to Fort Edward.

WHILE COMMANDING THE GREEN Mountain Boys, Seth Warner had been a leading participant in Vermont's move to independence. The Yorkers were outraged that such a figure should have been given command of the new regiment of the Continental Army, which was inaugurated on July 5, 1776. Thus Warner was now responsible to Washington or the commander of the Northern Department, not to New York. On January 20, 1777, the New York Provincial Congress demanded that Congress recall the commission of the outlaw Warner and his officers.[13] Recruiting for the regiment proceeded slowly. Many balked at the three-year term of service, or enlistment for the duration of the war, which was required. The Congress was hard-pressed to finance a regular Continental regiment since, as with the Canadian regiments of Livingston and Hazen, it could not rely on the states to provide pay, provisions and equipment. Warner pursued recruitment in the Grants and in Connecticut. He wrote to the Continental Congress on February 26, 1777, stating his difficulties over recruitment.[14] Schuyler had not released money to the regiment until November 16, 1776 and, even then, he was expecting a bounty from the New Hampshire Grants, "sufficient to compleat said regiment." Warner reported that the regiment was either at or on its way to Mount Independence, where conditions were appalling, as bad, it was said, as those at Valley Forge. By the spring, there were an estimated 173 Green Mountain Rangers at the Ticonderoga positions. The 350 said to be at the Battle of Hubbardton included militia under Warner's command, though probably not the Vermont militia, since the newly raised regiments of Colonels Benjamin Bellows and Joseph Olcott were not included in St Clair's rearguard.

On June 24, two days before Burgoyne occupied the abandoned post of Crown Point, the British raided the Vermont shore at the mouth of Otter Creek. The party of British, Germans, Indians and Tories under the command of Captain Alexander Fraser, included Justus Sherwood of the Queen's Loyal Rangers. St Clair sent Warner down from Ticonderoga with instructions to raise "a body of men," rout the enemy and return to Ticonderoga as soon as possible. After the raiding party was long gone, Warner wrote from Rutland on July 1 to the delegates of a convention, meeting in Windsor, who were working on a constitution for the new State of Vermont. He said that the commanding general had advised him that the enemy on the Lake were approaching and had ordered him to call out the militia "of this state" as well as those of New Hampshire and Massachusetts, to join him at Ticonderoga.

He also asked them to recruit militia from the east side of the Green Mountains and added that he hoped that recruiting would not be marred by the need to hoe "a few hills of corn."[15] Probably he remembered the mutiny of fifty Green Mountain Boys at Crown Point in 1775. The Convention forwarded Warner's letter to the General Court of New Hampshire on July 3.[16] By July 5, St Clair had about 900 Vermont militia at the Ticonderoga positions. Early on the next morning, they were in full flight down the wagon track to Castleton. The next day, St Clair wrote to the President of the Vermont Convention, reporting on the retreat and saying that, in view of the enemy occupation of Skenesborough, he was heading for Bennington. He asked that the militia be directed there as he was moving on to the Hudson "to place himself between the enemy and the inhabitants."[17]

The Americans were pursued by the British advance brigade under Simon Fraser, an elite force of 850 men brigaded with the 24th Regiment of Foot. Included were a battalion (actually closer to company strength) of grenadiers, strong men picked from the best of the other infantry regiments, under Major John Dyke Acland. The light infantry were led by the young Alexander Lindsay, the Earl of Balcarres. These first class troops were ideal for the pursuit as were, on this occasion, the advance party of 180 Brunswickers led by von Riedesel himself. Of these elite troops, about eighty were drawn from the Brunswick Grenadier Battalion "Breymann" under Captain Maximilian von Schottelius. The remaining hundred were from the *jaeger* (light infantry) company of the Battalion "von Barner." The men were former foresters and gamekeepers, equipped with rifles, under the command of Captain Clark von Geyso, who distinguished himself in the coming battle.

St Clair halted at Hubbardton and conferred with Warner. He told the Vermonter to pause at Hubbardton while he moved with the army to Castleton, seven miles down the road. The rearguard behind him consisted of the 11th Massachusetts regiment, 420 strong, under the command of an experienced soldier, Colonel Ebenezer Francis.

Warner was ordered to take command of the rearguard, strengthened by the 2nd New Hampshire Regiment, rising to about 360 men, under the veteran Colonel Nathan Hale (not to be confused with the Patriot spy). There would thus be three Continental Regiments in the rearguard, buttressed by the militia under Warner's command, a total of about 1,130 men, outnumbering Fraser's troops, even with the addition of von Riedesel's advance party. As soon as the two regiments arrived, Warner was to move to Castleton, to protect the main body north of the town.

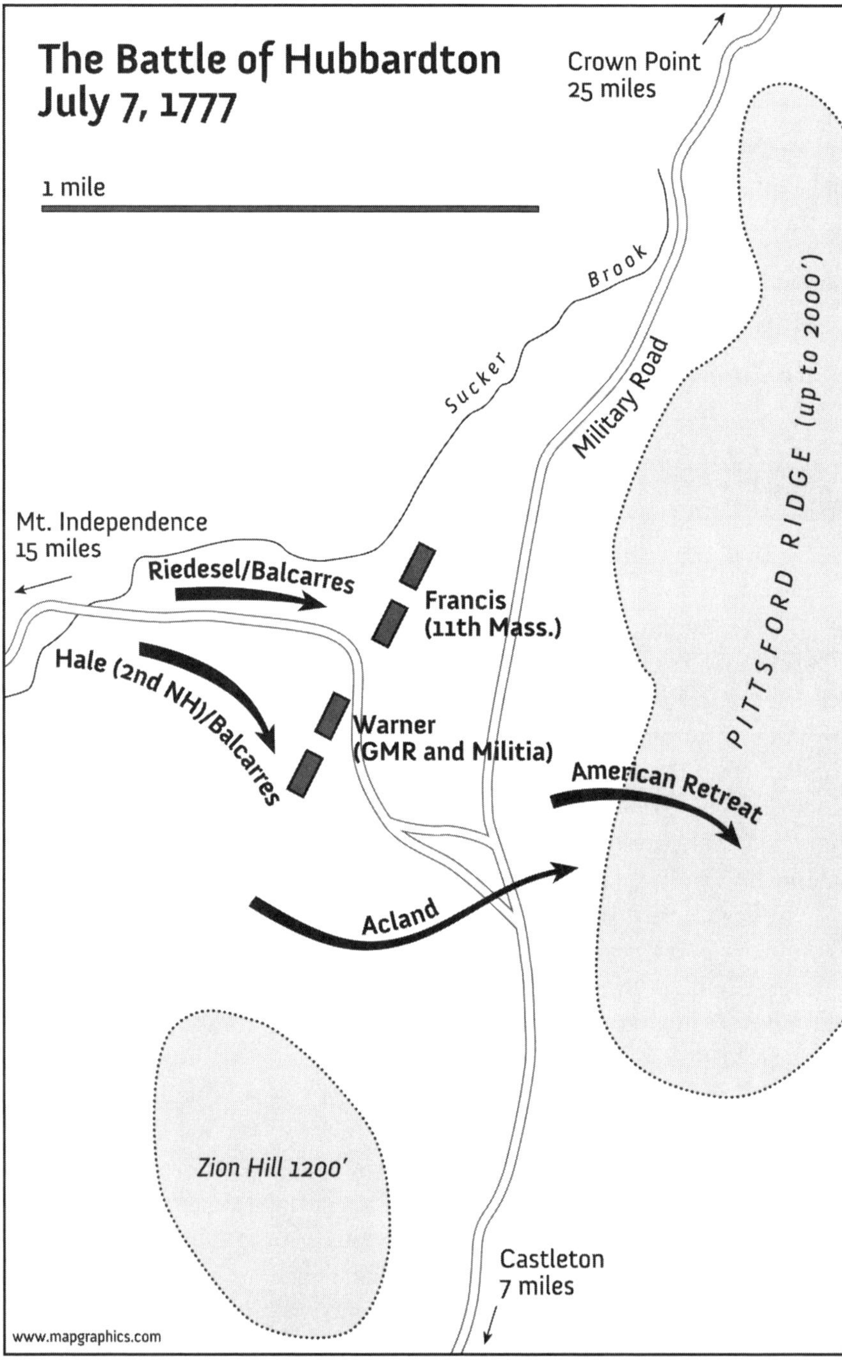
The Battle of Hubbardton
July 7, 1777
1 mile
Crown Point
25 miles
Sucker Brook
Military Road
PITTSFORD RIDGE (up to 2000')
Mt. Independence
15 miles
Riedesel/Balcarres
Francis
(11th Mass.)
Hale (2nd NH)/Balcarres
Warner
(GMR and Militia)
American Retreat
Acland
Zion Hill 1200'
Castleton
7 miles
www.mapgraphics.com

But Warner halted at Hubbardton for the night. Why he did so has given rise to a great deal of speculation. He was known for querying the directions of his superiors, but not for disobeying orders, nor, in the words used by Schuyler of Ethan Allen, of conducting his own "personal war." Possibly, the New Hampshires, burdened and delayed by stragglers and wounded, were disinclined to move. One probable motive, indeed, was the exhaustion of the two arriving regiments, which had made contact with Warner by 4.00 pm on the 6th. Another was that he had sent out patrols, warning Patriot families in the vicinity to disperse or to head south. One party of two hundred troops only arrived back at Warner's camp at 7.00 am on the morning of the 7th.

The Hubbardton position was intersected by the north-south wagon road from Mount Independence, which met with and terminated at the Crown Point Military Road, essential for the American retreat or retirement. This led to Castleton and points south. In the vicinity of Hubbardton, the Military Road ran northwest to southeast but at the junction with the road from Mount Independence, it ran west-east, behind the American positions. The center and anchor of these positions was Monument Hill, later named as such for the memorial to Colonel Francis. To the left and foot of the American positions were stationed the troops of Colonel Hale, along the Sucker Brook. In the center and on the left face of Monument Hill were Warner's troops; on the right face of the hill were the Massachusetts men. Behind and to the left (east) side of the Military Road rose Zion Hill, 1,200 feet at its summit, with the potential of outflanking the American defenses. To the right was Pittsfield Ridge, running north-south and consisting of a series of summits of around 2,000 feet.

Fraser's vanguard observed the campfires of Hale's regiment before dawn and bore down on them in daylight, while they were making their breakfast. The whole regiment bolted, though some were later rallied by Hale in bolstering Francis's Massachusetts troops. Hale himself came under a cloud from under which, in the absence of a court martial, he never recovered until his death in 1780. His troops did nothing different from what most others would have done and the worst that Hale could have been accused of was a failure to post enough sentries and actually leading the retreat instead of trying to impose some order upon it.

Warner and Francis watched the rout, then received the disconcerting news from St Clair of the disaster at Skenesborough, which would force them to detour through Rutland to the Hudson. Francis's men ascended to the ridge where they beat off an attack by the British light infantry. Even now, it is hard not to admire the soldiery of both sides, marching and fighting in the sweltering heat. While he was being repulsed, Fraser had his grenadiers under Acland drop their packs and scramble up the rocky face towards the summit of Zion Hill on his right. The Redcoats were not supposed to do that! They stopped short of the summit of Zion Hill, descending upon and severing the Military Road. On the British left, the light infantry and the 24th Regiment were again repulsed and Fraser, thinking himself grossly outnumbered, sent an urgent message back to von Riedesel. The Brunswicker had been camped about three miles behind the British; he had started his march at the same time as Fraser at 3.00 am, as promised.

Meanwhile, St Clair had heard the sounds of battle, seven miles away. He sent two officers to turn back to Hubbardton the two Vermont militia regiments that were camped four miles north of Castleton. But these were already in flight upon hearing the gunfire behind them.[18] The two officers rode on to the battlefield, arriving soon after Fraser's second assault on Monument Hill. Unaware as yet of the whereabouts of von Riedesel's troops, Fraser launched his third assault against the Massachusetts regiment and elements of Warner's formation. As the British prepared for a bayonet charge, dreaded whenever the Americans were in a traditional line of defense, von Riedesel led his jaegers and grenadiers, to the sound of a military band and German battle hymns, against the crest of the ridge, where it prepared to envelop the American right. Francis attempted to rally his men but was killed by a German bullet to the heart (recognizing his gallantry, the *Braunschweiger* gave him a solemn funeral). Unnerved by their great loss while faced with British bayonets and the volleys of the German grenadiers, the 11th Massachusetts faded away into the woods behind the open fields. Seth Warner was in the process of falling back in good order to the south side of the Military Road when the Massachusetts regiment broke. In a rare display of exasperation, Warner cursed the fleeing men, then calmly gave the order for his men to "scatter and meet me at Manchester."[19] And scatter they must, because the road to Castleton was barred. They moved over Pittsfield Ridge to the right and rear of the American lines. "A considerable part" of Warner's regiment joined with St Clair at Rutland and Warner arrived at Manchester with about ninety more, with others expected to follow.

Meanwhile, St Clair's two officers had managed to return to report on the American defeat. With Skenesborough occupied by the enemy, St Clair returned to Schuyler's camp at Fort Edward on July 12, via Rutland, Manchester and Bennington.[20] St Clair had lost 228 officers and men as prisoners at Hubbardton, among the total casualties of 370. The British and Germans suffered a loss of 174 in killed and wounded, but what came home to the British was that the Americans could be expected to fight as well as the British, in marked contrast to their performance at Ticonderoga.

From the time of Hubbardton onwards, Burgoyne was plagued by a shortage of supplies, for want of transport to move them, and the need to retain troops to secure his supply line, such as those at Crown Point, Ticonderoga and Skenesborough. His build-up of supplies was inadequate for the advance on Albany. The aim of the coming foray deep into Vermont was both to secure animals and carts for his supply train and to acquire foodstuffs for a stockpile at his supply base. On August 2, Burgoyne laid out his "Instructions for Lieutenant Colonel Baume (on a secret expedition to the Connecticut River"):

> The object of your expedition is to try the affections of the country, to disconcert the councils of the enemy, to mount Riedesel's dragoons, to compleat Peters's corps [The Queen's Loyal Rangers], and to obtain large supplies of cattle, horses, and carriages.[21]

Baum's route was to take him from the Batten Kill to Arlington, to await Sherwood's company of the Queen's Loyal Rangers coming up from the south, then to proceed from Manchester to Rockingham (Fort No. 2) on the Connecticut River, and from there back via Brattleborough to Fort Miller on the Hudson. Baum was expected to commandeer and pay for 1,300 horses, together with nearly two hundred mounts with saddles and bridles for the German dragoons, as well as carts, oxen and live cattle. Though von Riedesel had first proposed a raid for supplies in July, he came to have deep misgivings about the project, because it would take his troops into the heart of rebel-held territory. The whole expedition was to take "about a fortnight." The premise of such an ambitious exercise with its unrealistic aims and timetable was that Loyalists would rise up and support the expedition. This was the view of Colonel Skene, the political advisor on the march, whose projections over the pursuit of St Clair had not been fulfilled: even after the success at Hubbardton, only about four hundred Tories had rallied to the cause, half of them unarmed.

Just as Baum was about to move out of Fort Miller on the Hudson, he got word in person from Burgoyne, whose camp was at Fort Edward, that he was to proceed to Bennington. Captain Justus Sherwood, returning from a spying mission to Bennington, had informed him that there was a large stock of provisions, cattle and horses, inadequately guarded by three or four hundred men.[22] This should not have been a surprise: on May 20, while Burgoyne was still in Canada, Carleton had written to Germain, informing him that he had heard from a spy that "there is a great quantity of provisions at Ticonderoga and at Bennington in the Bay Province."[23]

According to von Riedesel, Burgoyne's thought was that the capture of the supplies would enable the army to subsist until a four-week stock could be built up. By this time, Burgoyne's logistics were in disarray: because of the state of the route from Ticonderoga and the lack of pack horses, he received only a trickle of supplies in August.[24] In the face of a skeptical Riedesel, Burgoyne also said that he could deter the Americans from attacking Baum by moving his whole army against Arnold (actually Schuyler) at Stillwater and he could prevent the Americans from raising St Leger's siege of Fort Stanwix.[25] Burgoyne even thought that with a good stock from Bennington, he could move on Albany right away, instead of the two to four weeks he had envisaged.

On August 11, Baum moved out of Fort Miller with a mixed force of Germans and Loyalists. According to Furneaux it consisted of:

> 175 dismounted dragoons; less than 200 German infantrymen, chiefly grenadiers and light troops; a squad of Hesse-Hanau artillerymen with two three-pounders; fifty of Fraser's marksmen; 300 Tories and Canadians; and a small number of Indians—a total, with officers, sergeants, and musicians of about 800 men.[26]

His opponents, meanwhile, had moved with great speed. On July 9, St Clair wrote to Jonas Fay, Secretary to the State of Vermont, from "Col. Marshe's," advising him that Warner's regiment and the Vermont militia had been directed by Schuyler to be "left for the Protection of the People." Warner was to remain at Rutland, carry off cattle and commandeer or destroy carriages (wagons) that may be of use to the enemy.[27] Warner expected the three battalions newly raised in New Hampshire to be sent without delay to his camp at Manchester.[28] Schuyler, however, changed his mind and directed Major- General Benjamin Lincoln, his deputy in the region since July 29, to order the Massachusetts and New Hampshire militia on from Bennington, to the Hudson, where the enemy was expected.[29] The approaching New Hampshire regiments were to "join the army at Stillwater" (on the Hudson);

the later order to Stark via Lincoln was only a confirmation of a move previously planned.[30]

The Vermonters had already acted upon the request for militia made by St Clair to Warner.[31] Early in August, Warner had about 600 militia at Manchester, along with the Green Mountain Rangers. Ira Allen was at the General Court of New Hampshire on July 18 when Schuyler's request for New Hampshire militia arrived. By July 24, the state had raised 1,492 officers and men, under the command of Major-General John Stark, a distinguished and popular soldier, appointed colonel on June 3, 1775.[32] Stark had resigned his commission as a Continental officer on March 22, 1776 when he had been passed over for promotion by more junior officers, among them Benjamin Lincoln.

There was an open split between New England on one side, and New York and the Continental Congress on the other. The New Englanders had no confidence in the leadership of the army after the evacuation of Ticonderoga and feared that their militia would be ordered to join Schuyler in Stillwater, which was what happened at one point in the changing series of orders from the Northern Department. So Stark was given a command independent of the Continental Army. Stark may well have heard of von Riedesel's plan for a foray into Vermont, which he put forward around July 22, though Stark thought (wrongly at the time) this was aimed at Bennington, to which Stark later directed his militia, ideally placed to face Baum's expedition. Stark first sent 700 men to Warner at Manchester; he then led another 300, meeting with Warner on August 7. Lincoln was also there and gave Stark the orders from Schuyler to join him at Stillwater.[33] The Vermont Council of Safety objected strongly, since it needed its militia and the newly raised Herrick's Rangers for its own defense. With the support of the Vermonters, Stark ignored Schuyler's order and rode out to Bennington with his New Hampshire troops, accompanied by Seth Warner (but not the Green Mountain Rangers), on August 8. He had apparently agreed that his force would harass Burgoyne's left flank, a plan that Lincoln promised to take to Schuyler for endorsement. The plan was pre-empted by Baum's approach and with Stark well placed to confront the enemy.

The Green Mountain Rangers were left at Manchester under the command of Lieutenant-Colonel Samuel Safford. The regiment was not numerically strong: a return of August 3 showed a total strength of 160; but by August 13, ten had deserted, one was discharged, five recruits were added but 56 were missing.[34] By the time of the Bennington battle, the Green Mountain

Rangers had expanded to about 150. The colonels of the Vermont militia, Williams, Robinson and Bellows, had already been ordered to send half their strength from Manchester to Bennington, where they met up with Herrick's Rangers, authorized on July 15 under their Lt. Colonel commandant, Samuel Herrick, a veteran of the Ticonderoga operation of 1775.[35] By the morning of the 16th, Stark also had a detachment of militia, about 250 strong, from Berkshire County, Massachusetts, part of the regiment under the command of Colonel Benjamin Symonds (Warner had sent an express to Symonds on July 1).[36] Stark had the three battalions (regiments) of New Hampshire militia and two Vermont companies from Bennington. Thus he had around 2,000 militia at Bennington, few trained and few who had been in action, under a soldier who had the confidence, affection and respect of everyone under his command. Of these, 1,350 were estimated to have taken part in the coming battle. The Green Mountain Rangers and the balance of the Vermont militia, estimated at two hundred[37] were still at Manchester, guarding against an attack there and what was to have been von Riedesel's original route through the Green Mountains to Rockingham.

In twelve hours, Baum marched the sixteen miles from the Batten Kill to Cambridge, where he clashed with the Americans on August 13, 1777. He also learned that the Bennington commissary was defended by 1,500 to 1,800 troops, but he pushed on, halting four miles short of Bennington on the Walloomsac River.[38] Since the enemy was gathering, Baum decided to establish a defensive position and, expecting reinforcements, to await orders from Burgoyne.[39] Lt. Colonel William Gregg's American expedition, retreating from the engagement at Cambridge, destroyed the bridge at San Coick (Saint Croix, now North Hoosick) at the confluence of the Hoosic River and the Owl Kill, impeding Baum's advance for a short time, while Stark withdrew from the place where Baum halted to positions a mile outside Bennington. At the same time, he summoned Warner's regiment and the militia to Bennington; they arrived wet to the skin and camped at nightfall on the 15th, a mile north of the town. As a result of Baum's intelligence on the strength of the enemy, Burgoyne sent Breymann's advance corps of 642 men to reinforce Baum. Beset by pouring rain, muddy tracks, unreliable guides, carts of ammunition and two four-pounder cannon, Breymann arrived seven miles short of Cambridge and seventeen miles from Baum by nightfall on the 15th. Skene rode back from Baum's camp to tell Breymann to get a move on.

Stark relied on reports from his skirmishers; he and Warner saw Baum taking up his positions on the 15th which Baum fortified on that wet day.

The center of Baum's position, looking towards Bennington, was a bridge over the Walloomsac at Hoosic, New York, taking the road from the north over to the south side of the river. This bridge was vital to Baum since he needed it to continue the advance to Bennington, eight miles away. He placed a detachment of 150 Loyalists to defend the bridge from the south side, adjacent to the road, but about 250 yards away from it. About 150 Canadians under Charles de Lanaudiere defended the bridge from the north side, close to the river. Behind the bridge were twenty of Captain Alexander Fraser's marksmen, with fifty Brunswickers and one of the two three-pounders. A mixed group of fifty Germans and the balance of the Loyalists were placed on a knoll about a thousand yards behind, on the south side of the road and river, to protect the force from an attack on the rear. This was the "Tory Redoubt," constructed under the direction of a Loyalist engineer, Colonel Francis Pfister of Hoosic, New York. Baum himself, with 170 of his Dragoon Regiment Prinz Ludwig, twenty of Fraser's men, some Indians under St. Luc de la Corne (the father-in-law of de Lanaudiere) and the other cannon, were positioned on a hill of 300 feet on the north side (the Dragoon Redoubt), about a thousand yards from the bridge. This had a commanding view of the ground to the south, east and west, but the shape of the hill obscured the forces on both sides of the bridge. Baum's tactics have been criticized. It is certainly true that the detachments on both sides of the river were too far apart to offer mutual support, but it is less clear that Baum was wrong to have occupied the hill on the north side, since it would have been an open invitation to the Americans to descend on the troops below. As to commanding the battle, Baum himself was ill-placed to direct the movements of the four detachments on the road and river; they could receive no central direction at all.

When Stark paraded his troops on the morning of the 16th, he harangued the troops in the traditional fashion which, being a case of preaching to the converted, was well-received. It was then that he is said to have uttered the famous line, "[Over] there are the Redcoats and they are ours, or this night Molly Stark sleeps a widow" (one of several versions). The plan of attack, devised by Stark, Warner and their officers, was to envelop Baum's rear, to his left on the hill of nearly a thousand feet (the Dragoon Redoubt) and on his right, the detachment of Germans and Loyalists positioned well behind the main positions. For the former, he sent Colonel Nichols with 2–300 New Hampshire militia to Baum's left, reinforced on request by a further hundred men. This force was complemented by the 300 men of Herrick's Rangers,

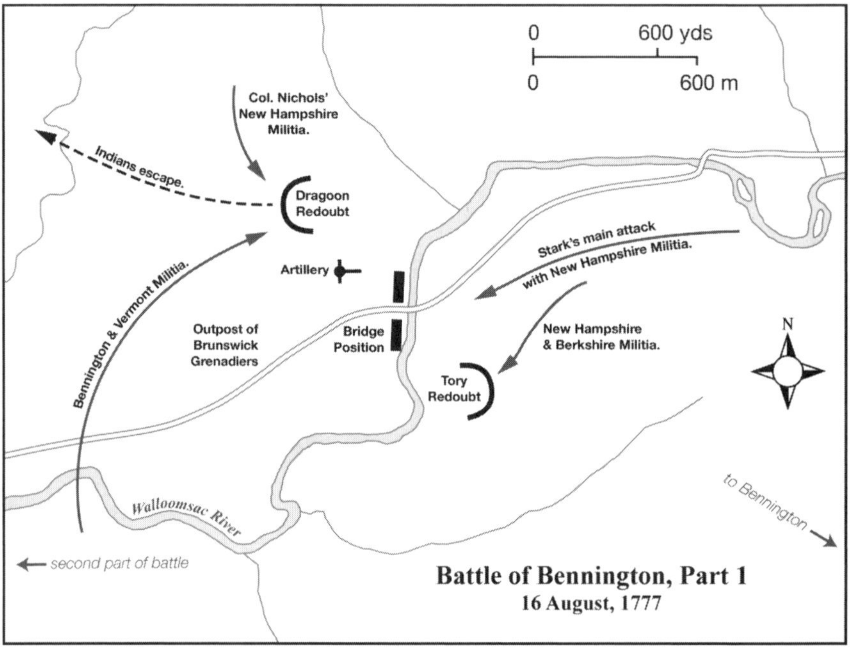
0
600 yds
0
600 m
Col. Nichols' New Hampshire Militia.
Indians escape.
Dragoon Redoubt
Artillery
Stark's main attack with New Hampshire Militia.
Bennington & Vermont Militia.
Outpost of Brunswick Grenadiers
Bridge Position
New Hampshire & Berkshire Militia.
N
Tory Redoubt
Walloomsac River
to Bennington
second part of battle
Battle of Bennington, Part 1
16 August, 1777

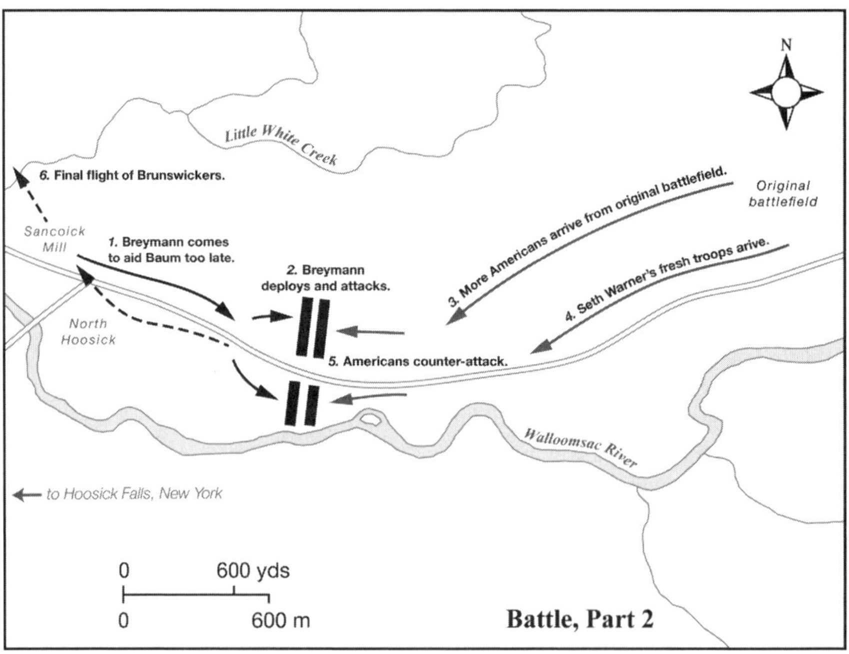
N
Little White Creek
6. Final flight of Brunswickers.
3. More Americans arrive from original battlefield.
Original battlefield
Sancoick Mill
1. Breymann comes to aid Baum too late.
4. Seth Warner's fresh troops arive.
2. Breymann deploys and attacks.
North Hoosick
5. Americans counter-attack.
Walloomsac River
to Hoosick Falls, New York
0
600 yds
0
600 m
Battle, Part 2

who were sent on a wide detour around the Tory Redoubt on the south side of the Walloomsac, to wade the shallow river onto the north bank. The two forces, "when joined," were to envelop Baum's troops in the Dragoon Redoubt. Captain Elijah Dewey's company of Bennington militia joined with the 2–300 men under Colonels Hubbard and Stickney to reduce the Loyalist Redoubt and perhaps advance even further to the west. What actually happened was that the forces of Nichols and Herrick drove Baum's dragoons off the hill and down towards the balance of Stark's troops in the center of his line.

The Tories on the south side comprised the 300 men of Colonel John Peters' Queen's Loyal Rangers, which now included Sherwood's company, about fifty Germans and Lieutenant Colonel Francis Pfister's Loyal Volunteers. This group was infiltrated by Patriots posing as Loyalists, partly as spies, partly to reveal themselves when the time came and attack the Tories from within their positions behind the breastwork. It was a good plan and it relied on the performance of the troops, in which Stark had a well-merited confidence.

The timing of the attack is not clear, with Stark claiming afterwards that the signal was to be firing from Nichols' militia, at precisely three in the afternoon. The other account was that he was waiting for Warner's regiment and, at 3:00 pm, could wait no longer. It was still raining on the morning of the 16th and Safford had first to dry his men and their weapons before moving through Bennington towards the battle front. Whether they took more time than was needed is not so important for, in one of those accidents of history, they arrived fresh and just in time to blunt Breymann's relief of Baum. At any event, the battle began with firing from Nichols' regiment and the rising of the Patriots in the Tory Redoubt, which was then attacked by the troops of Stickney and Hubbard. The Loyalists retreated from the Tory Redoubt at the first volley. In hard fighting, Nichols' troops drove the Germans off the hill and down its south face, where they met the forces of the center who, led by Stark himself, had crossed the bridge into the path of the retreating Germans. (The Indians in the Dragoon Redoubt retreated unopposed down the north face.) Baum's ammunition supply wagon blew up, leaving his troops in the terrible heat with only the ammunition in their pouches and weighed down by their parade-ground woolen uniforms, heavy boots, scabbards and swords. Only nine of Baum's 375 troops escaped; he was wounded in the stomach and died in captivity the next day. By the time the action was over at five in the evening, Warner's regiment of a hundred and fifty had arrived, along with two hundred Vermont militia.

Breymann and his Brunswickers had marched in the oppressive heat and reached the Van Rensselaer mills of San Coick at around 4:30 pm, taking 31 hours to march the 24 miles from the mouth of the Batten Kill. Still apparently oblivious of the battle ahead of them, they moved on, brushing off a party of Americans, forcing them to retreat further up the road. About a mile from the battlefield, they met Warner's troops on the north side of the Walloomsac and those of the Americans not engaged in plunder, caring for the wounded or rounding up prisoners. Stark was trying to rally the troops and, it seems, organizing a retreat when Warner came up and forcefully argued for a counterattack. The battle raged, obliging Breymann to retreat; the pursuit continued till nightfall. The performance of Herrick and Warner were especially commended to General Gates: "Colonel's Warner and Herrick, by their superior intelligence and experience, were of great service to me; and I desire they may be recommended to Congress."[40] The Continental Congress responded by making Stark a brigadier general of the Continental Army in October,[41] ignoring Stark's snub in reporting to Gates rather than the Congress.

Justus Sherwood had envisaged a lightning raid on Bennington, but the sluggishness of the expeditionary force enabled the Americans to organize their defense. Of the invading force, at least 207 were killed, among them Baum and Colonel Pfister, with Peters wounded. About 700 were lost as prisoners, as well as armaments and all four cannon. Heinrich Breymann, universally detested for his brutality and tyrannical command, was allegedly shot down by one of his own men, when he tried to prevent them from retreating in the Battle of Bemis Heights on October 7. Of the Tory prisoners, some were banished under pain of death; others were employed as forced laborers and the balance were sent to Newgate Prison, a dank copper mine in Granby, Connecticut. As for Burgoyne, he had lost a seventh of his army, now reduced to 4,500 men, with many of the Indians deserting. Without scouts, this left his army blind. He was later outnumbered nearly four to one. St Leger lifted his siege of Fort Stanwix and retreated on August 7. It was a good month for the Americans, who got their revenge for the defeat at Hubbardton, though the evacuation of Ticonderoga was much more ignominious.[42]

Baum's expedition had failed to bring in any supplies or transport. By the time Burgoyne had made a conditional decision to retreat to Ticonderoga in the second week in October, the road back was so hazardous as to be virtually closed. In mid-September, Lincoln sent three detachments of 500 men each from Pawlet towards Ticonderoga, to cut Burgoyne's lines of communication, to capture his base camps and, if possible, to take Ticonderoga and Mount Independence.[43] One contingent occupied Skenesborough, abandoned by the British, while the second tied down the garrison of Mount Independence in a cannonade. The third, led by Colonel John Brown with Herrick's Rangers under command, overwhelmed the garrison at Fort George, which meant that Burgoyne's two remaining supply routes were now, temporarily, cut. Brown moved on to Ticonderoga, where he lay concealed for two days. His men, led by Captain Ebenezer Allen's company of Herrick's Rangers, captured the landing to Fort George on September 18, rushed the defenses of the old French lines, captured Mount Defiance, took nearly 300 prisoners and released over a hundred Americans. These had been taken at Hubbardton and were now "acting in conjunction with Brown and Herrick." Brown's attempt to bluff the commander of Ticonderoga, Brigadier General Henry Watson Powell, into surrender, failed, as did a subsequent attack on Diamond Island to the south. Before Brown left Ticonderoga on the 22nd, he had taken, by his own account, 293 prisoners, 200 bateaux, an armed sloop, several large gunboats and a stock of stores.[44] When Burgoyne sent an expedition out to secure and improve his line of retreat on about October 7, he found even Fort Edward occupied by the Americans. The fort had been commandeered after Colonel Wallbridge had occupied Skenesborough in September. At about the same time as Burgoyne sent his troops up the road to Fort Edward, Colonel Bayley's Gloucester and Cumberland County militia moved from Castleton to occupy a fortified camp on the road, just north of Fort Edward. Burgoyne informed Sir Henry Clinton in New York that he had supplies enough to last until October 20, a fact known to Brown late in September.[45]

By mid-September, Burgoyne had built up a stock of supplies sufficient for thirty days; he had resolved to advance on Albany towards the end of August. His aim was to establish a fortified camp and hope that there were enough supplies in the vicinity to see him through the winter or until relieved by Sir William Howe. He decided to cross the Hudson with his whole army onto the western bank, then break up his bridge of boats This is what he meant when he said that he had "cut the communications" with his rear, not realizing that to all intents and purposes, the same would be achieved by General Lincoln's threefold foray a few days later. Burgoyne fought an engagement with the Americans at Freeman's Farm on September 19, which was followed by his defeat at the Battle of Bemis Heights on October 7. Upon this, he withdrew north to Saratoga, seven miles in the three days,

October 8–10. Soon afterwards, he found himself surrounded by a vastly superior American force and surrendered to Gates on the 17th.

The predicament of the three British commanders, Howe, Clinton and Burgoyne in September and October 1777 was one of poor communication, indifference to Burgoyne's situation on the part of the Commander-in-Chief, and frustration with the situation by Howe's second-in-command, Sir Henry Clinton in New York. Clinton had earlier warned Howe that his move south would ruin Burgoyne and he was sure that he could not assist the force from Canada. He told Howe, then on his expedition towards Philadelphia, that he had written to Burgoyne on about August 10, informing him that "it would not be possible for me to attempt any thing to favour his Operations but that I was determined if possible to try something *towards the close of the year*." This was in line with Howe's earlier plan to help Burgoyne after his expedition "to the southward" was concluded.[46] Despite being left in "so starved a defensive," Clinton undertook a foray into New Jersey "to favour the operations" of the armies of both Howe and Burgoyne and he even contemplated an expedition to Rhode Island under Major General James Robertson, the commandant of New York. His attempts to assist Burgoyne were in two phases. The first (which Howe had envisaged) was to send a raiding party up the Hudson late in September to take or invest several forts, including Montgomery and Clinton, so to take the pressure off Burgoyne, This might, as Burgoyne surmised, "draw away a great part of [the enemy's] force,"[47] but since Clinton only envisaged a foray, "not of long duration" it would, in Clinton's view, merely "facilitate your operations." Clinton sent a message by Captain Campbell on October 6, stating "General Burgoyne could not suppose that Sir Henry had an idea of penetrating to Albany with the small force he mentioned in his last letter." In the absence of instructions from Howe, Clinton "cannot presume to give any orders to General Burgoyne."[48] Throughout, Clinton never gave any orders or advice to Burgoyne.[49] In the second phase, Clinton, reinforced by 1,700 recruits, changed his mind, and on September 24[50] decided to send an expedition up the Hudson to effect a junction with Burgoyne at Albany.

Clinton did this with the best of intentions; but the project was beset by illusions on the part of both Burgoyne and the British in New York. Well aware that his supplies were running out, Burgoyne informed Sir Henry that, if he not heard from him by October 12, he would retreat back to Canada. After Brown had returned from his raid in mid-September, the cross-country route back to Fort George was still open, Baroness Riedesel recording that it was only closed on the 13th when Burgoyne had merely five days of provisions left.[51] Burgoyne could hold on until the 16th if a "cooperating army" could reach Albany by that date. Burgoyne said that he would not have given up his communications with Ticonderoga if he had not expected a communication (relief) on the part of a force from New York.[52] Burgoyne's contention has no credibility: he knew all along that he could expect no relief from New York in the foreseeable future. Clinton estimated that Burgoyne was besieged by 12–14,000 men with a "considerable body" of 4,000 "hovering about" or in his rear. Burgoyne had indeed decided to give up his line of retreat to Ticonderoga (by breaking up the bridge of boats across the Hudson, in his rear), but when he wrote to Clinton on September 20, he was unaware of the success of John Brown's raid and of the capture of Fort Edward, which was worse than merely "giving up" his communications.[53] Clinton gave orders on October 11 for six months' provisions for 5,000 troops to be loaded into small vessels in New York, and on October 15, Clinton sent Major-General Sir John Vaughan with 1,700 men up the Hudson to Esopus (Kingston), "ready to push for Albany."[54]

Clinton sent a message to Burgoyne from Fort Montgomery on October 10, saying that if on hearing of "our success" on the Hudson, "he had determined to push for Albany, we would do everything in our power to communicate with him."[55] Burgoyne did indeed hold on; but the timing of events shows the unreality of the plans: he expected a junction to be made in Albany by the 16th, when Vaughan only set out from New York on the 15th. A retreat to Canada, alternatively, should have started on the 12th. Clinton then got an order from Howe of October 9, received on the 17th, to send him 4,000 troops immediately—or within a few days, if a decisive move up the Hudson could be made right away. Clinton wrote to Vaughan on the 22nd, conveying Howe's orders. Since communication with Burgoyne was poor and Clinton, even before hearing from Howe, considered Vaughan's situation "desperate," Sir John was instructed to return to New York immediately, which he did, perhaps even before receiving Clinton's order and after burning Esopus.[56] In the American version, the reason for the recall was that four regiments had left New York to reinforce Howe, and Vaughan's troops were needed to replace them.[57]

Vaughan returned to join Clinton's force at Fort Montgomery on the Hudson, upon which Sir Henry evacuated the Highlands and sailed back to New York on October 26. When Vaughan moved north, Burgoyne was not even at Albany, where the "communication" was supposed to have taken place by the 16th. The closest that Vaughan got to Burgoyne was at Livingstone Manors above Esopus, forty-four miles from Albany and eighty from Saratoga. Burgoyne surrendered two days after Vaughan left New York for Albany. Any contact between Burgoyne and Vaughan was such an unlikely event, and relief with troops and supplies practically impossible, that Burgoyne's army was doomed to disintegration or surrender.

As for the Regiment of Green Mountain Rangers, a return of September 5 shows four sick, including Colonel Warner, and 102 present, a few more than the return of August 13, before the Battle of Bennington, but none of these were listed as fit for duty. If the Green Mountain Rangers took part in the siege of Burgoyne's army in mid-October, there could have been very few of them (some Vermont militia may have been at Saratoga). Warner was officially off sick for the remainder of the regiment's existence, though he was wounded in an inspection tour in 1779, at which skirmish Captain Gideon Brownson was captured. Vermont's part in the campaign of 1777 was not quite over: Captain Ebenezer Allen and about fifty of Herrick's Rangers harassed the enemy in the retreat from Ticonderoga in mid-November, capturing prisoners, boats and livestock.[58] Chittenden told Gates that he had, upon request, sent Warner's regiment to the vicinity of Albany, where it remained throughout 1778.[59]

The Battle of Bennington and the Saratoga Campaign

The Battle of Bennington has seen confusion over its tactics and a controversy over its place in the Saratoga campaign. In his letter to the New Hampshire Council of August 18 1777, Stark wrote:

> I divided my army into three divisions, and sent Lieut. Col. Nichols with two hundred and fifty men on the rear of their left wing, Colonel Herrick on the rear of their right, ordered, when joined, to attack the same. In the meantime I sent three hundred men to oppose the enemy's front, to draw their attention that way. Soon after I detached Colonels Hubbard and Stickney on their right wing, with two hundred men, to attack that part. . . .[60]

Commentators have not been clear as to what Stark meant. James E. Petersen depicts Herrick as moving to the left of Baum's defenses and Nichols to Baum's right,[61] the opposite of what Stark wrote. Michael P. Gabriel has Nichols moving to attack Baum's right rear, not his left.[62] But Gabriel also has the proposed encirclement of Baum by Nichols at the

Hessian left flank and Herrick at the right, the latter contention reflecting Stark's account.[63] Probably, the confusion arose because Stark referred to his own position as being at the center, in which case, the Dragoon Redoubt was on Stark's right and Baum's left. When he wrote of Herrick moving to the right rear of Baum's position and Nichols to the rear of his left, he meant, not the right and left of the American center, but the right and left of the Dragoon Redoubt. It is clear from the firsthand accounts reproduced by Gabriel that Herrick's troops were with Nichols when they began their attack on the Dragoon Redoubt.[64] What happened was that Baum was caught between the Nichols/Herrick forces and those of Stark in the center, obviating any need for envelopment by Nichols and Herrick. Yet even the best accounts of the battle are not quite clear; the late Richard M. Ketchum has Herrick's force fanning out to the south after it had crossed the Walloomsac to attack the Dragoon Redoubt, when he really meant north.[65]

The American aim was to defeat Burgoyne's army in battle, but retrospective analysis shows that there were other ways in which Burgoyne could be overcome. First, the Americans did not need to win a major battle; they had only not to lose one. Then they had two tasks: the first to cut off Burgoyne's supply routes and line of retreat. Burgoyne thought he might be obliged to retreat on October 12, when Brown's raid had shown the vulnerability of the escape routes and Fort Edward had fallen, compromising the road back through Skenesborough. Then the Americans had to prevent Burgoyne's relief by Sir Henry Clinton. Since this was not a serious possibility, it was in the event the easiest of the American tasks. The question can well be asked: how did Bennington contribute to the defeat of Burgoyne, over and above the retreat of St Leger from Fort Stanwix? Gabriel has noted, correctly, that Bennington cost Burgoyne a seventh of his army; undermined Loyalist support and disheartened the Indians; denied him provisions, cavalry mounts and draft animals, which postponed the advance to Albany for nearly a month and increased the confidence of the Americans enormously.[66] Burgoyne observed to Germain that the Americans could assemble three or four thousand militia in twenty-four hours at a critical point. He had a healthy respect for the Vermonters:

> The Hampshire Grants in particular, a country unpeopled and almost unknown in the last war, now abounds with the most active and rebellious race of the continent, and hangs like a gathering storm on my left. . . .[67]

Burgoyne can be forgiven for underestimating the strength and enterprise of the enemy.

Bennington was undoubtedly a great victory, greater than even Stark and Warner had imagined and the first victory in the Northern Department since November 1775. But if we look at Burgoyne's predicament and the sequence of events from mid-August, through the Battle of Freeman's Farm on September 19 and the surrounding of his army after Bemis Heights on October 7, Bennington seems to be but the first of several milestones rather than the turning point of the campaign, as Gabriel contends.[68] The main thing that the Americans had to do was to isolate Burgoyne from his supplies and his escape route, while preventing relief from the south. Bennington contributed to this eventuality but it was not a singular deciding factor; the vital task was to besiege Burgoyne's army. Once this was done, Burgoyne's position was hopeless.

There never was any clear set of orders coming from Germain to Howe and Burgoyne; there was also vagueness over what was meant by "effecting a junction" and "opening a communication" with New York. But the drift is clear and it was understood by all the players: Burgoyne could expect no practical help from the Commander-in-Chief until the end of the year at best and he would be isolated in Albany until this happened. In deciding to advance on Albany late in August, instead of retreating, Burgoyne was following orders; if the decision was also an act of folly, it was one whose implications had been known by all parties from the beginning. The role that Burgoyne's army was supposed to play was futile all along, the product of a harebrained strategy that could have had no prospect of success. All the more reason for contending that Sir Guy Carleton's conduct of the campaign in 1776 was thoroughly adept and realistic. But Burgoyne, having castigated Carleton for his retreat in the previous year, was in no position to eat crow and do the same in 1777.

Early in 1777, Burgoyne adumbrated a sound strategy: the sole purpose of his expedition was a junction at or beyond Albany of the forces of Howe, St Leger and himself. The strategy which Germain endorsed was vague about "effecting a junction" with Howe, and the plan did not take into account the prior plans of the Commander-in-Chief. By May, the plan sketched in February had been dropped: Howe was never to "effect a junction" with Burgoyne and St Leger. There was only a tentative plan to link with Burgoyne sometime in the future. So the common supposition that there was to be a three-pronged assault[69] is not correct: this had been only an initial thought at the beginning of the year, on the part of Burgoyne and Germain only, not including Howe. Even supposing that Baum had won the Battle of Bennington and was able to transport all the supplies in Bennington back to Fort Miller unmolested, this would still not have advanced Burgoyne's timetable enough to "effect a junction" with Sir Henry Clinton. For this to have happened, Clinton would have had to advance his own timetable, but he had neither the intention or orders nor the resources to do this.

Looking at the sequence of orders and responsibilities with the progress of operations is one thing, but there is also evidence that Burgoyne really had no serious purpose in the Saratoga campaign. Already, on July 11, 1777, Burgoyne was requesting leave to go to England, on the grounds that his health would not hold up in the winter and that he was not cut out to succeed Carleton in Quebec. He wrote that he was "confident of fulfilling the object of my orders," which was only to get to Albany. At the end of the month, he wrote that, despite his efforts, he had failed to open a correspondence with Howe and later observed that he had no cooperation from New York City, such as an expedition from there to the Highlands, which Howe had envisaged. In August, he wrote that despite the gathering strength of the enemy, he would push on to Albany and, if he found that his army could subsist there, he would fortify the town and await the operations of Sir William Howe. In the correspondence, there is no trace of any obligation to "effect a junction" with Howe.[70]

The roots of the British failure lay much deeper than the stance of Burgoyne and the defeat at Bennington: the key is the attitude of Germain. His plans for the 1777 campaign were the product of malice towards Sir Guy Carleton and strategic confusion. He allowed the British strategy to slip away, leaving Burgoyne isolated and adrift. Germain lacked appreciation of the British military predicament in North America. His experience was of warfare in western Europe, where the British fought on short, interior lines, not the vast distances, the difficulties of the weather and terrain and the eternal problem of supply in the North American theater. But nothing can excuse the sheer folly of Burgoyne's expedition, which put him in the same predicament as Carleton the previous year. When we consider that campaign of 1776, we have to conclude that the British knowingly brought on their own disaster. Germain, Howe, Burgoyne and Skene were all responsible for overestimating Loyalist support, which was supposed to sustain Burgoyne in Albany, but instead became the alibi for a botched campaign.

CHAPTER 7

The Republic of Vermont

ONE OF THE SOLUTIONS proposed by the Grantees to secure the New Hampshire titles was a new government, independent of both New Hampshire and New York, for what is now Vermont. The first tangible sign of this new direction was a convention at Manchester of "His Majesty's Loyal Subjects" on January 13, 1775, which, however, fell short of any goal of independence.[1] Delegates at the convention resolved to enter into a "temporary compact" to make rules of governance, the compact to be enforced by properly arming the Green Mountain Boys. This move was bold and radical; but the resolution was qualified and conservative, even more cautious than the resolves of the Continental Congress the previous October: the convention awaited the King's pleasure in resolving the issue of jurisdiction over the Grants and "will defer to him in all things." The convention further deferred to the New York authority in Albany and Charlotte counties, except in cases of land disputes or the taking of rioters (outlawry), which will be opposed by the three companies of Green Mountain Boys.

The first move specifically towards the independence of the Grants was the Dorset Convention of January 16–17, 1776, which thirty-two delegates attended, representing eighteen towns, all from the western side of the Green Mountains.[2] This was the result of a convention call on December 10 of the previous year. The Convention met to consider whether the jurisdiction of revolutionary New York was to be accepted in the Grants "where it doth [not?] infringe on our properties, or Title of Lands, or Riots (so called) in defense of the same"; to determine whether a remonstrance should be sent to the Continental Congress, protesting the refusal of New York to recognize New Hampshire titles; to move towards supporting the war under the Continental Congress and not under the Provincial Congress of New York; and, if Ira Allen's later account is to be believed,[3] whether a "new Government" should be established in the Grants[4] to make application "to the inhabitants of the said Grants to form the same into a separate District." No concrete action resulted from the Dorset Convention; but a petition[5] was presented to the Continental Congress by Heman Allen on May 8. The petition said that the Grants will fight the British but are "not willing to put ourselves under the honorable provincial Congress of New York in such a manner as might in future be detrimental to our private property." The response on May 30 was to advise the petitioners to submit to the Government of New York for the time being, pending a consideration of jurisdiction after the spat with the British was over; submission to New York was not to prejudice the claims of New York or the Grantees either way. When the "present troubles" are over, the "final determination of their right may be mutually referred to proper judges."[6]

In the confusion which followed, the Grantees were divided, some in fear that the Congress, influenced by New York, would rule against them, others that the Grantees should take bolder action to "Associate and unite" together.[7] The committee assigned in January to arrange for subsequent meetings, as necessary, called for a further meeting at Dorset on July 24, 1776. Forty-nine members, representing thirty-two towns, attended.[8] The purpose of the convention was to hear the report of Heman Allen's mission to Congress, to test the will of the delegates in relation to an association with New Hampshire; and, alternatively, to decide whether an association should be formed to perform military duty only with Continental troops as members of the District of Land (the Grants) and not, consequently, under the direction of New York.

Heman's report is instructive. As recorded by the Convention of July 24, Heman reported that the petition was read to the Congress, and that New York endeavored to oppose it, after which he was given leave to withdraw the petition (on the grounds that he had left some supporting documents at home!). This he did, fearing that New York would succeed in dismissing the petition, in the absence of a "proper Delegate" from the Grants Convention. Heman stated that he had many conferences with sundry members of Congress "and other Gentlemen of distinction," who advised him that the Grants should take part in the fight against the British but that the inhabitants should not "connect or associate with New York." They intimated that the said inhabitants should pursue "suitable measures to associate and unite the whole of the Inhabitants of said Grants together." While Heman was no doubt exaggerating, it does lend some weight to Ira's contention that independence was discussed in the first half of 1776.

The Grantees had already got some of what they wanted from the Continental Congress. In May, the Americans were in a full and disorderly retreat from Canada and the Congress was in desperate need of forces to counter Carleton's forthcoming invasion. Knowing full well that the Grantees and thus the Green Mountain Boys would not willingly serve under New York, the Congress on July 5, 1776 (the Day after the Declaration of Independence) voted, without reference to New York, to raise a regiment under Seth Warner.[9] The rationale was supposedly that there were a number of veteran officers without command who had served in Canada and were needed for the defense of the Confederation. Thus the Boys became a third regiment of the Congress (further to those of Livingston and Hazen) with a record of good service in Canada earlier in the year. There were also several hundred militia, raised in the Grants, on Mount Independence opposite Ticonderoga who, as it happened, played no active part in resisting Carleton's expedition of 1776.

In July of 1776, a movement had crystallized under the leadership of Heman Allen, Jonas Fay and William Marsh. Though there were differing degrees of enthusiasm for the various tenets of the movement, the drift of policy was to reject the jurisdiction of New York over land patents and titles; to serve in the Revolutionary War but not under the authority of New York; to form an Association of the "District of Land commonly called and known by the name of the New Hampshire Grants" and to recruit east-siders in these projects. On this last, the July convention was not successful: of the thirty-two towns represented, only one (Townsend) was on the east side of the Green Mountains. After determining that the Order in Council of 1764 was invalid (something that Ethan Allen had hesitated to do), the convention issued a draft of an Association to be signed by the inhabitants of the Grants as a "separate district." The convention also adopted a resolution that anyone who subscribed to the cause of New York should be regarded as an enemy of the new Association. Further, the convention set up a committee to hear appeals from the decisions of local committees of safety in the pursuit of the war, which was the origin of the Committee of War of September 1776, with the power to raise militia. The convention then adjourned on July 25, 1776 to meet two months later at the same place.

The efforts to recruit east-siders were fairly successful. Of the forty-four delegates at the September convention in Dorset, the west-siders represented twenty-five towns, while twelve delegates represented eight Cumberland County towns and two others sent letters of support.[10] The action of the New York Convention on August 2 to make quit rents payable to any new state gave further encouragement to the dissenting nationalists. On September 26, the July vote to form the Grants into a separate District was unanimously confirmed. The delegates then resolved to repudiate the jurisdiction of New York in all its aspects but not to act in a way repugnant to the Continental Congress in the "General Cause of America." Dr Reuben Jones of Rockingham on the east side joined Fay and Marsh as an emerging leader of the movement, with Captain Heman Allen, Colonel Thomas Chittenden of Williston, Ira Allen and Joseph Bowker of Rutland, president of the conventions, following close behind. No further petition to the Congress was presented as a result of the September convention and a subsequent convention at Westminster on the east side on October 30[11] was poorly attended and inconclusive, partly because of Carleton's expedition down Lake Champlain and the British threat to Ticonderoga. Under Bayley's influence and the Brigadier-General's preoccupation with northern defense, there were no delegates at all from Gloucester County.

The convention adjourned to meet again at the momentous Westminster convention of January 15, 1777. Twenty-two delegates represented seven west-side towns, ten towns in Cumberland County; there were letters from two other Cumberland towns and even one from Gloucester County (Royalton) favoring a new state.[12] As the delegates were aware, this was not an impressive turnout. That day, the convention voted unanimously in favor of independence:

> . . . that the district of territory comprehending and usually known by the name and description of the New- Hampshire grants, of right ought to be, and is hereby declared forever hereafter to be considered, as a free and independent jurisdiction, or state; by the name, and forever hereafter to be called, known, and distinguished by the name of New-Connecticut, alias Vermont.[13]

Delegates who were also members of the Convention of the State of New York as representatives of Cumberland County were requested to withdraw permanently from New York.

The Petition to the Honorable Continental Congress cited the Declaration and requested that "the district [of "about one hundred and forty four townships"] described therein be ranked by your honors, among the free and independent American states, and delegates therefrom admitted to seats in the grand Continental Congress."[14]

Though there was no explicit reference to a constitution for the new state, the convention determined to establish at the next session of the convention a bill of rights and a form of government which, with a preamble, comprised the constitution that emerged in July 1777. On April 8, representatives of the new state presented a revised petition to the Continental Congress, minus the signature of a reluctant Jacob Bayley, though Ira Allen's covering letter included Bayley's name.[15] The petition recapitulated the differences between the Grants and New York, a central theme of all the deliberations of the new state, its constitution and its relations to the Continental Congress.

The reaction of New York from January onwards, was predictable. The President of the Convention of the State of New York, A. Ten Broek, wrote to the Congress on January 20, protesting the move "to revolt, and disavow the authority of [New York's] legislature."[16] The Convention blamed the Congress for conferring a commission on Seth Warner, who "hath been constantly and invariably opposed to the legislature of this State" and demanded that the commissions of the officers of the Regiment be rescinded. Further strong letters followed on March 1 and May 28, part of a campaign to have the acts of the Grantees declared unlawful and to restore the jurisdiction of New York in the Grants. Congress considered the petition as well as letters in support of the separatists from Dr. Thomas Young dated April 11 and 12.[17] In his letters, Young had recommended independence under a constitution similar to Pennsylvania's, asserting that Vermont would be accepted into the confederation in line with the resolutions of the Continental Congress.

The Congress came to a series of resolutions on June 30. Well aware of the danger of a civil war between New York and "the Green Mountain Men," it dismissed the petition presented by Jonas Fay for Vermont to be "a free and independent State" and asserted that neither the appeal of the Congress of May 15, 1777 for the former colonies to "exert their own governments"[18] nor the Declaration of Independence of the previous year could warrant an independent government in the Grants. The fact that Warner's Continental regiment was free of New York was not to be construed as a right to the Grantees' independence. The Congress declared that it could not do anything "injurious to the rights and jurisdiction of the several communities" which the delegates to the Continental Congress represented.[19] Young's letters were dismissed as "highly injurious to the Honor and Dignity of Congress" and a gross misrepresentation of its resolutions. The news of the Congressional resolutions did not arrive at the Grants until after the adoption of the Vermont constitution early in July, but what did arrive in time was the news of the conservative New York Constitution with its denial of the New Hampshire titles.

Prior to mid-1777, representation at the conventions had been thin, partly because of opposition in Charlotte and Cumberland Counties and partly because of the impending threat of Burgoyne's expedition from Canada, which only receded with his defeat at Saratoga in October. When the convention reassembled at Windsor on June 4, it attracted seventy-two delegates, twenty-two from the west side and a remarkable twenty-six from the east side,[20] with two more towns sending letters endorsing the idea of a government following from independence. In order to legitimize the acts of the convention, it sent letters to every township in the Grants, advising freeholders to meet on June 23 and choose delegates for the resumed meeting of the convention on July 2. This would form a constitution for the new state, appoint a committee of safety and elect delegates to the Continental Congress.

The convention of June 4 adopted the new name of Vermont, in view of the fact that lands claimed by Connecticut along the Susquehannah River in Pennsylvania were known as New Connecticut. The new name been proposed by Dr. Young, though he was not its originator. The most urgent issue was to put the new state on a war footing, in view of Burgoyne's expedition up the Champlain Valley. The delegates pledged to play a full part in the war. The convention redrafted the passages in the Declaration of Independence of January justifying the separation from New York, and Ira Allen later reported that a committee was designated to prepare a draft of the constitution that would be debated at the July meeting.[21] The early June convention also took the first step in administration, directing the committees of safety in Cumberland and Gloucester to cease action under the authority of New York, and authorizing local Committees of Safety to sequester the estates of "enemical persons," Tory and Yorker loyalists, for the use of the state. The Commissioners of New York were also required to desist from the same. Local committees were also to arrest enemical persons for trial.[22]

When the convention assembled again at Windsor on July 2, Burgoyne's expedition was just outside Ticonderoga and attendance was less good, with about fifty delegates representing thirty-one towns. Among the delegates to the convention were Jonas Fay (Bennington), Heman Allen and Ira Allen (Colchester); Jacob Bayley (Newbury) and Ebenezer Allen (Tinmouth). The convention dealt with a letter from Seth Warner in Rutland, relaying St. Clair's order that the convention turn out the militia in view of Burgoyne's naval threat to Ticonderoga, as well as ensuring that New Hampshire and Massachusetts did the same. Warner also requested supplies. The convention passed on St Clair's order to New Hampshire on July 3.[23]

On July 8, the news came that Ticonderoga and Mount Independence had been evacuated. General St Clair, writing from Otter Creek on July 7, said that he was planning to move to Skenesborough via Castleton but since the former had been occupied, he was now aiming for Bennington, ordering the militia to do the same. Warner, commanding the rearguard, had been attacked six miles short of Castleton and, St Clair believed, the losses had been heavy on both sides.[24] By that time too, the delegates had received a copy of Lieutenant-General John Burgoyne's Proclamation of June 24, 1777.[25] Burgoyne offered protection to those not joining "the present unnatural rebellion" but promised "devastation, famine, and every concomitant horror that a reluctant but indispensable prosecution of military duty must occasion" to those who would not return to loyalty. Among these concomitant horrors was a passage in the Proclamation calculated to strike terror in soldiers and civilians alike: "I have but to give stretch to the Indian forces under my direction, and they amount to thousands [an exaggeration], to overtake the hardened enemies of Great-Britain and America. . . ."

The imminence of the enemy prompted the delegates to adopt the constitution which had already been considered in draft form. The Vermont Constitution of July 8, 1777 is quite a long one, but since the format and much of the language was the same as the Pennsylvania Constitution of 1776, little had to be changed between the decision of June 2 and the adoption of the constitution on July 8.

Before adjournment, the July convention chose a Council of Safety for the provisional administration of the state.[26] The names of the twelve members, as later recorded, indicate the leading lights of the independence movement: Thomas Chittenden (the first Governor of Vermont), Ira Allen (State Treasurer), Nathan Clark (to become the Speaker of the General Assembly), Joseph Fay (Secretary of the Governor and Council, then Secretary of State), Heman Allen (died May 18, 1778), Jacob Bayley, Jonas Fay, Benjamin Carpenter, Jeremiah Clark, Matthew Lyon, Moses Robinson and Paul Spooner. The most immediate task of the Council was to continue the work of putting

Vermont on a war footing, such as the recruitment of a militia. From July 8, 1777 to March 12, 1778, the Council was engaged in raising and organizing the militia.[27] Samuel Herrick continued his distinguished career in the service of Vermont when he was appointed Colonel of the Vermont Rangers; he was later Colonel of the southwestern regiment of Vermont militia.

In regard to the Constitution, there was no provision for public consultation. The reason was that the towns were regarded as representing the will of the people and there were provisions in the Constitution, through the septennial Council of Censors, for ensuring that the decisions of the Assembly were both constitutional and equitable. That Council also had powers to set a process in motion for amending the Constitution. The Preamble to the constitution with its anti-Yorker manifesto, was published only in December; Ira later claimed that, had it been published in July, the Constitution would never have been adopted, on account of Yorker opposition on the east side. The date for an election was postponed to March, 1778[28] after which the Assembly met for the first time, officers were elected, the Preamble was adopted and the government of Vermont was inaugurated. The fact that Vermont was ruled by the Council of Safety till mid-1778 gives us a clue as to how the Allens proposed to govern Vermont. They would rule as an oligarchy, the Arlington Junto, centering on the Governing Council but not coterminous with its membership.

The adoption of the Constitution did not mean that the independence of Vermont was to remain a fait accompli. A resolution of the New York Council of Safety on July 17, 1777, cited the Congress resolutions of June 30 and said that it would reassert jurisdiction in Cumberland County.[29] Vermont was to face threats from Massachusetts, New Hampshire and (especially) New York, with, at times, a hostile Congress and a constant military threat from the British in Canada. There was also an internal threat. At various times, "Yorkers living in Guilford, Brattleborough, Putney, New Fane, Hinsdale, Rockingham, Westminster and Weathersfield declared that they refused to acquiesce in independence" and advocated compromise with revolutionary New York.[30] At other times, if only briefly, the eastern towns advocated reunion with New Hampshire. Then again, the "college party" centered on Dartmouth College, advocated a separate state straddling the Connecticut River: the early years of the Republic were a complex mixture of various factions, at times allied with each other and at other times exhibiting a pattern of rivalry and dissent, with differing attitudes toward the Allens on the west side.

Dr. Thomas Young had proposed the radical constitution of Pennsylvania (September 28, 1776) as a model for the new state; subsequently the Vermont Constitution was similar to Pennsylvania's in many ways. It was also very different from New York: unlike the Constitution of revolutionary New York, the Executive had no legislative powers and it could not veto legislation. There was no separation of powers between the judiciary, the executive and the legislature in the sense that an individual could hold office in all three, and all Council members were simultaneously justices of the peace. There were provisions giving substantial protection for the persons and the property of debtors, which addressed the concerns of the east-siders. The provisions governing religious diversity were similar to Pennsylvania, except that in Vermont, no one could be deprived of rights if they were of the protestant faith[31] and the Sabbath had to be observed in one form or another. The protestant requirement for office was abolished in the revised constitution of 1786 but in the constitution of 1793, after Vermont had joined the Union as the fourteenth state, members of the Assembly had to declare that they were protestants (Section 12th).

There were also significant differences from the Pennsylvania Constitution. In Pennsylvania, voters had to have paid public taxes in order to vote,[32] as in New York, where in the neighboring counties, the franchise was restricted to a figure as low of 10% of the adult male population. In Vermont all freemen over the age of twenty-one had the vote. Vermont was the first jurisdiction to institute this universal manhood suffrage,[33] which divorced matters of liberty from those of property. Vermont's move was radical in its effect but not in its origin: since there were no public state taxes in Vermont at the time of the Constitution, the fathers had little choice but to open the field to everyman.

A second big difference lay in the Preamble. Both constitutions asserted that the King had "withdrawn his protection" and attacked the colonies, not only with his own troops, but with "foreign mercenaries, savages and slaves." But the Vermont Constitution makes as much of the hostility of New York as it does of the British, particularly New York's continuing claim to the legitimacy of land patents, as reflected (here Vermont is explicit) in Section 36 of the Constitution of revolutionary New York. This language survived the revision of the constitution in 1786. But the biggest difference was in the first section of The Declaration of the Rights of the Inhabitants of the State of Vermont. Whereas the Pennsylvania Constitution, in an echo of John Locke, spoke of the right to life, liberty, happiness and property, Vermont's referred briefly to these, then made a bold and blunt inference in the declaration outlawing the slavery of males over twenty-one and females over eighteen. The result, with certain important provisos, would be to abolish slavery within a generation, a matter which is discussed below in *Slavery and the Vermont Constitution.* Again, we can point to expediency, in that there were few African-Americans in the state in 1777, as well as radicalism, since Vermont was the first of several states and provinces to adopt similar provisions in the coming decades.

The Constitution of the Republic of Vermont was the culmination of a decade of political aspiration, during which the idea of a separate state was only one of several options, the most popular of which was re-annexation to New Hampshire. Vermont independence was not the creation of Ethan, nor of Ira or Heman, but from the time of his return from captivity in May 1778, the prime mover in maintaining Vermont's independence was Ethan Allen.

Slavery and the Vermont Constitution

In the draft Articles of Association of the United Colonies, October 20, 1774, Section 2 reads, "We will neither import nor purchase any slave imported after the 1st day of December next; after which we will wholly discontinue the slave trade," to go into effect if the Coercive Acts were not soon repealed. They were not of course repealed and the Articles were overtaken by the Revolution; slavery became lawful and entrenched in the American Constitution of 1787. Vermont was the first of the North American States to outlaw adult slavery. The very first article of the first chapter of the Constitution of the Republic of Vermont (July 8, 1777), A Declaration of the Rights of the Inhabitants of the State of Vermont, reads:

> That all men are born equally free and independent, and have certain natural, inherent, and unalienable rights, amongst which are the enjoying and defending life and liberty; acquiring, possessing, and protecting property, and pursuing and obtaining happiness and safety. Therefore, no male person, born in this country, or brought from over sea, ought to be holden by law, to serve any person, as a servant, slave, or apprentice, after he arrives to the age of twenty-one years; nor female, in like manner, after she arrives to the age of eighteen years, unless they are bound by their own consent, after they arrive to such age, or bound by law for the payment of debts, damages, fines, costs, or the like.

It was not a greatly difficult thing to outlaw adult slavery in the Constitution—there was no slave-owning class in Vermont to oppose it. The Constitution became a reality right away. Ebenezer Allen, the cousin of Ethan, for instance, captured a slave, Dinah Mattis, and her child on his raid into New York. He had them declared free in all of the American provinces by the Town Clerk of Bennington on November 27, 1777, since it was "not right in the sight of God to keep slaves." Ebenezer was clearly an abolitionist.

There are two interpretations of Vermont's prohibition.[34] The first relies on a plain reading of the text: slavery of minors was permitted, but adult slavery not. This was far from the abolition of slavery and the break-up of slave families was inevitable. There would have to be rules and court cases preventing the migration of minor slaves to and from the Republic and the extradition of African American adults; there would also have to be effective enforcement of the terms of the Constitution (there was no provision for a criminal law against slaveholding). That all of these took a long time was the reason why slavery persisted in Vermont long after the theoretical termination date of 1798, when all existing minor slaves would have reached adulthood.

The second interpretation holds that the article made no particular reference to black slaves, only instituting a qualifier or reservation of freedoms: minor servants, slaves and apprentices are still bound by rules superseding normal contracts of employment. On this view, the article only deals with rules of employment, irrespective of color.

As to which of these interpretations is correct, it is very difficult to say: there is no surviving record of the deliberations of the Constitutional Convention, nor was there any public consultation before the document was adopted. We simply do not know why the fathers decided to compress the sentiments of the Pennsylvania Constitution into a single sentence, then make stipulations about servants, slaves and apprentices. A strand of argument over the second interpretation would be that anti-slavery sentiment in the Grants was not yet strong and the main concern of the drafters was to institute rules over child labor and the work of young adults, which were no less common than elsewhere in New England. So when anti-slavery or abolitionism became stronger in the 1780s, Vermont could point to the Constitution as outlawing adult slavery while making rules over the migration of African-Americans to and from the Republic.

The law of October 30, 1786, "An Act to Prevent the Sale and Transportation of Negroes and Mulattoes Out of This State," claimed that "the idea of slavery is totally exploded from our free government."[35] This law made it impossible to retrieve slaves from outside the state, as Levi Allen had tried to do when he offered a reward for a runaway slave from Dutchess County, New York, on November 24, 1778. It is worth noting that this Act does not provide a weight of evidence in favor of either of the two interpretations of Article 1: the claim that slavery was totally exploded was made in spite of the fact that there were still rules over minor servants, slaves, and apprentices.

Similar legislation to that of Vermont was passed in Pennsylvania (1780), Connecticut and Rhode Island (1784), New York (1785), Upper Canada (1793—with some very big reservations) and New Jersey (1804). The fact that slavery persisted in Vermont until the early nineteenth century does not detract from the fact that, whether by accident or design, Vermont had led the way towards its abolition.

Despite the rules outlawing slavery, the part played by African-Americans in the saga of the Vermont Republic has been hidden from history. Ethan Allen owned or rented three slaves when he "took possession" of the lead mine in Northampton;[36] negroes were also among those captured at Ticonderoga in 1775.[37] Justus Sherwood, as much a hero of this tale as any Patriot, owned two slaves, and Upper Canada allowed him to keep them. Ethan hired two mulattoes on his farm in Burlington, one of whom accompanied him on his last ride home from South Hero.

CHAPTER 8

Defending the Republic: New York, New Hampshire and the Continental Congress

ETHAN ALLEN, FRESH FROM British captivity, arrived in Bennington on the last day of May 1778. He moved on to Arlington, where he met with the Governor and Council. There he also got word of his brevet colonel's commission from the Continental Congress and the promise of back pay, at the rank of lieutenant-colonel, for his years in the hands of the British. His exchange had been blocked by the royal governor Tryon while Gouveneur Morris of New York claimed credit for the fact that Ethan did not get a full colonelcy on the active list. Ethan was honored for his service to the American Republic but no more than that, for he never got an active command, nor did he accompany any troops in battle as he had done in 1775. From Arlington, Ethan and the Council proceeded to Bennington early in June, where the Assembly was beginning the second session of its existence. Though Ethan resumed his leadership in what was now Vermont, both within and without its institutions, he was never a member of the Council or the Assembly, nor did he hold any offices of pivotal importance. Ethan was appointed to the Court of Confiscation after the Assembly had passed the Banishment Act. He was later appointed what he described as "agent for the State of Vermont at Congress"[1] and from mid-1779 he was Brigadier-General of the Vermont militia, with specific commissions from time to time to quell internal disorders.

The Republic of Vermont had been born in war and, on the presumption that Burgoyne would have fulfilled his plan to reduce New England, had survived only because of his defeat at Saratoga in October 1777. The Republic was still in a perilous position, with British raids starting in July 1778.

Politically, the state of the Republic was precarious. Congress had "peremptorily dismissed" the petition for recognition at the end of June 1777.[2] There was a fear of an invasion by the provincial troops of New York to claim its jurisdiction, which the Republic was ill-equipped to resist: Warner's regiment had been withdrawn to Albany, away from the most likely invasion route, and such militia that Vermont had mobilized were engaged in garrisoning a rough and thin defense line against the British from Castleton to the Coos Country around Newbury. This fear of action by New York was at the time nearly groundless, since Governor George Clinton was engaged in resisting Burgoyne's invasion and he actually fought in the battles for the Highlands. It was not until December 1781 that Governor Clinton sent troops eastwards, not into Vermont, but to reclaim New York territory east of the Hudson, which Vermont had annexed. Vermonters still had reason to believe that they were under siege.

Economically, the Republic was poverty-stricken. Ira was the state Treasurer, but the Treasury was empty and no system of taxation or revenue in the form of fees had been established. A first round of confiscation and auctioning of vacated Tory property, to finance Herrick's Rangers,[3] had begun in mid-1777 and the proceeds were all spent. The new Banishment Act went further and authorized the expulsion of those found guilty of disloyalty as well as the confiscation and sale of their property; those disloyal included, in effect, Yorkers as well as Tories, as Ethan intended. This enabled the Republic to get by without a taxation system until 1781 and was one factor in the desire of the western New Hampshire towns to join Vermont. It also increased the enmity of Governor Clinton, who relied on Yorker loyalty in Cumberland County to reclaim jurisdiction and to raise militia for the state.

By the time Ethan arrived home, Clinton had already begun his attempts to bring Vermont back into the fold. He issued his first Proclamation, dated February 23, 1778,[4] offering to confirm titles to lands in the Grants in return for the acknowledgement of the jurisdiction of New York but denying confirmation to those expressing allegiance to the "pretended state of Vermont." He required all four counties of Vermont to "yield allegiance and obedience . . . to this state." Clinton followed this up with a further Proclamation of October 31, 1778.[5] Critics have taken it that the Proclamations offered to confirm titles free of charge and that Clinton's move was "not an ungenerous gesture."[6] This was not true of the first Proclamation, where there was a whole complex system of confirmation fees, quit-rents and commutations. The second Proclamation referred to the first but was silent as to whether there would be any charge for confirmations. Ethan, naturally enough, did not refer to these fees in his two responses, confining himself to the denial of New York's jurisdiction and commenting that Clinton could not offer to annul the attainders of royal New York, since these were invalidated at the collapse of royal authority.

Vermont was bent on recognition and acceptance into the Continental Congress, so Clinton's overtures were bound to fail. Where he could succeed was in blocking Vermont's aspirations in the Congress. Initially, the New England states were pitched against New York, but the latter had allies in those states, such as Virginia, Pennsylvania and the Carolinas, which faced separatist or secessionist movements. As Vermont's agent, Ethan made three visits to the Continental Congress in Philadelphia to lobby on behalf of the Republic. The first of these, in September 1778 was to undo the damage done by the first Eastern Union of Cumberland County towns, with sixteen of those in New Hampshire, to be discussed below. In the course of this, Ethan had a private conversation with Henry Laurens, the President of the Congress. Ethan claimed, with how much truth is not known, that Laurens had said that if the union were dissolved, he would have no objection to the recognition of Vermont and its admission to the Confederation. There were no other signs of promise or success.

The purpose of Ethan's second visit, from late November till December 4, was to announce the good news of the union's dissolution. Before this visit, he had got from the third session of the Assembly the title of "Agent to the Honble Congress when the Governor and Council Shall Judge Necessary." The Congress was not impressed either with the title or with the news that Ethan brought; he was all but ignored and the mission was likewise a failure. George Clinton's proclamations had not been met with any favorable response from Vermont, and New York remained as hostile as ever to the Republic's admission. Ethan, with Jonas Fay, visited Philadelphia for the third time early in. July 1779 to make amends for the suppression of a Yorker insurrection in Cumberland County that spring. Clinton was so outraged by the foray that he threatened to send a thousand Continental troops into Cumberland County if Congress did not retaliate in some effective way. He also intimated to Washington that recruits and provisions might have to be diverted from the war effort to the suppression of Vermont. Congress did indeed apologize for the delay in attending to the business of Vermont and it appointed a five-man commission to investigate the true situation of the district "known as the New Hampshire Grants"[7] But Clinton was not assuaged;

the Vermont emissaries did not succeed in getting a hearing at the Congress. The situation for Vermont had gone from bad to worse and from this time can be dated the first thoughts that Ethan had of a strategy that did not aim for the admission of Vermont into the Continental Congress. Certainly, at this time, the British in New York had some reason to believe that Ethan could be turned towards a reunion with Great Britain, as will be seen.

IN MARCH 1778, BEFORE Ethan's return, sixteen New Hampshire towns on the east bank of the Connecticut River applied for admission into Vermont, a case of voluntary annexation.[8] This was not welcome news for the Governor and Council but they were faced with a pro-Yorker and secessionist movement in Cumberland County. So emboldened, some towns wrote to the Assembly on March 4, protesting the request of the Council to disavow allegiance to New York. On April 15, the protest was adopted by a Convention in Brattleborough with representation from that town as well as Guilford, Putney, Newfane, Hinsdale (Vernon) and Rockingham, with letters of support from Westminster and Weathersfield, all of whom affirmed allegiance to the State of New York.[9] The threat was that if Vermont did not submit to New York, the dissenters would form a separate state with as many towns as will join us—including those in New Hampshire. On the other hand, an increase in the number of seats in the Assembly by the admission of New Hampshire towns would, as Colonel Bayley knew, eventually increase the strength of the opposition to the Allens to the point of outvoting them. Chittenden was aware of this, but he had little choice. When the Assembly voted to admit the towns, Chittenden invited the towns straddling the Connecticut River to hold referenda and to send delegates to the next session of the Assembly, which would lay a foundation for more towns to unite.[10] The towns voted in the affirmative and, upon a recommendation from the Governor and Council, the Assembly voted on June 11, 1778 in favor of a union with the Sixteen Towns.[11] Further, the Assembly invited any New Hampshire towns contiguous to the sixteen to enter in the same union. In a move that was to have repercussions over the next year and more, the Assembly called for a convention to be held on December 9 at Cornish in New Hampshire, on the east bank of the Connecticut River.

Delegates at Cornish, one of the Sixteen Towns, could attend from the towns on *both* sides of the river. The mandate of the convention was to provide for the "amicable agreement and quiet settlement of the *whole* of the

Grants in a regular state of Government."[12] The convention was to "consult and agree upon measures "whereby we all may be united together, by being or remaining a distinct State," facilitating admission by Congress. Alternatively, the convention could "claim the antient Jurisdiction of the Government of New Hampshire" . . . "to defend ourselves against the pretended right of any other State" [New York] and thereby become one entire State as it stood before the decree of 1764. This was only to be done if New Hampshire laid claim to all of Vermont.[13] The mandate was ambiguous. The terms of reference included a settlement of the whole of the Grants, so a "distinct state" evidently meant an extended Vermont and not a new state straddling the Connecticut River. But the second option seemed to leave open the possibility of a union of all of Vermont with all of New Hampshire, as was the case before the decree of 1764. In other words, a sectional interest was to "agree upon measures" for all of Vermont.

The revolt of the Sixteen Towns had long been brewing. In November 1775, New Hampshire abandoned the property qualification for suffrage in favor of determining that all taxpayers would get the vote. In keeping with New Hampshire tradition, the revolutionary Constitution of January 5, 1776 laid down that the terms of elections would be determined by the Council and Assembly:

> The precepts in the name of the Council and Assembly, signed by the President of the Council, and Speaker of the house of Representatives, shall issue annually at or before the first day of November, for the choice of a Council and house of Representatives to be returned by the third Wednesday in December then ensuing, in such a manner as the Council and Assembly shall hereafter prescribe.

The eastern seaboard establishment was determined to keep political power in its own hands, at the expense of the Connecticut River towns. The way to do this was to allot seats in the Assembly on the basis of population. Already, in the Constitution, representation in the Council had been stacked in favor of the seaboard: Cheshire County on the Connecticut River to the south got only two seats out of twelve, while Grafton County to the north, adjacent to Colonel Bayley's fief in Gloucester County, got a single one. So intense was the desire to retain seaboard hegemony that some thought it would be better to let the western counties go, thus according with the aims of the western separatists.

So the first fear of the western towns was under-representation in the Assembly. When it was proposed that towns with a hundred or more taxpayers would get a seat in the Assembly, the first response of the Connecticut River towns was to contend that all towns should get a seat, irrespective of population. Alternatively, some westerners contended that towns with fewer than one hundred could combine to get a shared seat[14] The Vermont Constitution, by contrast, laid down no restrictions on the size of an incorporated town to qualify for representation (Plan or Frame of Government, Section XVI) and all freemen over the age of twenty-one could vote, taxpayers or not (Section VIII). Thus, if the western towns joined Vermont, they would get representation in the Assembly, regardless of size.

A second issue was taxation. Settlers in the western townships already had a grievance in that the burden of taxation fell entirely upon them, while absentee title-holders got off scot-free. They were subjected to quit-rents at the rate of a shilling a year, lower than the New York rate in the Grants of half a crown, but a burden none the less. There was no state taxation of course in the Grants and none when the Republic was inaugurated in July 1777. The Constitution provided for state taxation explicitly (Plan or Frame of Government, Section XXXVIII) and implicitly when it laid down that the Council of Censors was to "enquire whether public taxes have been justly laid and collected" (Section XLIV). But the early years of the Republic were financed through the sale of Yorker and Tory properties; it was not until 1780 that a system of state taxes was inaugurated; they were collected a year later. So when the first revolt of the Sixteen Towns took place in 1778, the residents would pay no state taxes if they joined Vermont. The standing grievances of the Sixteen Towns over taxation and representation meant that the issue was unlikely to go away, even if the union of 1778 were reversed. (The case was altered at the second Eastern Union of 1781, when the New Hampshire towns were subjected to Vermont's taxation, one reason why it did not last.)

A third factor comprised the vicissitudes of Vermont politics, such as the revolt against the power of the Allens all along the west bank of the Connecticut River which initially and at times gave the dissenters a common set of aims with the New Hampshire east bank. What rankled in particular was Ira's confiscation and sale of Loyalist properties in Cumberland County. In 1781, however, there was something of a reversal: the western New Hampshire towns initially wanted to share in the benefits of the truce with the British that the Allens had secured.[15]

On August 22, Meshech Weare, President of the Council of State of

New Hampshire wrote to Chittenden, explaining that the Sixteen Towns were indubitably a part of New Hampshire and that Vermont should "relinquish every connection, as a political body, with the towns east of Connecticut River."[16] The tone of the letter is courteous, expressing sympathy with Vermonters' aspirations to statehood, merely deploring the union as "supplying their enemies with arguments against them." However, his letter of August 19 to the New Hampshire delegates at Congress is very different.[17] He told the delegates that the "pretended state of Vermont" has extended jurisdiction to the "revolted towns," where a majority of the inhabitants were against the union and were threatened with the confiscation of their estates. He added that Colonel Timothy Bedel "has occasioned a great share in the disorder in those towns." Bedel was disgusted at the disbandment of his regiment after its two years patrolling the Canadian border; he joined in political alliance with his old comrade, Colonel Bayley. The delegates were advised to call on the aid of Congress; if not, bloodshed was sure to follow. In the previous winter, the New Hampshire delegate at Congress, William Whipple, had warned that recognizing Vermont would encourage "many towns on the Eastern side of the River" to join the new state.[18]

When Ethan returned to Windsor from his first mission to Philadelphia early in October 1778, he reported that "except this state recede from such union, immediately, the whole power of the confederacy of the United States of America will join to annihilate the state of Vermont."[19] A complex series of maneuvers followed. On October 19, the Assembly voted for a union with all the New Hampshire towns west of the "Mason claim," a far greater number than the first sixteen. But on the 21st, under pressure from Ethan, the Assembly implicitly dissolved the union by voting to exclude all New Hampshire towns from Cumberland County and prohibiting the formation of a further county for those towns.[20] This was despite strong opposition from the delegates from Cumberland County. The Vermont government was in an uproar. Twenty-seven members representing towns straddling the Connecticut River withdrew from the Assembly, claiming that their exclusion from the Assembly was unconstitutional. In Ira Allen's words, the members present who represented ten of the Sixteen Towns "withdrew from the Assembly, and were followed by the Lieutenant Governor, three members of the Council, and fifteen members of the Assembly, who lived near Connecticut River."[21] Chittenden and the Assembly tried in vain to mollify the opposition by getting the Assembly on October 23 to refer the question to the people for instructions to their representatives. This was akin to the Cornish resolution of June 11.[22]

Ethan wrote to Weare on October 23, saying that in his opinion, the union "is now entirely Dissolved" and counting on New Hampshire to "Accede to the Independency of the State of Vermont as the last Obsticles are Honourably removed."[23] Weare replied on November 5,[24] saying that New Hampshire would endorse any acknowledgement of Vermont's "Independency" by the Continental Congress; but he had reservations about Vermont's claims to have excluded the New Hampshire towns. The trouble was that the dissolution of the union was not quite final. Chittenden had informed Weare that Vermont would not exercise jurisdiction east of the Connecticut River "for the time being." To which Weare observed that this "by no means expresses their future designs or intentions in the matter." This was a pertinent observation, for Weare knew full well that the status of the union was still the subject of ongoing public discussion.[25]

The convention of "protesting members" duly met at Cornish on December 9, 1778 and repudiated the royal order of 1764. Four options were proposed, apparently in descending order of preference. The first was to get an agreement on a dividing line between New Hampshire and the Grants; the second was to appoint commissioners from Connecticut, Massachusetts and Rhode Island to determine the same; the third was to refer the matter to the Continental Congress for its prescription; and the fourth option, in the event of the failure of the first three, was to consent to form one state as it was before the "arbitrary line" drawn on the Connecticut River in 1764.[26] This arbitrary line was contrary to the view of the delegates that the river was not a natural boundary dividing a single area of commercial and economic activity. The "one state" was union with New Hampshire, one of the options in the June 11 mandate: "Or 4: If the controversy cannot be settled on either of the forgoing articles, and in case we can agree on a plan of government with New-Hampshire, inclusive of extent of territory, that we unite with them, and become with them one entire State, rejecting the arbitrary line drawn on the western bank of Connecticut-river, by the King of Great-Britain in 1764."[27]

The Cornish convention invited the non-protesting members of the Vermont Assembly to rescind their vote for the dissolution of the union and join in pursuing the four options. The towns in the Grants who were not represented at Cornish were asked to send their votes for and against the four options. The votes were to be sent to a committee which included Colonels Jacob Bayley and Davenport Phelps. If this did not happen, the fourth proposal was to be sent directly to New Hampshire for a joint plan of union. It was these "Subscribers" from the towns that Bayley and Phelps (representing the New Hampshire east-siders) claimed to represent when at Newbury they signed and then presented a petition to the New Hampshire Assembly on March 17, 1779.[28] Having set down the four options, "we the subscribers, being duly authorized for that purpose, do now propose to this honorable Court, that the whole of the said Grants be connected and confederated with said State of New-Hampshire."

The June 11 resolution did not require the Cornish convention to refer their findings back to the truncated Assembly, whose constitutionality the "protesting members" did not in any case recognize. Otherwise, Bayley and Phelps had violated the June 11 resolution in several ways. Not least of these was the supposition that the Cornish convention had the authority to "make an offer" to New Hampshire. Nor is it clear how much of an attempt there was in undertaking the formidable task of winning over the towns and Assembly members to the Cornish cause, in other words, how far the first three options had been pursued. Ira, who had been at the Cornish convention and attended the New Hampshire Assembly, protested in vain. The New Hampshire Assembly "allowed" that Congress might recognize Vermont but referred to the petition, asserting that New Hampshire had a right to all of the Grants. The state would exercise jurisdiction only east of the Connecticut River until the dispute was settled by Congress.[29] The question was referred to a committee, which reported to the New Hampshire House of Representatives on June 24 and 25, 1779. The Committee's report was accepted: New Hampshire, it was implied, claimed all of the Grants, subject to a settlement by the Congress, until which time the state would exercise jurisdiction only to the east of the Connecticut River. Bayley, whose case was a shaky one, had achieved his long-held ambition of union with New Hampshire. This would of course settle the issue of the Sixteen Towns, whether they liked it or not.

We have only the documentary evidence, a skeletal compendium of Assembly proceedings, with the letters and the writings, not always reliable, of the Allens. For instance, Ira claimed that it was the dissenting members and not the Assembly who had decided to hold the convention at Cornish, and that this was decided in October, not in June.[30] The details of the interplay of personal interests and the complex maneuverings at the Vermont Assembly in March and October, 1778 are not known. Nor are the machinations that took place between the Cornish convention and the petition of March 17, 1779. Clearly, there were pressures on Chittenden and the Allens which they could not completely or successfully resist. It is all too easy, over two centuries later, to cast judgment on the players, when we can only make inferences from the written record. Yet it is hard to escape the conclusion that the Allens lost control of the events that led to the claim of New Hampshire to Vermont. The Cornish convention was allowed to convene without terms of reference, and a vagueness as to the convention's mandate: the delegates had only to "agree upon measures," with no indication as to what was to become of the agreement. Colonel Bayley then proceeded, apparently without seriously pursuing the first three options, and without any reference to the truncated Vermont Assembly, to petition New Hampshire for union of the two states. Had the Vermont Assembly, instead of the Cornish convention, appointed commissioners to look into the issues on both sides of the Connecticut River, then report back with their findings, there would have been a better chance for the Sixteen Towns remaining within the grasp of the legislators. The rationale for New Hampshire accepting union was that it was "to help the inhabitants, in case the Yorkers should hinder said state from being established by Congress."[31] This reflected the sentiments, but not the political strategy, of the Vermont Assembly. It was indeed true that the New Hampshire government had received reports from its delegation at Congress that New York was about to have its jurisdiction confirmed at the expense of the Granite State. The move of New Hampshire was traditional in that the province had asserted jurisdiction, without much publicity, even after the royal order of 1764.

The Allens responded through their various vindications and pamphlets in a number of ways. In some writings, they asserted the validity of the 1764 decision which removed jurisdiction from New Hampshire but, seeing that this would legitimize New York's claim, they contended that the extinction of royal authority had invalidated all previous decisions. Thus the status of the Grants was an open question to be decided by the Grantees themselves. Many of Ira's arguments concerned the internal deliberations of the Vermont decision-makers: the rulings of the truncated Assembly were valid and there were "but eight towns represented on the west side of the river" in the Cornish convention.[32] (The Resolves of the convention stated that a total of twenty-two towns were represented, fourteen of New Hampshire.) This convention was in any case not a legitimate decision-making body.

Meanwhile, the Vermont Assembly had resolved at Bennington on February 12, 1779, that "the said union is hereby dissolved and made totally void, null and extinct."[33] Ethan wrote to Weare on March 4, stating that the union has been "in the fullest and most Explicit manner Disolved."[34] This did not prevent the New Hampshire House of Representatives from pursuing union in the following months. President Weare was right to have been skeptical: the Sixteen Towns had a standing grievance against New Hampshire, which was not resolved by the reiteration of the state's claim from the Mason line to the western borders of the Grants, and jurisdiction east of the Connecticut River. For instance, John Wheelock (the son of Eleazer, the founder of Dartmouth College and the leader of the Sixteen Towns) had shown up at Congress during Ethan's visit in November 1778, asserting that the towns were still in revolt against New Hampshire and Ethan had no authority to give them back.[35]

The resolve of New Hampshire to "help the inhabitants" of the Grants was soon to be tested. Yorker sentiment and protests at the confiscation of their property increased in the wake of the dissolution of the union, while others who resented the dissolution and the Allens' part in it, joined those already disaffected. This came to a head in the Cumberland County insurrection of May 1779. The insurrection was actually more of a series of protests in Putney and the neighboring towns of Guilford, Brattleboro, Westminster and Hinsdale. The disturbances were caused by resistance to the attempts of the Council to recruit men to "guard the frontiers of this State" rather than serve in the New York militia.[36] The Yorkers responded by setting up committees opposing "the pretended state of Vermont" and appealing to Clinton to take immediate and effective measures to end "the lawless rule of riatous men."[37] On May 6, Ethan was authorized to lead an expedition into Cumberland County with a hundred men to assist the County Sheriff in enforcing the law.[38] He arrived in the county in mid-May with more than double that number, many of them former Green Mountain Boys. There was no resistance to the huge, blustering figure who headed the expedition. About three dozen were arrested, tried and found guilty, most at the insistence of Ethan, who intervened quite improperly in the trial at Westminster. The punishments were fines for the breach of public order. In response, the Vermont Assembly decreed corporal punishment and mutilation for "opposers of the Republic and, especially, those who claimed to hold office under any government except that of Vermont or the Continental Congress." Then on June 3, Chittenden issued a pardon for past offences but not capital crimes, thus exonerating the Westminster protesters.[39]

Ethan, as a reward, was elected Commanding General of the Vermont Militia on June 2, with the rank of Brigadier-General; the appointment was evidently uncontroversial. At the same time, Ira was appointed Surveyor-

General, in addition to his office as Treasurer and member of the Council. He was to draw up a General Plan of the State and to ascertain the location of vacant lands.[40]

The reaction of an outraged Clinton has already been discussed. He openly encouraged the residents of Cumberland County to resist the authority of Vermont and told the Continental Congress so.[41] Clinton was satisfied neither with the apology from the Continental Congress for being so sluggish in dealing with the business of Vermont, nor with the dispatch of the five-man commission to report on the true situation in that "certain district known as the New Hampshire Grants."[42] Vermont offered conciliation in that Chittenden issued the pardon of June 3, 1779. Limited and bloodless though the Cumberland County insurrection was, it signaled the virtual end of Vermont's attempts to get recognition from the Continental Congress. A letter from Ethan and Jonas Fay to the Continental Congress, requesting that discussions of Vermont's application be resumed, was to no avail.[43] Massachusetts, well aware of the declining position of Vermont in the light of the New Hampshire claim, asserted that it would reclaim the towns in southern Vermont over which it had once had jurisdiction.[44] By October 1779, there was an open, four-way conflict between Vermont, New York, Massachusetts and New Hampshire, with the Congress in an impossible position, one reason why it declined to move to a resolution.

Chittenden wrote to the Continental Congress on August 5, 1779, renewing the application to join the Confederation, saying that Vermont would pay its "just portion" of the war in which the state had played its full part. He observed (no doubt with relish) that some in Cumberland County needed to be "roused to do their duty."[45] Over the Massachusetts claim, Chittenden wrote a conciliatory letter to Samuel Adams, President of the Council, on October 28, 1779. Soon afterwards, Adams replied, rejecting the royal boundary decision of 1739 (actually 1740) and laying a claim to part of the Grants, as well as some of central and western New York.[46] On December 28, 1779, the General Court of Massachusetts declared that it had "a clear and indisputable right" to the southern part of Vermont.[47]

Just how much of Vermont was not clear. In 1740, the King in Council determined the boundary between New Hampshire and Massachusetts. Early in the next year, New Hampshire surveyed the boundary, but Massachusetts declined to take part, so any claim by Massachusetts to townships north of the survey line would have meant disputing the boundary as ascertained by New Hampshire. The towns north of that line, granted by

Massachusetts prior to 1740, were Hinsdale and Winchester (both reconfirmed by New Hampshire in 1753, the latter renamed Vernon in 1802); Bernardston (overlapping Hinsdale and Guilford); Brattleboro; Fulham (later Dummerston) and Putney (all three chartered by New Hampshire in 1753); New Taunton or "Number One" (rechartered as Westminster in 1752) and "Number Two" (rechartered in 1752 as Rockingham) and possibly also Coleraine, which, being absorbed by other towns, was not chartered by New Hampshire.[48]

In a memorial of Charles Phelps of Marlborough, Vermont on June 23, 1774, "about fifty towns" were mentioned, which would have meant the most populous parts of the state up to the Castleton-Newbury line.[49] This was far more than the seven towns chartered by New Hampshire in 1752 and 1753. Phelps was an obtuse and eccentric Yorker who, in the words of Benjamin H. Hall, was engaged in a "scheme to effect the annexation of Vermont to Massachusetts . . . with a singularity of behavior not easily to be accounted for."[50] Again, Phelps had actually been commissioned, with Ethan, to prepare the remonstrance *against* New York in the meeting at Westminster on April 11, 1775. Fifty towns were mentioned in a further memorial of October 27, 1777[51] and Phelps was actively pursuing the issue in the summer of 1779. Ethan, in his *Concise Refutation,* evaded the issue by defending the royal decision of 1740 and illustrating the point by reference only to Fort Dummer, for which Wentworth had been given responsibility.[52] There seemed to be no happy medium between the seven towns, aptly described by Chitttenden as a "snack," and the grandiose claims of Charles Phelps.

There the matter stood for a year. Chittenden contended that Massachusetts had not "as a legislative body" laid claim to the territory of Vermont,[53] though in its deliberations of September 1779, the Congress had clearly recognized the fact of the Massachusetts' claim. Chittenden wrote from Arlington to Governor Hancock of Massachusetts on December 12, 1780,[54] demanding that the Commonwealth relinquish all claims and jurisdiction to any and every part of the State. In view of the British attacks on Vermont, he wrote that unless the state were "admitted into Union," it might be "under the disagreeable necessity of making the best terms with the British that may be in their power."[55] Also on December 12, Chittenden wrote to Governor Trumbull of Connecticut.[56] He demanded that New Hampshire, New York and Massachusetts relinquish their claims of jurisdiction over Vermont, saying that this impeded Vermont's admission to Congress. He offered an alliance with Connecticut.

To anticipate: the Yorker threat to Vermont receded. Early in 1781, the New York legislators came close to recognizing Vermont and by August, New York was isolated in the Continental Congress over the future of the Republic, since at that time, New Hampshire was not actively pursuing its claim. The General Council of Massachusetts responded to Chittenden's letter of the previous December and passed a resolution on March 8, 1781, stating that if Congress acknowledged the independence of Vermont and admitted her to the union, Massachusetts will relinquish claims to jurisdiction over Vermont.[57] In other words, Massachusetts would continue with its claim until that of New York were extinguished. The only condition was to reserve right and title of those towns from the Province/Commonwealth of Massachusetts: Vermont could not invalidate those titles that had been issued, then confirmed by Governor Wentworth. There the matter rested. When motions for the recognition of Vermont came up in Congress early in 1782, Massachusetts voted in favor.

While the claims of New Hampshire and Massachusetts stood, neither of these two states were prepared to see a state "already Troublesome to her Neighbors and Tyrannical to the last degree over all such as are the unhappy victims of their resentment"[58] swallow up the Yankee territory of the Grants. In principle, they were as hostile to New York as the Vermonters, lacking only the direct confrontation with Yorker power, actual and potential, that Vermont experienced. What followed was a flurry of pamphleteering by the Allens. Confronted by enemies on both sides, they sometimes saw New Hampshire and New York as colluding in the destruction of Vermont. Indeed, at one point there were rumors that the two states would divide up Vermont along the Green Mountains; but the main thing that the Allens had to do was to resist the claims of New Hampshire, Massachusetts and New York alike.

Governor Clinton's insistence that the Congress pursue a resolution of the Vermont question was not the only pressure on that body. He pulled the strings on the Yorkers in Cumberland County. On July 23, 1779, the committees of ten towns in Cumberland County, still smarting over the May insurrection, sent a petition to Congress, asking for "the speedy interposition of the Congress in settling the disturbances upon the New Hampshire Grants."[59] A Congress Committee of the Whole reported on September 24.[60] The Committee noted the Cumberland County petition and the claims to jurisdiction of New York, New Hampshire, Massachusetts and "the pretended State of Vermont." The Congress recommended that Massachusetts, New

Hampshire and New York pass laws, authorizing Congress to determine their boundaries, which the latter two did.[61] (The Articles of Confederation, granting the Congress the power to settle right of soil, had not yet come into force.) The five-man committee investigating the issue was discharged. The four parties were enjoined to appoint agents for hearings to begin on February 1, 1780, at which time "the Congress will, on said 1st day of February next, proceed, without delay, to hear and examine into the disputes and differences relative to jurisdiction . . . and will decide and determine the same according to equity."[62] Vermont was directed to refrain from the granting or sale of confiscated lands, understandable in that some of the lands in question were confiscated from Yorkers who had denied Vermont's legitimacy.

In one other respect, however, the terms of the interim settlement went against Vermont. New York, New Hampshire and Massachusetts could exercise jurisdiction over towns on both sides of the Connecticut River if those towns had professed allegiance to one of these three. Thus New Hampshire was enabled to do what it had conceded it would not do, namely to exercise jurisdiction west of the Connecticut River. New York was not entirely happy, because it considered that the fate of Vermont was the business of New York alone. It was obliged to recognize the other two states on grounds of equity, but it was confident that the decision would favor New York because of the state of jurisdiction at the outbreak of the Revolution.[63] New York also got a part of what it wanted: to subject Yorker towns to the authority of New York. Vermont could exercise jurisdiction only over those towns "who have affirmed a separate jurisdiction."[64] Charles Jellison's comment that "in effect, Congress was ordering Vermont to stop functioning as an independent state"[65] is an exaggeration, yet Vermont's authority was severely truncated. Ethan Allen could well assert that the ruling was outrageous.

Ira Allen in his *History* considered that, in Ethan's absence, the delegates to the Assembly in Manchester, held in October, were deeply concerned; "nine-tenths were for suspending the sale of confiscated property, and the granting of lands till after the 1st of February."[66] Then came Ethan's finest hour. It took him nearly two weeks, single-handedly, to turn the Council and Assembly around. He had himself appointed to a committee of the Assembly to work with the Council on a plan to counter the aspirations of New York, New Hampshire and Massachusetts alike. This took five days, after which a grand committee of the whole, comprising the Governor, Council, Assembly and a few outsiders such as Ethan, voted *unanimously* to assert Vermont's independence and freedom from outside interference. By the time the

Assembly adjourned on October 27, 1779, it had delegated the power to Ethan, with two associates, to determine the implementation of petitions for grants of wild lands, which he then did.[67] Confiscations of Tory property were also to continue.

Ethan then got the Manchester Assembly to send him as an agent of the Council to the General Court of Massachusetts "and other places contiguous to negociate the public business."[68] Ethan's attempt before the General Court in November to have Vermont buy out the Massachusetts claims to Vermont was a complete and abrupt failure. This was in the context of a rumor that there was a secret agreement between New York and New Hampshire to divide up Vermont at the Green Mountains, at the expense of Massachusetts, and it was not helped by Ethan's tirade and invective against greed and stupidity of the members of the General Court. He could hurl abuse at the officers of the Vermont courts and the Cumberland County rioters; but there was no way this could work in Boston. The result for Ethan was the pamphlet already cited, the *Concise Refutation,* endorsed by the Governor and Council of Vermont on January 1, 1780.

There was nothing more to do but shore up the defenses of Vermont. In his capacity as Commanding General of the Vermont Militia, Ethan attempted to build up the militia, hampered by the inability to pay and equip them and by the fact that many of the remaining young men would serve only New York. Early in 1780, he reinforced what came to be known as a front line, which was really only a line above which the safety of the residents could not be guaranteed. Starting in the west, Sergeant Elisha Towner and a few privates garrisoned Skenesborough; Fort Vengeance at Castleton, authorized in April, got a lieutenant and nineteen men; Ebenezer Allen and four companies camped at Pittsford, with a larger force in the Coos Country on the Connecticut River to the east.[69] All told, Ethan had a maximum of 500 men under command, of whom few were fit and properly equipped. Warner's regiment was out of the state in the region of Fort George and, obviously, it was out of the question to request the Continental Army to come to the aid of Vermont. There was a further blow to this sorry state of affairs when, early in 1780, Congress forbade the Continental Commissary at Bennington under Isaac Tichenor from issuing any more supplies to Vermont and its militia. Ethan was forced to go to Boston and Hartford several times to buy ammunition. The Assembly retaliated, forbidding the export of food from the state. To the north and west, Vermont was besieged, with New York threatening to withhold taxes from the Confederation unless it resolved the Vermont issue and with claims to Vermont still emanating from the east and south. In view of Vermont's defiance of the terms of the interim settlement, the deadline of February 1, 1780 passed without Congressional resolution or action; further deadlines came and went. For instance, Ira Allen and Stephen R. Bradley presented a remonstrance to Congress on the Vermont question. The Congress heard evidence from New Hampshire, then resolved that further consideration of the subject be postponed.[70] Within the state, the issue of Cumberland County and the Sixteen Towns continued to simmer, while on the west side, there were the beginnings of an anti-Allen party, favoring conciliation with the states of the Continental Congress and starting to assert itself in the Assembly. The events of early 1780 reinforced Ethan's premonitions of 1779 that, if Vermont was to survive, there had to be a resolution that depended on parties other than the predatory states and the Continental Congress.

There was one last chapter in the episodes of the Sixteen Towns and it occurred when Ethan and his faction were in discussions with the British over a truce, the exchange of prisoners and, secretly (as will be seen) the return of Vermont to the British Empire.[71] (The truce came into effect at the end of October 1780; when the Assembly gave its approval, Ethan resigned as Brigadier-General of Militia on November 7, 1780[72]). The truce was popular in many quarters, initially covering northern New York state, while the secret Loyalists and the conservative Yorkers of Cumberland County welcomed it. A beleaguered Vermont got relief from one of its enemies.

The Sixteen Towns were again asserting themselves, with the result that the grouping of townships, larger than in 1778, both east and west of the Connecticut River, were bent on a political union, either with Vermont, New Hampshire or in a state of their own. Bezaleel Woodward sent a letter "in behalf of the people on both sides of Connecticut river" to the President of the Continental Congress. The letter asked for no more delay "on whether a new State be allowed in the Grants" and, if this were not permitted, union with New Hampshire.[73] A group of Cumberland County delegates met at Hanover on October 31, 1780 to organize a convention for the inhabitants of Cumberland, Gloucester and Grafton (N.H.) counties "from the Mason's Line to the Heigth of land on the West side of said [Connecticut] river"... "to unite in one Political Body."[74] The activists met in a Convention at Charlestown, New Hampshire on January 16, 1781, with delegates from forty-three towns on both sides of the river. This convention first voted on union with New Hampshire, then at Ira Allen's intervention, reversed itself and voted the next day on union with Vermont. Unlike the first Eastern Union, the Allens supported the second: Ira's motive was to counter New Hampshire's claim to Vermont, reasserted at Congress on January 13, while dampening the risk of losing the most populated and prosperous part of the state, which had been on the cards at Hanover in October. On the recommendation of a Committee of the Whole, the Assembly agreed to the annexation of the Sixteen Towns, on February 12, 1781.

> . . . the Committee of the Assembly recommends that the Legislature of this State. . . . lay a jurisdictional claim to all the lands situate east of Connecticut River . . . and that they do not exercise jurisdiction for the time being.[75]

But the new Eastern Union was also a threat to the future of the Allens' negotiations with the British: the state was to be expanded among parties, some of whom were largely hostile to the Allen faction, including Loyalists, Yorkers and revolutionaries opposed to the truce. So at the same time, the Allens (Chittenden was lukewarm) began to work for the incorporation of a tract of land in New York on Vermont's western border, into the state. This was an area, twenty miles broad, from the border to the Hudson, and eighty miles in depth, the northernmost part of a region from New York City to Lake Champlain known as The Oblong. Culturally, the settlers were Yankee with economic ties to Vermont through a network of family holdings on either side of the border; some were democrats opposed to the manorial and county government of New York. They had a grievance in that both New York and the Continental Congress had given up on the defense of the region, as was clear from response to the British raids of October, 1780. They were also pro-Allen, since they benefited from the truce with the British. Ethan, for his part, could offer the British an unopposed approach to Albany, on the assumption that neither the Continental Army nor the New York militia would move to oppose them. The Assembly voted soon after the inauguration of the second Eastern Union to "lay a jurisdictional claim" to the region. Ethan worked the region tirelessly in the spring of 1781. On April 11, the Vermont Assembly voted to send delegates to a convention at Cambridge and on May 15, the convention voted to join Vermont as the West or Western Union. The Articles of Union fixed its boundaries and called for the defense of the district by the military force of Vermont from internal and external enemies, which clearly included New York.[76]

On June 15, 1781, the Vermont Assembly agreed to an "Annunciation of the boundaries of this State" in the form of the Articles of Union. It further proposed that whenever Vermont becomes united with the American states, boundary disputes will be submitted to Congress. On the following day, all this was approved, 53-24. Since the aim of the Allens was to balance the representation from the Eastern Union, it was natural that three-quarters of the nays were from New Hampshire towns and all were from the Connecticut River Valley.[77] New York and New Hampshire were, predictably, in an uproar, possibly as Ethan had intended, since it would increase support for a rapprochement with the British.

But the support that Ethan expected from the Assembly, as will be seen, did not materialize. Congress appeared again to offer recognition and admission early in August 1781 if only Vermont would give up the Eastern and Western Unions. This was prompted by the interception of a letter from Germain to Sir Henry Clinton of February 7, 1781 in which the British expressed their clear intention to bring Vermont over to the Empire, including British garrisons in the state and the supply of troops for further offensive action.[78] The Congress resolution of August 20 was not definitive: the delegated ruled only that an "indispensable preliminary to the recognition of the independence of Vermont" was its acquiescence in the boundaries of New York and New Hampshire as they were prior to the two unions.[79] The offer was not a firm guarantee of independence, and the Allens had no difficulty in getting the Assembly to reject it. What the Assembly did not know was that the Allens had been engaged in secret discussions for nearly a year with the British, relations with whom they did not want to compromise. In the Congress, New York in the persons of Messrs Duane and L'Hommedieu alone opposed the resolution of August 20, partly because it implied recognition and partly because New Hampshire had no business being a party to the issue. For Congress to act on the August resolutions was an "assumption of power" and contrary to the Articles of Confederation.

From Vermont's perspective, the situation was no more favorable than it had been at the inauguration of the two unions. Chittenden wrote to Washington on November 14, 1781.[80] He rehearsed the history of the British offer to make Vermont a colony under the Crown, the truce and the exchange of prisoners. New Hampshire was again threatening to use force in the settlement of disputes at the eastern border, allegedly "for the protection of some persons who professed allegiance to that state."[81] Chittenden wrote that he had spent the last winter in fruitless attempts to form alliances. The only good news for Vermont was that Massachusetts would withdraw its claim on condition that the United States concede the independence of Vermont; if not, it would "have its snack at the south end of [Vermont's] territory." In view of the claims of New York and New Hampshire "as well as to quiet some of her internal divisions occasioned by the machinations of these governments" and "to strengthen this state against insult," the Vermont legislature had extended jurisdiction from the old Mason line to the Hudson.

Chittenden concealed from Washington all of the secret dealings that Vermont had with the British over the past year: the letter must rank as one of the most mendacious diplomatic letters even written in the revolutionary era. He made it clear without explicitly saying so that the two unions were a bargaining chip, to be traded for recognition. Of the two unions, the situation in the Eastern Union was somewhat less dire, since it was essentially a tussle between two powers who claimed authority and civilian jurisdiction on both sides of the Connecticut River.[82] (By October, Vermont had admitted thirty-five New Hampshire towns to the Eastern Union). Each side arrested the officials of the other and, though it never came to confrontation, New Hampshire authorized the use of troops against the "usurped authority of Vermont" and Vermont threatened to "repel force by force." The controversy in the Western Union was, on the other hand, military as well as civil: whether it was Vermont or New York which had the authority to raise militia for the Northern Department. Here, Chittenden's enemies did not hold all the cards, since the position of New York in and around the Western Union was not strong.

> In the [late] spring of 1781 [Brigadier-General John Stark] was ordered once more to assume command of the northern department, and fix his head quarters at Saratoga. Some feeble detachments of militia from New-York, Massachusetts and New-Hampshire constituted all the disposable force for the protection of this extensive frontier. If the country was in a sad condition in 1778, it was tenfold more so in 1781. It was overrun with spies and traitors. Robberies were frequent, and many inhabitants (non-combatants) carried prisoners to Canada.[83]

Stark was joined by the two Continental Regiments of the New Hampshire Brigade but his military resources remained appallingly low. His letters to Washington and Governor George Clinton are a constant catalogue of complaints about the severe lack of clothing, cooking utensils, food, rum, writing paper and money, so much so that Stark could not even pay his messengers and dispatch riders. He wrote to the President of the Congress on September 1, 1781, saying that he had received no pay for over two years; his means and his credit were exhausted. New Hampshire had loaned him cash in the form of paper money, of which some remained in hand. "There it must remain, for I can get nothing for it."[84]

The region was under threat from the British on Lake Champlain and along the Mohawk River as well as internal weakness. The Albany County Militia (ACM) was potentially mutinous[85] and the Western Union about to erupt in a rebellion against what was left of the Yorker authority. Stark's military position was so poor that he considered evacuating Albany and retreating even further south.[86] This was in response to a threat from the British supposedly on Lake George, when in fact it was from Jessup's corps (the King's Loyal Rangers) operating just south of Lake Champlain.

When Washington appointed Stark Commander of the Northern Department on June 25, 1781, he was directed to "draw forth the force of the country from the Green mountains and all the contiguous territory."[87] But on December 21, Stark wrote to Washington, telling him "I have been promised everything from their government and their leading men that I could wish for; but they have taken particular care to perform nothing."[88] The only troops that Vermont sent west were to assist the insurrection in the Western Union. Arrests by New York of insurrectionists and civil servants of "the pretended state of Vermont" started immediately after the declaration of the Western Union and they continued right up to the dissolution of the two unions in the following year.

Chittenden issued a Proclamation on July 18, 1781 telling the residents of the Western Union to submit to the laws of Vermont and requiring all officers, civil and military, to execute the laws of Vermont. Several incidents followed, in which Chittenden protested the recruitment of residents into the New York militia and the Yorkers recruitment by Vermont.[89] Then in mid-October, a violent confrontation occurred at San Coick. In accordance with the Proclamation, a former ACM private, Samuel Fairbanks, commissioned Lieutenant-Colonel by Chittenden, had attempted to raise militia for Vermont under what was Stark's mandate. On October 15, Peter Gansevoort, commander of the First Brigade of the Albany County Militia, notified Governor Clinton of the arrest of Fairbanks and some of his associates. According to Samuel Safford, by now a Brigadier-General of Vermont militia,

"Colonel [Henry] Van Rensselaer came with a party of men from Albany and its vicinity, and took them prisoners, broke open their houses, and much distressed their families." Both Samuel Safford and Samuel Robinson wrote to Stark from Bennington, threatening to use force if the Yorkers persisted in their conduct.[90]

The second episode grew out of the first, due to the continuing need to protect the person and the home at San Coick of Lieutenant-Colonel John Van Rensselaer of the 14th ACM. In an account of the incident, relayed to Stark, a party of men and acting under the command of a former 14th ACM Captain, John Abbot, "assaulted a public house at Hoosac." Abbot was one of fifteen Vermont Assembly members from the Western Union, representing Hoosic.[91] They carried off several men to Bennington, principally John Van Rensselaer. There the magistrates declined to try them and they were released. Rensselaer wrote to Gansevoort on December 4, appealing for protection.[92] The next day, Gansevoort sent troops from the militia regiments of Henry K. Rensselaer (6th ACM) and Peter Yates (14th ACM) to John Rensselaer's house. The insurrectionists responded by collecting their force and by about the 7th, the two parties were drawn up on each side of the Walloomsac River. Stark reported this to Major-General William Heath, Washington's surrogate for Commander-in-Chief in the Northern Department, on December 12, saying that there were about two hundred on each side, the rioters not yet joined by any from "old Vermont," that is, Vermont troops from outside the Western Union.

On December 8, 1781, Ira Allen wrote from Sunderland to the Board of War, requesting that the Vermont militia move to the Western Territory to affirm Vermont's jurisdiction against that of New York and "to suppress some internal divisions."[93]

By mid-month, Chittenden had sent a cannon and militia under the command of Lieutenant-Colonel Ebenezer Wallbridge to assist the insurrection. Both sides offered to negotiate, pending a settlement by Congress, the Yorkers because of the extreme weakness of their military position: when Gansevoort appealed in person to Stark on December 16, he found that the New Hampshire troops were in such poor condition that they were unable to march from Saratoga. Gansevoort proceeded the next day to the line of confrontation and found Yates' troops, menaced now by the "old Vermonters," in full retreat from the Van Rensselaer house to the Hudson. Yates had only eighty hungry men from four regiments as against 146 indigenous insurgents and considered that even with the full complement of the two New York militia brigades, he would be unable to suppress the insurrection. On about December 20, Gansevoort dismissed his men, who were in any case about to vote with their feet, unwilling to fight either Vermonters or the British.[94] Wallbridge, with no enemy to face, also withdrew.

Stark was thoroughly disgusted with the stance of Vermont. He had a high opinion of their troops and, in true Yankee fashion, he sympathized with their political dilemma. On August 27, he had written to Chittenden, saying that "the people of your State, by their utter detestation of the management of New-York, must have been wretched under their government."[95] But by the end of the year, his attitude had changed completely, complaining to Meshech Weare about their annexations in the Eastern Union and to Washington about both.[96] But what concerned Stark the most was the state of the northern frontiers. He had been obliged to send home the 10th Massachusetts Regiment and stand down the New York militia for want of provisions, while the two emaciated New Hampshire regiments had still not been supplied with new uniform. Conditions in the Western Union were so chaotic that he told Washington

> . . . I may venture to predict that unless something decisive is done in the course of this winter, with respect to these people [the Vermonters], we may have everything to fear from them that they are capable of, in case we are under the disagreeable necessity of making another campaign.[97]

By then, the suspicions of all the leading players were thoroughly aroused, that Vermont was in league with the enemy—Washington, Stark, Schuyler (still holding a senior military command) and Governor Clinton—and concrete evidence from Clinton was about to emerge. For Washington, it was a matter of the utmost urgency that the issue of the Western Union be resolved. Washington's motives have received different interpretations. When Eli Brownson went to Philadelphia in the summer of 1781 to seek the exchange of his cousin, Gideon Brownson, Washington refused the because of rumors that Vermont was conspiring to unite with Great Britain; if Vermont persisted, he "threatened to destroy it entirely."[98] Though he was suspected of trying to cause divisions in Vermont because of his suggestion, held by his critics to be disingenuous, that Vermont would be recognized on annulment of the two unions, his military predicament in the region suggests that he wanted a resolution at all costs. George Clinton too was alarmed, demanding the return of New York's two Continental regiments to the front line in the north. At times, Vermont had an unlikely ally in New York in the person of Philip Schuyler. He had exerted pressure on the New York Assembly to recognize Vermont, which came close to success. Schulyer later advocated the recognition of the Western Union on the grounds that the dissention and migration of population out of New York, which it occasioned, was detrimental to the war effort.

In Ethan's absence, Chittenden received a private letter from Washington, dated January 1, 1782, urging Vermont to accept the Congress's resolutions of August 7 and 21.[99] Washington said that if Vermont annulled the Eastern and Western Unions, Congress would recognize Vermont, which would deter the enemy "from their expectations of disunion." He took Chittenden at his word (the November letter) in saying that the negotiations with the enemy were "innocent," though privately he was convinced of the opposite. The issue of the two unions came together when on January 12, a Proclamation by President Weare of New Hampshire gave forty days for Vermonters to leave the Eastern Union or take an oath of allegiance to New Hampshire.[100] Exactly forty days later, on February 23, 1782, the Assembly dissolved the two unions, much to the disgust of the delegates from the marches. It did so by determining that the Congress resolutions of August 7 and 21, 1781, guaranteeing the borders of New Hampshire and New York, also delineated "the boundaries of this State." The Assembly agreed to "relinquish all claim and demand to and right of jurisdiction outside the boundaries of Vermont, as they were before the two unions."[101] These boundaries were the west bank of the Connecticut River to the east and, to the west, a line north from the north-west corner of Massachusetts, twenty miles from the Hudson. The Assembly resolved to transmit the dissolution to the Congress, New Hampshire and New York. Chittenden wrote to Washington from Arlington on March 16, saying that Vermont had withdrawn our jurisdiction to the confines of our own limits, so we expect "an acknowledgement of our independence and sovereignty."[102] During March, several towns in the Western Union declared submission to New York.[103] As to admission to Congress, this was to be achieved by negotiation. But the impact of Cornwallis's defeat at Yorktown had sunk in: settlement of the Vermont question was among the lowest of the priorities of the Continental Congress. More important was the fate of the western lands, which would likely revert to American control.

This was not the only reason for Congressional inaction. On January 21, 1782, Governor George Clinton of New York wrote to Washington, saying that he had two affidavits proving "a traitorous correspondence between the leaders on the New Hampshire Grants and the enemy."[104] The dissolution of the unions was followed the day after by a revelation from Governor Clinton that "Vermonters had been treasonably communicating with the enemy" and on March 21, Clinton divulged the contents of the traitorous correspondence to the New York Assembly.[105] In addition, there was a whole spectrum of delegates at Congress who held New Hampshire or New York titles or who had been granted rights in the new townships created by the Allens, which divided the inclinations of the representatives between those two states and the aspirations of Vermont. Those states that faced secessionist movements of their own would not encourage them by recognizing Vermont, nor did they want to increase the influence of the New England bloc in Congress (despite the resumed opposition of New Hampshire to recognition). Following the refusal of Ira Allen and Jonas Fay at the Congress early in February to rescind the unions, the former never returned to Philadelphia; but lobbying by Vermont continued until it fizzled out in mid-April, owing to the "unexpected delay" of the Congress in reaching a decision on Vermont.[106]

In result, the Allens became even more convinced that their singular future lay with the British, with explicit hostility to the Congress and the project of recognition. Ethan Allen had declined to serve when he was elected as Brigadier-General of the 1st Brigade of Vermont Militia on April 12, 1781;[107] his role in the Western Union affair was as a back seat driver in Bennington, despite his appearance on the Walloomsac in military finery towards the end of the confrontation. His influence was now in radical decline, due to the vote, in his absence, to dissolve the two unions. What would have meant a corresponding victory for his enemies, the acceptance of Vermont into the Union, was to remain elusive for another decade.

If the defeat of Cornwallis removed the urgency in resolving the Vermont question, it also reduced the tensions on the issue among the rival states. In a shrewd set of "Observations" on the issue of Vermont independence of May 1, 1782, James Madison noted that

> New Hampshire having gained its main object by the exclusion of its territory east of Connecticut River from the claims of Vermont, is already indifferent to its independence, and will probably soon combine with other eastern states in its favor.[108]

He observed that the other New England states were not prejudiced against New York, that the citizens of those states had an interest in lands granted by Vermont and (especially) that the accession of Vermont would increase their weight in Congress. The second of these—offering rights of land to citizens of other states—shows that the policy of the Allens in winning influential friends was, belatedly, paying off.

Madison also observed that the Assemblies of Maryland, Delaware, Pennsylvania and New Jersey were inclined to the Vermont cause: these were all states whose members at Congress had been lobbied in February by Jonas Fay, Abel Curtis and Ira, who gave them copies of Ethan's lengthy pamphlet, *A Vindication of the Opposition of the Inhabitants of Vermont to the Government of New York and of Their Right to Form Into an Independent State.*[109] Yet even at the end of the year, Vermont was faced with the threat of "effectual measures" to enforce compliance with resolutions of Congress against banishments and confiscations.[110]

CHAPTER 9

Defending the Republic: The British Raids from Canada

THE IDEA OF A ROAD from the Coos Country to points in the province of Quebec long predated the Bayley-Hazen Military Road of 1776–1779. In 1753, the Assembly of New Hampshire funded a party of pioneers to survey and mark a road from what is now Concord up to the Coos, on the east side of the Connecticut River.[1] In about December 1760, Samuel Sleeper of Gloucester County sent a petition to Cramahé and members of His Majesty's Governing Council.[2] Sleeper (who later held civil offices under royal New York) advocated a road from Gloucester County on the Connecticut River to the northern limit of the Lake Champlain-Richelieu River waterway at St. John's for trade between "the lower parts of New England" and Quebec. In February 1761, Gloucester and the surrounding counties were deserted, but nine years later there were eight hundred settler families in place. Sleeper sought a subsidy for opening a "wagon road" to connect the two centers. Carleton and Lord Hillsborough, the Secretary of State for North America had already expressed interest in a "route into New Hampshire or the New England governments." Since this was in the context of the defense of Quebec, their interest was clearly military: the route to the fortress of Quebec from New York via Lakes George and Champlain was too "tedious and uncertain."[3] In 1764, both Moses Hazen and Jacob Bayley, veterans of the French and Indian War, acquired New Hampshire titles to Haverhill on the east bank of the Connecticut River and Newbury on the west. They were among the first to see the value of a road between the Coos and St. John's, where Hazen held half a seigneury, while Bayley thought of an import route for Canadian furs. When the revolution came, Bayley continuously urged the conquest of Canada and the building of a road between Coos and St. John's.

Nowadays, it's customary to see men such as Hazen and Bayley either as soldiers or as civilians—landholders, settlers, lawyers, artisans or merchants. But for the revolutionaries at the time, this division was hardly valid: soldiers needed a means of support other than military pay, while civilian leaders often held military rank and divided their time between politics and campaigning. So questions of motive, military or commercial, are not pertinent unless one is entirely at odds with the other. For instance, there were several possible end-points to the military road: Missisquoi Bay of Lake Champlain, St Francis on the St. Lawrence, or St. John's. The fact that Hazen favored St. John's because of his business interests was unremarkable; Colonel Skene urged a land route for the progress of Burgoyne's army in 1777 because it would develop his estate between Skenesborough and Fort Edward, even though this was probably not the best path for Burgoyne to take. In the most notorious case of all, the Allens were accused of a pro-British bias because they needed a free trade route between the Onion River settlements and Montreal, then down the St. Lawrence to the ocean.[4]

In the spring of 1776, Bayley got authorization from Washington to build the road, and by June he had built a thirty-mile bridle path from Wells River above Newbury to Cabot, six miles beyond Peacham. Washington then told Bayley of the disastrous retreat from Canada, and warned him against developing a fast invasion route for the British.[5] Late in the following year, the Americans planned an invasion of Canada, in a move led by Bayley, Hazen and Horatio Gates. One possible invasion route was from the Coos Country to St. John's, to St Denis on the Sorel or to Odanak, where Bayley had long been friendly with the St Francis Abenaki. This Washington eventually described as a "child of folly" and, by the end of the year, the project was dead.

Hazen, like Bayley, never lost the idea of an invasion of Canada. Washington thought that an invasion from the Coos could be at best a feint or a diversion, so he authorized Hazen, with Timothy Bedel's New Hampshire regiment, to extend the road towards St. John's, or at least to develop that stretch of the road already completed. This Hazen did in the summer of 1779, taking the road as far as Hazen's Notch in Westfield by August, before his regiment was withdrawn to join the main army on the Hudson.[6] The Notch was close to the Canadian border but still forty miles short of St. John's. In departing, Hazen, a quarrelsome man, picked a fight with his associates, including Isaac Tichenor and Colonel Bayley, charges which were overruled or which came to nothing. As Washington had feared, the road became a potential invasion route for the British[7] and, as it transpired, a route for raiding parties to capture Colonel Bayley. The departure of Hazen's troops and the disbandment of Bedel's regiment caused consternation in Vermont, New Hampshire and Massachusetts, since the northern frontier was now exposed—one reason why the truce that the Allens secured with the British late in October, 1780 was so popular on both sides of the Connecticut River. As for Hazen, the commander of the 2nd Canadian Regiment of the Continental Congress, he was important enough for the British to want him eliminated, a main purpose of the British raids of 1778.

From the time of the raid at the mouth of the Otter Creek, which Warner was ordered to counter early in July 1777, there were small, sporadic but lethal Tory and Indian raids until mid-1981. The exceptions to this pattern in terms of size or significance are dealt with in some detail below. They are:

1. Two raids in 1778, one led by John Peters and the other known as Carleton's Raid.
2. Lieutenant Houghton's second raid of October 1780. This followed his first raid of November 20, 1779 towards today's Brandon, which fell short of its aim of "making a stroke at Hazen's [Road]."[8]

These raids of 1777–1781, often led by British regulars, mostly originated from the Lake on the west side of the state, some down the Connecticut River valley, or the Bayley-Hazen Road. Two Indian raids took place in September 1777. Then in March 1778 a force of Vermonters, said by Ethan to have been Green Mountain Boys, defeated a party of British regulars and Indians at Shelburne.[9] The mandate of Major-General Sir Frederick Haldimand, who replaced Sir Guy Carleton on June 26, 1778, was to raid into Vermont and New York wherever possible. The raids would disrupt the potential invasion route up the Connecticut River from the Coos and create a diversion from the campaigns further south. It was unlikely, however, that he could undertake a major expedition such as that of Burgoyne in 1777. By 1782, Haldimand had a total of 10,573 troops in the province and on the frontiers—British, German and Loyalist, not counting several thousand Indians, of varying degrees of loyalty, within Quebec.[10] Before the defeat of Cornwallis in October 1781, a major expedition would have been as risky as that of Burgoyne; after that, it would have been suicidal.

Though the American invasion of Canada had been called off, officially only in March of 1778, the British still feared an invasion, which was indeed the ambition of Moses Hazen, despite Washington's extreme skepticism. On July 25, Haldimand wrote to Germain, requesting help against an American invasion.[11] He wrote again three days later, telling Germain of his plans to attack along the Onion River, to disrupt the building of the Bayley-Hazen Road, to rid the region of rebels who might subvert the *habitants* or the Canadian Indians and to capture Hazen, reported to be in the area.[12] This was correct: Haldimand had learnt from informers that Hazen had left Albany and in fact he arrived at Newbury on July 12, with a price of $200 for his capture.[13] The raid was to be led by Lieutenant-Colonel John Peters, who was actually more interested in apprehending Colonel Bayley than Hazen: Bayley, sitting on the Court of Confiscation, had taken Peters' lands and, allegedly, used them for his own purposes. However, the expedition along the Onion River Valley, at the end of the month, got nowhere near its main objectives. The raid succeeded in destroying the Allens' blockhouse at the mouth of the river and taking some prisoners, and Peters arrived back at St. John's on August 3.[14] The project was clearly unrealistic, one reason why the subsequent expedition, known as Carleton's Raid, was less ambitious than the first.[15] The purpose of the second raid was only to neutralize the "many conveniences and necessaries which would facilitate the approach of an enemy." The aim of disrupting the Bayley-Hazen Road, the projected American invasion route, was quietly dropped.

Haldimand gave his orders to Major Christopher Carleton on October 17, 1778.[16] Carleton was now only to destroy provisions, animals, boats and mills on the shores of Lake Champlain, to take prisoner all those who had sworn allegiance to the Continental Congress and to expel their families. On October 24, Carleton's fleet left the Ile-aux-Noix with 354 officers and men, along with about a hundred Indians.[17] Three weeks later, the expedition returned with thirty-nine prisoners (useful for exchange), having destroyed food stocks, enough for 12,000 men for four months, animals (some "brought away"), dwellings, barns and mills.[18]

There was one notable achievement—the capture at Monkton of Winthrop Hoit, under the name, variously, of Wintress Herrick or Howick and Winter Howett, an "Indian interpreter."[19] The raid increased the fear of Indian raids and also caused much devastation in the towns of Monkton, Ferrisburgh, Middlebury and Bridport. But when we look at the aims of the expedition, even as they had been scaled back, the raid must be accounted a failure. The Vermont Council of Safety had ordered the evacuation of the region in April and was not counting on any supplies being brought down to the Castleton-Newbury line. Even the Peters expedition was unrealistic and highly risky: the expedition route to the Coos from the Lake had its limitations. It was also a long shot to have tried to capture Hazen, who had in fact left the region for White Plains, New York by the time that Peters launched his raid at the end of July.

Apart from Houghton's first raid of November 1779, there was no major raid on the territory of Vermont for the next two years, despite raids and ferocious battles in New York and the Indian Territory west of the Hudson. There was also the raid on the Connecticut coastal towns and ports by the royal Governor of New York, Sir William Tryon, in July 1779. But two raids took place in October 1780, one virtually destroying Warner's regiment west of the Hudson and the other deep into northern Vermont, causing consternation throughout the state.

The Regiment of Green Mountain Rangers left for Albany in the spring of 1778 and patrolled up and down in the turbulent region of the Hudson, before being stationed at Fort George. Near there a party was ambushed by twenty-four Indians and three British regulars on July 15, 1779, killing seven of the regiment and two women. A report of the incident on July 20 gave the strength of the regiment at nearly 200, of which thirty-four were at Saratoga, sixteen at Bennington and the remainder at Fort George, under the command of Lieutenant-Colonel Safford. Warner himself was officially off sick and spent much time at Bennington, though this did not prevent him from being ambushed and wounded in an inspection tour from Fort George some months later.[20] Worse was to come. Early in October, 1780, Major Carleton led a raid on the Mohawk Valley, with a mixed force of a thousand regulars, Indians and Loyalists, by far the biggest of the war to date. From this force, sailing up Lake Champlain, Carleton detached a party of the 1st Battalion, King's Royal Regiment of New York (KRRNY), to raid Ballstown, led by Captain John Munro, the Allens' old enemy of pre-revolutionary days. This detachment left Crown Point on October 6, while Carleton disembarked his force on October 8.

The region towards which these two forces were advancing was not well defended, the only regulars being two understrength New Hampshire regiments and Warner's Rangers. The New York militia was in a poor state, ill-equipped and badly provisioned, prone to desertion and unwilling to serve beyond the strict terms of service. So grim was the situation that regiments were stood down for want of pay and provisions. Governor Clinton pleaded for reinforcements in mid-October, saying that he was preparing to retreat to Schenectady; even in the following February, he was requesting the return of his two New York regiments to the region, along with food and ammunition.[21]

On October 10, Fort Anne surrendered, Warner giving a figure of about fifty lost, the British seventy-five, of whom fifteen were New York militia.[22] One party then proceeded south, destroying the towns of Kingsbury, Queensbury, Fort Edward and Fort Miller, then branched off at the bend of the Hudson and proceeded to Fort George, garrisoned, in Warner's account, by between sixty and seventy men under Captain John Chipman. The latter had sent out a patrol under Captain Sill to pursue what he thought was a small body of the enemy; of these eight were captured, twenty seven killed and thirteen escaped (Warner's figures are lower, compensated by a higher figure for the Fort George surrender).[23] Upon this, Chipman surrendered Fort George on October 11, with a total of forty-five troops.[24] Fort Edward was abandoned by its garrison of New York militia in mid-October.[25] The British sources list a total of 148 prisoners taken in Carleton's expedition (not all of them Green Mountain Rangers), plus those taken by Munro.

Before reaching St. John's on November 14, Carleton arrived back at Crown Point, where he was joined on October 24 by Captain Munro and his battalion of the KRRNY. Munro had burnt Schoharie and part of Ballstown.[26] Justus Sherwood, the Supervisor of Spies and Prisoner Exchanges, was en route to a meeting with Ethan Allen[27] and encountered Munro. The meeting was no doubt a frosty one, as Sherwood was in the party that had rescued Remember Baker from the clutches of Munro, who was doubly outraged at the very idea of treating with the Green Mountain Boys. Munro remained hostile to Sherwood, trying to deny him political office when both were settled in what became Upper Canada after the war.

The end of Warner's regiment was in sight. In the return to Washington of October 27, 1780, Warner listed only 101 troops who were dead, sick, captured or on furlough, and none "on duty." However, many Green Mountain Rangers were left of the nearly 200 of the previous year. Warner had furloughed them all, believing that the Boys were no longer an effective fighting force. At this, Washington expressed his perplexity when he replied on November 12 to Warner's dispatch of October 30, announcing the disbandment of the Green Mountain Rangers (along with Livingston's 1st Canadian Regiment) on January 1 and saying that the men would be transferred to the

"Regiments of those States to which they properly belong."[28] It was a sad end to a proud regiment, whose awesome reputation was to last into the Civil War, when the valiant Vermont brigades were still saluted as the Green Mountain Boys. Warner himself, officially off sick since November 1777, was promoted Brigadier-General by the Vermont Assembly in March 1778.

Why Washington disbanded the Rangers is not entirely clear, but it seems obvious that he could not rely on the regiment in the light of the truce that the Allens had secured with the British. The answer may be, simply, that Warner had effectively disbanded his regiment and Washington accepted the fait accompli. As to Warner himself, Washington need not have doubted: in the middle of 1782, Sherwood still believed that, along with Samuel Herrick, he was a rascal, "best put nicely out of the way."[29]

For Vermont, Houghton's Raid of October 1780, was even more important. Answering a call to arms, about 300 Indians, Caughnawagas and Kanesatake, assembled at St. John's late in September for Carleton's expedition up the Lake. But Captain Munro, under pressure from his superiors, declined to take any of them with him, since it was thought they would be unreliable if faced by their Oneida enemies. So Carleton took 108 with him, leaving two hundred eager warriors anxious to see action and the plunder that went with it. In Carleton's expedition of 1778, his orders from Haldimand had been transmitted through Brigadier-General Watson Powell, the commandant of St. John's. This time, Powell acted on his own initiative, ordering an expedition along the Onion to "the Head of the Connecticut River" under the command of Lieutenant Richard Houghton, seconded from the 53rd Regiment to the Quebec Indian Department. The purposes of the raid were similar to that of 1778, to cause terror and devastation but also to provide a diversion for Carleton and Munro.

By the night of October 12, the raiders were on the Onion, heading east and somewhat south towards the source of the White River. On the 15th, they burnt Tunbridge on the First Branch of the White River, as well as, notoriously, Royalton the next day, followed by Randolph on the Third Branch the day after that. About three hundred Gloucester County militia, under the command of Colonel John House of Hanover, New Hampshire, organized a half-hearted attack on the Indians' camp at Randolph but, instead of a pursuit, House disbanded his loose formation on the 17th. The Americans feared that, if threatened, the Indians would kill their prisoners. The attacking party returned with the usual great speed and were back in St. John's by the 21st. In his letter to Germain of October 25, Haldimand passed on

Major Carleton's report: the destruction of the towns, dwellings, barns, food and livestock and the taking of thirty-two prisoners.[30] As an operation of the Revolutionary War, the raid was of no great significance, but politically and psychologically, its importance was immense. Vermont had been threatened by the raids on its western border and its territory in the north invaded, penetrating the rough defense line established earlier in the year. Above all, this was an Indian raid with its devastation and plundering, the murder and scalping of male civilians, the killing of fugitives and escaping prisoners, the sudden and silent assaults of which the people lived in constant fear. Lest this appear as a slur on the Indian nations, it should be remembered that the creation of terror was a British policy (Sir Guy Carleton excepted) which had been explicitly threatened by Burgoyne, mitigated only at times by such orders as a prohibition on the scalping of wounded prisoners.

In the space of a few weeks, the raid recreated the terrors of the French and Indian War, in which even the most remote south-east corner of Vermont and western New Hampshire were unsafe.[31] It was no wonder that the Allen's truce of late October was initially welcomed, by and large, in most parts of the Republic, including the Sixteen Towns of New Hampshire.

The truce was also welcomed in the region of New York that had been subjected to the raids of Carleton and Munro. This was something that Ethan Allen had envisaged and possibly planned, in view of the forthcoming Western Union. When the raids began, the only troops in the area were the fortress garrisons and Warner's sole Continental Regiment. The Yorkers mobilized two companies of the 12th Albany County Militia and three hundred men of Colonel Alexander Webster's Charlotte County Militia, but the resistance at Ballstown to Munro's raid was feeble and the two parties moved north, only to find that the British were gone. With Warner's regiment dissolved, the region was almost defenseless, so much so that Webster requested more troops from Vermont.[32] The failure of protection from British raids was one factor leading to the Western Union of the following year.

While the truce lasted, formally and otherwise, there were no British raids on Vermont; it will be argued that the Allens had effectively taken Vermont out of the Revolutionary War. Lieutenant-Colonel Barry St Leger's expedition up Lake Champlain, from October 17 to November 10, 1781 (to be discussed later in the context of the Haldimand Negotiations) was not aimed at Vermont, though it naturally caused alarm in the military commands of New York. After Cornwallis's defeat at Yorktown in October, the British feared a multi-pronged invasion of Quebec and, to this end, scouted the possible invasion routes, which were also routes for a counter-offensive. Much of the scouting was done by the Loyal Rangers, authorized by the amalgamation of several Loyalist units on November 12, 1781. Among its components were Adams' Rangers, led by Samuel Adams, whom the Green Mountain Boys had humiliated at the Catamount Tavern in Bennington. In October, the British planned scouting expeditions to make note of any tracks along the Missisquoi River and to mark the routes to the Bayley-Hazen Road. The "Grand Scout" to the Hazen Road took place early in February 1782, but it was abortive. An expedition from St Francis, March 11–24, aimed at a reconnaissance as far as possible along the Road, failed even to locate it, but in mid-April, another patrol found Hazen's Notch and penetrated several miles down the road. Early in June, these findings were confirmed, when a party of St Francis Indians moved from the Notch and found the northernmost of Hazen's blockhouses burnt; it did the same for the next one south. In August, the British looked for alternative routes to the Bayley-Hazen Road; the various "scouts" reveal the uncertainty of British intelligence regarding the location, state and access to the Road.

The most celebrated raid was the attempted abduction of Colonel Bayley on June 15, 1782. The abduction had been planned as early as July 1781, but it was postponed owing to the delicacy of the Haldimand Negotiations: even though Bayley was an enemy of the Allens, his abduction would be seen as an attack on Vermont.[33] The abduction party was led by Captains Azariah Pritchard and James Breakenridge Jr, with Corporal Abner Barlow, Levi Sylvester and five Loyal Rangers. It failed because the kidnappers had been betrayed and Bayley forewarned;[34] that night, he crossed the Connecticut River to safety.[35]

Ethan Allen; statue by L.G. Mead, ca. 1874–1875.

Top left: Sir Frederick Haldimand, Carleton's successor as Governor of Quebec. His ideas of what he was empowered to offer to, and accept from, Ethan Allen in the Haldimand Negotiations differed from that of his superior, Sir Henry Clinton. *Library and Archives Canada, Copy C-010966072*

Top right: Sir Guy Carleton, Governor and Captain General of Quebec: the outstanding British soldier and statesman of his day. *Library and Archives Canada, Copy C-002833*

Left: Sir Henry Clinton, British Commander-in-Chief in New York and as such, responsible for the initiation, course, and outcome of the negotiations with Ethan Allen. *Library and Archives Canada, Copy C-010965956*

Ira Allen, Ethan's youngest brother and Vermont's chief negotiator in the Haldimand Negotiations. *Special Collections, University of Vermont*

Thomas Chittenden, first Governor of Vermont, a close ally of the Allen family and the state's official spokesman in dealings with General Haldimand. *Special Collections, University of Vermont*

A depiction of Ethan Allen surpring the commander of Fort Ticonderoga and demanding his surrender.
Library of Congress

Below: Ethan Allen and the Green Mountain Boys, examining a map.
Library of Congress

Above: Another portrayal of Ethan Allen's daring, early morning surprise assault on British-held Fort Ticonderoga.

Engraving depicting Ethan Allen being held captive before General Prescott in Montreal, 1775. *New York Public Library*

The Battle of Montreal at which Ethan Allen, depicted here at center with upraised rifle, was captured. *U.S. Army Center of Military History poster series*

Right: Zion Hill from the Hubbardton battlefield: British grenadiers scrambled up the slope, then descended to the left to cut the American escape route behind their lines.

The key bridge over the Wolloomsac on the Bennington battlefield as it is today: Colonel Baum, commanding the troops from the Dragoon Redoubt behind the bridge was unable to see the center of the battlefield and the American General Stark's breakthrough.

Left: The statue of Ethan Allen at the statehouse in Montpelier, Vermont. No likeness of Ethan Allen has survived. Here he is wearing the uniform of an officer of the Continental Army, to which he was entitled, but it is unlikely he wore such a uniform: his favored dress was a gaudy mixture of military finery.

Ethan Allen Monument, Burlington, Vermont

CHAPTER 10

The Haldimand Negotiations, Phase 1: July 1780 to December 1781

THE MOTIVE OF THE Allens in the Haldimand Negotiations has always been controversial, at the time and ever since. Michael A. Bellesiles (1993) considered that the Negotiations were aimed at what they were declared to be: a prisoner exchange. Samuel Williams (1794) followed Ira Allen's *History* in stating that their aim was "the cessation of hostilities." Major Dundas, present at the meeting with Ira Allen in May 1781 on the Ile-aux-Noix, but ignorant of "the business [of reunion]," thought that all the Allens wanted to do was to impress the Continental Congress into the acceptance of Vermont in the American Confederation. Ira's presence was to "alarm the Congress and the particular states." Unbenown to Dundas, this contention had some foundation, if only as the rationale or the potential cover for something less than proper. In 1853, Henry Walter DePuy reproduced two internal memorials, signed by several of those privy to the Haldimand Negotiations at a time when "the people at large were in entire ignorance concerning the negotiations."[1] The first, of June 1781, claimed that the prisoner exchange was aimed at "a cessation of hostilities with Great Britain on the northern frontiers." In the second, dated July 10, 1781, the Junto stated that it had approved the letters of the same date from Ira Allen to Haldimand and to Captain Sherwood, "purporting an intention of this State's becoming a British province." The memorial claimed that the aim was to preserve the state and that the moves were merely a lever for Vermont to obtain a seat in Congress. DePuy took these claims at their face value, dismissing the allegations that the Vermont leaders wanted to join the enemy as "grossly unjust." But if the Allens were serious about reunion with the British, as will be argued, these memos were written as a secret cover, to be revealed if there were ever an embarrassment comparable to the revelation of Beverly Robinson's letters to Ethan, which had been exposed in the previous March. The conspirators were being very cautious: as will be seen, Ira's letters reeked of treachery but they were not definitive enough to allay the British suspicions of duplicity. It was not until September that the Allens became forthright in aspiring to a change of government.

At times, Haldimand suspected the same as Dundas, considering that the prime aim of the Vermonters was to join the Congress, which Ethan had put forward in his secret meeting with the British in October, 1780. Alternatively, Haldimand thought that Vermont aimed to join the party with the most power or which was in the military ascendancy. The contention that the Allens wanted "a separate government under the Crown" does not necessarily exclude any of these possibilities: they achieved the cessation of hostilities and a prisoner exchange, and on occasion moved the Continental Congress in the direction of Vermont's union with the Confederation. At other times, however, they positively worked against an association of Vermont with the Congress.

Prolegomena: 1775–1779

Ethan Allen had already gained public notoriety in England as the captor of the 'Gibraltar of America' when he landed at Falmouth early in December 1775, but he had long been known to the British political establishment as the chief troublemaker in the New Hampshire Grants. His fate had always been uncertain: unless Ethan were killed upon capture, it was impossible that he should have been executed in Canada since Carleton would absolutely have forbidden it. Despite Prescott's prediction that Ethan would be hanged at Tyburn, it was not obvious that he would be transported: Cramahé claimed that the only reason that the captives were sent to England was for want of a prison and guards in Montreal.[2] Despite Ethan's fears, it was not beyond doubt that he would be executed: the Administration was "embarrassed" at the arrival of its uninvited guest; his friends were surprised when he was "unexpectedly removed" back to North America[3]. Unbeknown to Ethan, the government had several options, all of them pointing to his return to North America. John Wilkes, the mayor of London and an outspoken opponent of the government's American policy had at least intended to obtain a writ of habeas corpus "early in his eleven-day imprisonment at Pendennis Castle in

Cornwall." But despite official denials, there was skepticism as to whether a trial of British subjects was lawful and, in any case, some doubted whether a jury would convict a folk hero like Ethan.[4] Primarily, the government feared retaliation by the Americans, "should any accident befall him," principally against General Prescott. This had been threatened by the Americans since October, initially by General Montgomery.[5] Washington took up the cause, threatening to Sir William Howe that any treatment meted out to Ethan would be reciprocated exactly on Prescott. He conveyed the same to Schuyler on the same day, blaming Prescott for Ethan's harsh treatment.[6] Then again, Ethan could be exchanged for the likes of Prescott; in fact, the Congress instructed Washington to work for an exchange in December.[7]

Already, the British envisioned a more ambitious plan. A cabinet meeting on December 23 indicated that Ethan should be returned, for fear of retaliation, and a few days later the King advised Germain that the captives be returned to America as prisoners of war[8] On the morning of December 27, the rabidly anti-American Solicitor-General, Alexander Wedderburn, wrote a letter to a senior bureaucrat, William Eden, Undersecretary of State and the head of the British Secret Service.[9] "Something more might be done than merely return him as a prisoner to America"; a 'person of confidence' was to propose to Ethan that his case had been favorably presented to the government. If he were inclined to return to his duty, his past conduct would be forgiven, he would be given command of a company of rangers and assured title to his lands. Thus the Green Mountain Boys would form a Loyalist corps with Ethan in charge. Though nothing came of the plan, the seed had been sown. Ethan's case came to be rather different from the other individuals whose loyalty the British proposed to buy, since (unlike Benedict Arnold or Philip Schuyler) he could bring a whole province over to the British.

The beginnings in 1775 developed into a consistent and well-founded policy, based squarely on an appeal to Ethan's political and economic interests which at one point (October, 1781) seemed to come close to success. Ethan was well-known to the British as the leader of the revolt against Yorker authority in the Grants; after the Revolution had broken out, the feud with New York continued unabated. Ethan had a further potential enemy in the form of the Continental Congress. Even at the war's end in 1783, Germain was still advising Haldimand that the return of Vermont to its former loyalty was a matter of the utmost priority.

Sometime after the Battle of Princeton and before the end of November 1776, the captive Ethan Allen was approached in New York by a senior

British officer. According to his own account, he was offered the command of a regiment of "new levies" to serve with the British and a large tract of land in the Grants or in Connecticut.[10] Ethan angrily rejected these offers. He may have been correct in these contentions, but it is also quite possible that the "new levies" were in fact the Green Mountain Boys, and that the large tract of land was really the Grants as a "separate Government under the Crown." The references to Connecticut and the "new levies" could have been designed to throw the suspicious off the scent.

On March 3, 1779, Germain wrote to Sir Henry Clinton, the Commander-in-Chief in New York, directing him to open negotiations with the Vermonters. "The separation of the country they style Vermont from the provinces in which it was formerly included is a circumstance from which I should hope much advantage might be made. . . . I see no objection to your giving them reason to expect that His Majesty will erect their country into a separate province." He wrote similarly to Haldimand on the same day.[11] Germain wrote further to Haldimand in April, enclosing an extract of his letter to Clinton of March 3, saying that the King was instructing him to try to open negotiations with the Vermonters since he had more ready access to them. Haldimand's agents were to correspond with Sir Henry Clinton and to act in concert with those of the Commander-in-Chief.[12] Haldimand was skeptical about his prospects of success. He wrote to Germain in September, observing that he would do what he could to reclaim the Vermont people, but they are "a profligate banditti," and no improvement on the lawless vagabonds of earlier times.[13] Both Germain and Clinton were more optimistic, citing the attractiveness of the British offer. "I will give Allen all he has demanded of Congress," the former wrote.[14] In other letters to Clinton of the same date, September 27, Germain expressed his general support of moves to buy the opposition to the King's side, sparing no expense.[15] In December, Germain reiterated his support for moves to bring in the Vermonters, supposing that they would need to be protected in their allegiance.[16]

Germain reconfirmed the dual mandate in a letter to Haldimand of February 7, 1781. He repeated the line which he pushed forward consistently from 1779 to 1783: "the return of the people of Vermont to their allegiance is an event of the utmost importance to the king's affairs," then said that "General Haldimand has instructions to draw them over and give them support." At the same time, he wrote to Clinton, saying that Haldimand has the same instructions as you.[17] Dutifully, Haldimand always tried to get the prior approval of the Commander-in-Chief in New York before taking action.

The dual mandate caused the British great difficulty. Germain never gave his commanders any guidance as to the extent of their powers to negotiate and they had different views on the limits of their authority. When the negotiations with Ethan Allen started in October 1780, it was not clear to Haldimand what he was empowered to offer the Vermonters. Over the next year, the needs of day-to-day negotiations were compromised by the poor and slow communications between Quebec and New York and the slowness of contact between Quebec and the Ile-aux-Noix, where negotiations took place. The difficulties were only concealed by the failure of the British to have the Allens publicly adopt a concrete plan for Vermont; it is hard to believe that the British difficulties over the negotiating mandate would not, in that event, have led to a very great obstacle to the implementation of a plan that had been agreed by both sides.

One aspect of the plan gave the British particular trouble. The two principals, Clinton and Haldimand, had different ideas as to how to dispose of land titles in Vermont granted by New Hampshire and New York, and the extent of their powers to settle land issues in any accommodation with Vermont. Germain had evaded the issue in his letter to Clinton of March 3, 1779 by suggesting that title to land was not to be a consequence of Vermont's becoming a separate province under the Crown. Instead, residents who gave proof of a return to duty would be confirmed in the possession only of *ungranted* lands. Thus the old controversy over the New Hampshire and New York titles, involving the British power, continued for the duration of the Revolutionary War.

By August, Sir Henry Clinton had made his first moves to win over Ethan Allen. On August 21–22, he wrote a confidential letter to William Eden, who had arrived in New York as a Peace Commissioner in 1778. He informed Eden of what he had done with the mandate ("approbation") that he had received from Germain in March.[18] Clinton said he had seen the "moment for tempting EA"; had made the attempt, and believed his offer had been accepted. He had sent a messenger with a proposal to Ethan, but this man fell sick and had entrusted the message to a second agent, who twice made contact with the Vermonter. The response from Ethan was that he could raise 4,000 troops to take Albany, then strike at the New York army of Governor George Clinton. Sir Henry, on the contrary, tried to send a message to Ethan, advising him to fall back on Canada to cooperate with Haldimand. Alternatively, he could join Sir Henry (on the Hudson), who would confirm Ethan's officers and troops as members of the King's Army. The Commander-in-Chief had not heard further from Ethan and his intentions were uncertain; the measures taken should not be conveyed to Ministers of the Crown. If the project should not yield any tangible results, nothing would be lost as Allen had not asked for any reciprocal action on the part of the British.

That Clinton should have decided it was time to tempt Ethan Allen was born of military necessity. His army in New York was laid low by disease and he could expect no reinforcements from the West Indies. Haldimand in Quebec is "alarmed for the fidelity of the Canadians" and was pressing Clinton for two thousand men. These Clinton would not refuse but could not send them right away for want of a proper convoy. This is why he advised Ethan Allen to move with his four thousand into Canada to cooperate with Haldimand. Sir Henry wrote to Haldimand on September 9, conveying that Ethan had said he would attack the forces of Governor George Clinton (Sir Henry's first cousin) in New York with four thousand men. For this, Ethan would be offered a "separate province," something no doubt contained in the various messages carried, abortively, to Ethan. The British Commander-in-Chief related how he had advised Ethan to fall back on Canada or join Sir Henry's forces if he thought it expedient.[19]

With Congress putting off consideration of the Vermont question till February, Clinton wrote again to Eden on October 10.[20] He said that his messenger (presumably the second messenger who had not yet reported back by the time of Sir Henry's August letter) had met with Allen and Warner north-west of Albany on August 10. Ethan had 1,500 men under arms and the numbers were rising fast, while Warner could raise about 700, "ready to join any body of men in opposition to the Congress, but particularly Colonel Allen." According to the messenger, the whole of the northern frontier in and around Vermont was in a state of turmoil, ready to desert the rebel cause, and General Schuyler was "at bottom a friend to Government." Clinton was still not ready to have Eden pass on the news to Ministers "as there is no being sure of a man of Allen's character, nor can we expect him to . . . show himself without we are in a situation to give him support." Though Clinton made no such observation in his letter to Eden, the messenger's report showed signs of telling the Commander-in-Chief what he thought he wanted to hear. For in doing so, he shows his ignorance of the military situation in Vermont. The impression that the messenger gave is that there were two loose bodies of rebels in Vermont, one commanded by Ethan and the other by Warner, who was prepared to join him. The reality of course was that the Green Mountain Rangers were a regiment of Congress, nowhere near seven hundred strong, and Ethan was the Brigadier-General of the Vermont militia, with at most five hundred men under command. There was no way that Warner would flirt with the British.

That the whole thing was a fabrication was reported by Clinton on December 11, when he told Eden that the messenger had not been able to meet with Ethan and had invented the whole story. He had, however, sent other messengers to Allen since he was still persuaded that the Vermonter would join with the British. Seen in this light, the letter that Beverly Robinson sent secretly to Ethan from New York in March of the following year was part of a continuous campaign to bring Vermont over to the British side.[21] When Clinton left New York by sea for Charleston on December 26, he turned the Vermont negotiations over to Robinson, who was working under the Adjutant-General, Major John André, in the Central Department of His Britannic Majesty's Secret Service.[22]

1780: The Subversion of Ethan Allen Begins

Haldimand was less optimistic than Clinton. He told Clinton on April 13, 1780 that if the Commander-in-Chief could bring Ethan over and he proved faithful, it would be a great event. He said that Ethan's joining the British or even remaining in possession of Albany would open communications between us and secure Quebec and the Upper Country. But he feared that if Ethan were allowed to enter Quebec (as Clinton had suggested the previous September), he would seize the province with the help of the *habitants*, especially if the European French were at their head. Haldimand was afraid that Clinton's messenger to Ethan had fallen into enemy hands, since Ethan's "intention of joining our Army" is publicly known, and he had collected a force to defend his own state from both King and Congress. He was adamant that Ethan had made no overtures to the command in Quebec. All told, it was a thoroughly ambivalent letter, but if Clinton made progress with Ethan, "you may depend I will improve [it]."[23] Germain too wrote to Haldimand on April 12: he had hopes that Allen and Vermont "will come in," to be joined by our numerous friends at Albany, so "the whole district will return to obedience." He seems to have forgotten that his strategy to have Burgoyne supported by his numerous friends at Albany in 1777 was a total disaster.[24]

Beverly Robinson had been a wealthy landowner in both New York and western Massachusetts; he was known to Ethan as a Yorker who had tried to enforce the province's titles in Massachusetts, a part of the whole controversy centering on the Grants. He had been formally banished and his estates confiscated in New York's Act of Attainder on October 22, 1779.[25] Robinson wrote to Ethan on March 30, 1780.[26] Ethan received the letter late in July and discussed it in secret with Chittenden and a small number of government leaders. The letter invited proposals from Ethan in regard to separating Vermont from the American Revolution:

> . . . I think upon your taking an active part & imbolding the Inhabitants of Vermont in favour of the Crown of England, to act as the Commander in chief [Sir Henry Clinton] Shall direct that you may obtain a seperete Government under the King & constitution of England & the men formed into Regts under such officers as you shall Recommend & be on the same footing as all the Provential Corps are here . . .

On the assumption that no copies of this letter had reached Ethan, Robinson wrote again on February 2, 1781,[27] again offering terms, but strengthening the conditions: "provided you & the people of Vermont take a decisive and active part with us." Ethan, it is said, was confronted by Seth Warner, who forced him to reveal the existence of the two letters.[28] With the cat out of the bag, and with the approval of the Assembly,[29] Ethan wrote on March 9 to Samuel Huntington, President of the Continental Congress, enclosing the two letters and denying that he had answered them, nor, he said, had he had any form of contact with Robinson. (He omitted, of course, to mention that he had already engaged in secret discussions with Justus Sherwood, to be examined later.) Ethan recorded that a truce had been made with the British for a prisoner exchange and that, unless Vermont were admitted to the Union, it had "the Indubitable Right to agree on terms of a Cessation of Hostilities with Great Briton."[30] This is to anticipate, for we have to understand how this truce came about. Robinson, for his part, seems to have been happy to hand over the conduct of negotiations to Haldimand, without sending any agents north from New York, even though Germain had envisaged this possibility. Robinson advised Haldimand to allow the "Junto" to play a double game and to accede to delays "to prevent a determination against us," i.e. of Vermont joining the Congress. It was clear enough that the reunion would not take place in a couple of months; Haldimand, despite his impatience with the Allens at the time, soon grasped the reality.[31]

In the course of the three-way relationship between Vermont, Great Britain and the Continental Congress, Robinson's second letter is less important than the first, since the first led directly to the Haldimand Negotiations and the initial encounter between Justus Sherwood and Ethan Allen in October 1780. There had been hints in mid-1779 that Vermont would go its own way and distance itself in some way from the revolutionary cause: "... let New York remember, we have a northern as well as they a southern key, and are determined to maintain and support our independence and freedom."[32] This premonition of what came to be known as the "northern door" strategy was publicized at the time when the British in New York were convinced that Ethan Allen could well be turned to an active alliance with the British. Not so Haldimand, who wrote to Sir Henry Clinton on April 30, 1780, saying that he suspected that Ethan Allen was attempting to deceive both the Congress and the British[33] On July 25, 1780, soon after Ethan had received Robinson's first letter, Chittenden wrote to the Congress that Vermont in its own defense was at liberty, unilaterally, "to offer, or accept, terms of cessation of hostilities with Great Britain." Chittenden dismissed the validity of the claims of New York, Massachusetts and New Hampshire alike.[34]

In the same month, Chittenden wrote to Haldimand, "on the subject of an exchange of prisoners," as he recorded in the letter to Washington of November 14, 1781.[35] This letter, which has not survived or was never sent, has given rise to much controversy, mainly because of a frantic attempt to deny that Vermont was the first to open the matter of a prisoner exchange and, through that, an accommodation with the British. There is a reference to a letter from Chittenden to Haldimand in July, but no indication of what it said, nor whether it was actually sent, then a skepticism on the part of the editor of the VHS *Collections* (1924) about Chittenden's letter to Washington of November 1781, on the grounds that it was likely drafted by Ira.[36] Nor is there a copy of the July letter in the Haldimand Papers. The timing of the putative letter to Haldimand is indeed curious, because it was only in the following month that Ethan's request to exchange his wife's cousin, Gideon Brownson, and three other Green Mountain officers, captured by the British in 1779, was turned down by General Washington.[37] Possibly, all that Ethan aimed to achieve was to get Washington used to the idea that Vermont would engage in a prisoner exchange and that there was nothing suspicious about his forthcoming contacts with the British. But Washington and the Congress had every reason to be suspicious, because both Ethan and Chittenden had already asserted Vermont's right to make peace with the British.

Naturally enough, there is no written trace of a positive response to Robinson's proposal, since the Allens were always careful not to put anything incriminating in writing. Yet all the evidence points to the conclusion that, right from the beginning in July 1780, both the British and the Allens were bent on discussing the terms under which Vermont would return to the British Empire, and that the prisoner exchange was merely a cover for more momentous matters. There are gaps in the record, to be sure, such as the period between late August, when Ethan was secretly invited by the British in Quebec to take up Robinson's offer, and Ethan's meetings with Justus Sherwood late in October. There is no record of Sherwood's correspondence from August 24 to the beginning of his Journal recording his meetings with his former comrade in arms[38] In the presence of "ten field officers," Ethan asked Sherwood for a private meeting on the feeble pretext that since he found Sherwood's proposals "somewhat discretionary" he needed "to clearly understand" his proposals. He had altogether three private meetings with Sherwood on October 29 and 30, before he left Castleton for Bennington on the 30th.[39]

On the British side, there is no continuous narrative leading to Sherwood's meetings with Ethan, but the evidence that does exist is convincing enough. On August 24, Sherwood wrote to the officer commanding at St. John's, Brigadier General Watson Powell, the same man who had refused to surrender Ticonderoga to John Brown in 1777.[40] He enclosed a letter he had written to a Mr Hawkins the same day.[41] From the documentation, it is clear that Sherwood was familiar with Hawkins, but who he really was remains a mystery. Possibly, he was actually a member of the large Anglican, Loyalist family, the Hawleys of Arlington, the unofficial seat of the Vermont Council and known, by contrast, as Tory Hollow. Sherwood told Powell that he had received intelligence that

> Ethan Allen is actually got a number of men Enlisted for the Service of Government if Congress Refuses to comply with his Demands . . . in order to bring about a Revolution in favour of Government. . . . I Beg Leave to Propose to send three or four men acquainted with the Country and People as a Flag of Truce to Mr Allen for the Exchange of Prisoners, or some other public business, and let them communicate the secret proposals to Allen under pretence of public business.

Sherwood had gotten the news a few days before from an agent, Thomas Fraser, that Ethan Allen had raised a force to defend Vermont against both

King and Congress. He expressed none of the skepticism about the success of the project that he later displayed, but he did say that Governor Chittenden, Colonel Bayley and Major (Ebenezer) Allen would first have to be gotten out of the way, on account of their hostility to the British and their influence with the Vermont public. (Despite the work of the British Secret Service from the Mohawk Valley to western New Hampshire, Sherwood was quite wrong about Chittenden.) Sherwood thought he could win over the leading men by offering them positions in the King's Army. The rank and file could expect to be assisted in defending their frontiers and thus be convinced of the advantage of a "separate Government under the King" and "be confirmed in their landed Property as Granted under N. Hampshire." Hawkins was told that "the leading men of Vermont will be bountifully rewarded if they bring back the people of Vermont, the inhabitants secured in their property, and Vermont recognized." He was advised to make personal contact with Ethan; but among the other delegates, Fraser or Mr William Marsh would be suitable. This was the same Colonel Marsh who had thwarted Ethan over the command of the Green Mountain Boys in 1775. Since Marsh had family in the area, he would have a "plausible excuse for going down." Sherwood asked Hawkins to find out "when and where a negotiation may be opened with him" and let him know the result as soon as possible. All this was to be done in strict secrecy.

What happened next is uncertain. On August 25 an agent, Samuel Sherwood, left St. John's with the letter to Hawkins. Samuel Sherwood was the son of Justus, a private in the Queen's Loyal Rangers and in later life a member of the Assembly of the new province of Upper Canada. Samuel was anxious to find out the response of Ethan Allen to his message to Congress. He speculated that if the Congress rejected the latest demand from Vermont, the rebels would defend the frontier posts rather than succumb to New York. He listed the defenses, held by the Green Mountain Rangers, at Fort George, Fort Anne, Skenesborough and Fort Edward. By September 23, Justus Sherwood had also got word of the enemy dispositions from New York, over the Green Mountains to the Hazen Road, including the detachments commanded by Captain Ebenezer Allen and Major Samuel Safford.[42] Of the greatest importance was the news from Samuel Sherwood on September 23 that Hawkins, "a friend to Government," was taken prisoner to Albany. Sherwood destroyed the papers entrusted to him by Justus "for fear of accident," but he did send a reliable man to try to find out what response Ethan Allen had to his message to Congress.[43]

Rumors abounded. Samuel Sherwood heard that Congress had refused the demands of Vermont and that leading rebels would agree to support Ethan Allen in support of Government rather than yield to New York. A paper of intelligence by Thomas Taylor from Charlestown, on October 10, speculated that the Congress would award Vermont to New York, in which case Vermont would immediately apply for assistance from H.M.'s troops; Colonel (Ira) Allen was thought to have gone to Canada already.[44] On the other hand, a letter from Hudibras (Dr. George Smyth) in Albany to Haldimand, sent on September 30 and received on October 18, made no mention of conditions in Vermont, nor any speculation as to the future turn of events.[45]

Chittenden at Arlington wrote a letter to Haldimand on September 27, "suggesting that they arrange a cartel to exchange the Vermont prisoners,"[46] and Haldimand responded on October 22.[47] The fact that Haldimand now saw a prisoner exchange as a cover for other negotiations, implies that he had received no letter from Chittenden in July. Haldimand asked Chittenden to send someone to Crown Point or St. John's to confer with Major Christopher Carleton on "this business"; he would authorize Carleton to receive him, but no exchange of prisoners was yet authorized. This in turn enabled Major Christopher Carleton, the British commandant at Pointe au Fer, to empower Justus Sherwood to treat with Chittenden and Ethan Allen on the subject.[48] But the date of Haldimand's letter to Chittenden makes it unlikely that Ethan was alerted to a forthcoming meeting only in late October. It seems certain, indeed, that the agent sent by Samuel Sherwood—or someone—had actually made contact with Ethan, since Allen conveyed a letter from Chittenden to Haldimand by a certain Captain Wright, known to be a British scout (that is, a spy) but the date makes it certain that this was not the letter of September 27. (Reports from a Major Wright are frequently cited by Justus Sherwood in 1781–82, though this was likely the George Wright who appears later in this story or, alternatively, Joseph Wright, commended by Sherwood for his "stability, secrecy and knowledge of the leading men of Vermont."[49] Yet again, the Captain in question could have been Samuel Wright, sometime of Jessup's corps, later stationed at the Loyal Blockhouse.[50]).

On Chittenden's order, Ethan escorted Wright to Lake Champlain, where they met with British agents. John Pell wrote that it was possible that Justus Sherwood actually made personal contact with Ethan.[51] This would make the date of the meeting late in August. But Justus Sherwood stated in his letter of August 24 that he had already received word of Ethan Allen's proclivities, making it virtually impossible that the meeting had taken place in August, and impossible that Sherwood had actually met with Ethan. Sherwood's meeting with Ethan was yet to take place. Ethan was paid forty-eight pounds in September for "conducting Captain Wright and others to Lake Champlain by the Governor's Orders."[52] This was unusual, since expenditures were authorized by the Council, the Treasury, or the Board of War. Pell dates the receipt as September 12, when in fact it is undated; but the most likely sequence of events is that the Allens made contact with the British, after which Chittenden wrote his letter to Haldimand on September 27, requesting a prisoner exchange.

There is one other small piece of relevant evidence: Powell reported to Haldimand at the end of September that one of his agents in Vermont, a Mr Johns, had left Bennington on September 4; perhaps he was one of the "others" that Ethan had escorted to Lake Champlain.[53] Powell also reported that the Green Mountain Boys were not making preparations for an attack, nor were they expecting one. As well as reporting that Major Carleton had set off, he also said that Lieutenant Houghton's expedition had been authorized to move against Vermont territory, so it cannot be established whether the Vermonters knew at the time that Carleton had been ordered not to attack Vermont. On the other hand, if Ethan knew that there was to be a meeting with Sherwood, it was a virtual certainty that he knew that Carleton would not attack Vermont.

Sherwood was ahead of the game. William Marsh sent a letter to Haldimand from St. John's on October 10, proposing a plan of correspondence with Ethan and Chittenden, believing that "these people" could be brought back to their allegiance. Marsh knew that Sherwood had departed on a mission but was unaware that Justus was already engaged on the very project that he was proposing to Haldimand. The Governor sent a sympathetic reply to Marsh on the 16th, without divulging that the project was already in the works. Haldimand had by then received Chittenden's letter of September 27. Captain Robert Mathews, Haldimand's Secretary, wrote to Sherwood on October 16, saying that Chittenden's proposal for a prisoner exchange gave them a good opportunity for discussing questions relating to the reunion of Vermont, the "material business" of accommodation.[54] From the letter, it may seem that Mathews, like Marsh, was unaware of Sherwood's activities, but since it is clear from Haldimand's letter to Marsh that the Governor was very well acquainted with Sherwood's project, it is a certainty that the Governor's Secretary (no less) knew that Sherwood had been working under the authority of Brigadier General Powell in St. John's.

On September 27, Major Carleton left St. John's for his expedition to New York, deliberately avoiding hostilities with Vermont. On October 24, Sherwood got instructions from Powell to leave for Miller's Bay, about five miles north of Crown Point, to make contact with Carleton, then to proceed to Castleton, to meet with Ethan. In his letter to Ethan of October 26, stating that Sherwood was authorized to treat with him and Chittenden, Carleton suggested his own personal intervention, should any difficulty arise (on the 16th Sherwood had been given verbal instructions as to how to treat with Ethan). Carleton offered to suspend hostilities during the negotiations and requested Ethan to make every effort to ensure the same. Ethan agreed.[55] Sherwood, with a servant, six soldiers, and Captain John Chipman (on parole) landed at Miller's Bay, about twelve miles from Castleton, on October 26. Less Chipman, they proceeded to Colonel Herricks's camp at Fort Vengeance near Pittsford, where about 300 men were stationed. Fort Vengeance had been authorized on April 7 by the Board of War but was incomplete in October. Herrick escorted them to Ethan's headquarters at Castleton, about four miles away. There, on October 29, the negotiations began.[56]

Ethan opened by saying that he would take part in no damned Arnold plan to sell his country. Sherwood replied that General Haldimand was well aware of Vermont's difficulties with Congress and things could only get worse. Now was the proper time for Vermonters to cast off the Congress's yoke and resume their former allegiance to the King of Great Britain. Thus they could secure for themselves those principles they had so long contended for with New York. Ethan said that he would take Sherwood's proposals into very serious consideration. He would lay the proposals of Haldimand and Major Carleton for the prisoner exchange before the Council (of the officers present), but the truce for that purpose would have to include the "frontiers of New York," and no offensive was to be made by Major Carleton. Joseph Fay was dispatched to Bennington, with news of the truce.

Ethan lost no time, declaring a cessation of hostilities in the letter to Carleton, and expecting to extend the truce to the "Northern posts and frontiers of the State of New York during this Negociation," which Carleton confirmed.[57] At the same time, he wrote to Colonel Alexander Webster, the commander of the Charlotte County, New York militia, informing him of the extension of the truce to the New York frontiers and instructing him to stand on the defensive. The tone of the letter was due to the fact that Ethan, as Brigadier-General, outranked him.[58]

The next day, October 30, Ethan told Sherwood that his prime concerns were the "liberties and properties" of the inhabitants of Vermont. Ethan said he would send Colonel Ira Allen and Major Joseph Fay to apprise them of Haldimand's proposals. His interest at this stage was the neutrality of Vermont, the first of two lines of approach in Ethan's strategy. Sherwood was not to communicate to them the whole of their conversations, nor to give them an idea of anything but neutrality, and even then, only if Congress forced them into it by refusing Vermont's just and rightful claims.

Ethan was extremely cautious, saying that it was not currently in his power to desert the cause and turn to Great Britain; if he "now made a declaration of that nature, his own people would cut off his head." Nor was Haldimand able right now to send a force sufficient to protect the Vermonters. Ethan said quite candidly that his aim was Congressional recognition of a fully independent Vermont with all its liberties and properties, including those claimed by New York: negotiations with Canada would end if Vermont got a seat in Congress, and would be kept secret (as Robinson had proposed). Ethan had written to Governor Trumbull of Connecticut and to Governor Hancock of Massachusetts, asking them to lay Chittenden's letter to the Congress of July 25, 1780 before their legislators; just as in his letter to Governor George Clinton, Chittenden had appealed to New York to relinquish its claim of jurisdiction and join with Vermont in a union versus Great Britain.[59]

But with all these caveats, Ethan put forward his tentative proposals. He would prepare the ground and work for a Declaration of Neutrality, in the event of Congress's rejection of Vermont's admission. Then, as soon as he found the Congress raising a force against him, he would march to take possession of Albany (which Sir Henry Clinton had thought was his intention in 1779). He would be assisted by troops from the borders of Vermont, and near four thousand men from Berkshire County, Massachusetts. If driven out of Albany, he would move back Ticonderoga and call on help from Haldimand, who should take post at No. 4 (Charlestown) or Bennington. This would need at least twenty thousand troops (actually more than double the number that Haldimand had available for the defense of the whole province from Quebec to Michilimakinak). In this event, Ethan laid down to Sherwood the terms he would require for Vermont's rejoining Great Britain. These were (i) that he would command his owns forces; (ii) Vermont would become a "separate government" under the Crown, with all the attendant privileges; (iii) Vermont would choose its own civil officers and troops; and (iv) the British would confirm the New Hampshire titles. All this would take time; meanwhile negotiations would continue, not by letter but under a flag. Both lines of approach (neutrality and reunion) were taken up by Ira at the Ile-aux-Noix in the following May: neutrality was discussed but without the proviso that Congress should first reject Vermont's admission, and reunion without the precondition that Vermont should first be threatened by Continental forces.

Meanwhile, Sherwood's mission had aroused great suspicion. Carleton's raid on the New York frontiers had concluded, but his force was still on Lake Champlain with such numbers of ships and boats that "the lake looked black for a mile in length." So the Ranger Captain Ebenezer Allen wrote to Webster on October 30, advising him of the possibility of a further raid on the New York frontiers. Apparently perplexed and suspicious, he detained Sherwood's party and told Webster that Ethan was on his way home: "I am afraid the Enemy have out-Generaled him."[60] It was not until November 6 that Chittenden ordered Ebenezer, in a cold letter, to facilitate Sherwood's departure, escorted by Captain Eli Brownson. Ira and Joseph Fay went along, but on the 14th they turned back because of the ice on the lake, saying that they would come to St. John's as soon as possible. Sherwood related that he had shown them the General's proposals (contrary to Ethan's stipulations), and was told that, when they met, they must be shown "all my authority and instructions from General Haldimand." He arrived back at St. John's on the 26th and delivered his dispatches to Major Carleton; they set out for Quebec to meet with Haldimand on the 28th. Unless Sherwood's Journal is wildly inaccurate, the proposal to make Vermont a separate government under the Crown was a central and growing concern, to be advanced in a concrete way at the meeting in Quebec, as soon as the weather permitted.

Back in Vermont, things did not go smoothly for the Allens. On October 31, Chittenden read to the General Assembly Haldimand's letter offering a prisoner exchange and Carleton's letter to Ethan of October 26. There was an uproar: remonstrances against Ethan were tabled by William Hutchins and Simeon Hathaway, no doubt protesting the truce for the exchange of prisoners. The Assembly dismissed the charges of Hathaway and allowed Hutchins to withdraw his complaint. Despite the furor, it is clear enough that the members saw that a decisive move had been made and that they supported the work of the Allens. They approved the cartel for the exchange of prisoners and requested Chittenden "to discharge the militia and the Volunteers raised for the defence of the Northern Frontiers," which Ethan proceeded to do.[61] The Act of February 26, 1779, preventing the return of Loyalists to the state (Colonel William Marsh was named as one), was repealed on November 8.[62] The British also got a report that a committee of the Vermont Assembly had recommended that no credit for Continental Army provisions should be extended to Colonel Udney Hay, as this would be a case of taxation without representation.[63]

Though Ethan survived the attacks on him in the Assembly, he did have to resign as Brigadier-General on November 4, saying that there was unease among some of the people on account of his command.[64] This may be true, but there would have been something incongruous about continuing to command without any militia to direct. Also, quite possibly, he did not want to be in the position to fight the British, in the event the truce miscarried. If the Assembly offered him the command at some future date, he would "endeavor to serve the State to the best of his ability." When Ethan wrote again to Major Carleton on November 4 from Bennington, confirming that the truce was extended to the frontiers of New York, he notified Carleton that the commissioners for the prisoner exchange were Ira and Fay, who had been appointed by the Council two days before.[65] Chittenden confirmed this in a letter to Haldimand on November 6.[66] A further letter to Carleton went out on November 24, with the news that the two commissioners would be in Montreal or St. John's on about the first of the year, but that the extension of the truce to the New York frontiers had proved controversial and was at an end.[67]

The British prepared for the meeting in the New Year and were optimistic about their prospects. After he had reported to Germain, on October 25, that negotiations with Vermont were proceeding, Haldimand wrote again on December 16, saying that Robinson's offer to Ethan Allen had been or may be accepted.[68] At the same time, Sir Henry Clinton expressed the belief that Ethan Allen had joined the King's troops.[69] On December 20, 1780, Haldimand sent his instructions to Sherwood for negotiating the "accommodation" with the Vermonters, variously described as reunion, reconciliation and return to allegiance. The instructions showed that Haldimand had taken careful note of the terms of accommodation that Ethan required.[70] Sherwood was to convey the General's sincerity and patience to the Vermont commissioners and he trusted that they too were sincere. Haldimand indicated no skepticism about the motives of the Vermont leaders that he expressed both before and afterwards. He had earlier described Ethan's followers as "a collection of the most abandoned wretches that ever lived, to be bound by no laws or ties," with the double-dealing Ethan at their head.[71] As well as abandoned wretches, Haldimand had several choice phrases to describe the Vermonters: lawless vagabonds, inveterate rebels, profligate banditti, etc. It is to Haldimand's credit that he never allowed his personal feelings to compromise his efforts to neutralize the Vermonters in the Revolutionary War.

When Haldimand appealed to the interests of the Vermonters in his instructions to Sherwood, he deplored the efforts of the New York government to deprive the Vermonters of the fruits of their labor and industry, a sentiment that both he and Sherwood continued to hold throughout the negotiations. Haldimand conveyed to Sherwood that he would grant a separate jurisdiction, even though he has no power to settle land titles; the separate jurisdiction would "appear sufficient to secure the property of every person belonging to the state of Vermont." Sherwood was to give the "most positive assurances" that Vermont would be erected into a Separate Province. Haldimand appreciated the delicacy of the situation, and that it would take time to convince the population of the advantages of reconciliation with the Mother County. Should Vermont join the Congress, he thought that time and "other methods" would bring about reconciliation. Vermont was to be promised 3,000 of the King's troops "when they declare for neutrality or for the King." Haldimand observed that "a truce cannot be privately continued or trade granted"; in other words, that there was to be no informal exemption from trading with the enemy. This showed at least that free trade with Canada was early on the Allens' agenda. The most specific part of the instructions concerned the armed forces of the separate province. Haldimand was prepared for Vermont to raise at least two battalions, each of ten companies with Ira Allen and Chittenden (or whomever the Governor and Council nominated) as Lieutenant-Colonels, and himself as Colonel commanding. As was usual in the Provincial corps, the officers, to be confirmed by Haldimand, were to be on half pay.

On December 31, 1780, Haldimand authorized Major Alexander Dundas, the commandant of the Ile-aux-Noix, to conduct the prisoner exchange, which he supervised well beyond the end of the summer of the following year.[72] To have kept Dundas in ignorance of the much larger project at hand was a remarkable feat, especially as negotiations were to take place for eighteen days under his very nose on the Ile-aux-Noix.

The Negotiations of 1781

On January 1, 1781 Chittenden wrote to Haldimand, saying that Ira and

Fay were unable to come to Canada because of the ice.[73] He wrote again on April 26, saying that Ira and his party were unable to cross the lake in February; Ira with Major Isaac Clarke (his son-in-law) would now be sent with full powers, as soon as the road were safe.[74] Ira Allen, without Fay or Clarke, finally arrived at the Ile-aux-Noix on May 7, 1781, with an escort of Lieutenant Lemman and fourteen privates of the Vermont militia, ostensibly to discuss the prisoner exchange, but actually to further the negotiations to bring Vermont back into the British Empire.[75] The next day, Ira sent off a letter to Haldimand via Dundas, stating that "The Legislature of Vermont stands adjourned to about the Middle of June next when it is expected that the People East of Hudson's River and West of our former Line will be represented in the Legislature." Then a prisoner exchange would take place with the emissaries empowered to "Transact such other Business that may be Then Judg'd Proper."[76]

The negotiations took place in an atmosphere of mistrust. Haldimand had written to Germain on April 30, claiming (in the absence of any appearance of the Vermonters) that "Ethan Allen is endeavouring to deceive both the Congress and us."[77] Ira wanted to know what Haldimand's official position was, for instance, through seeing his instructions to Sherwood of the previous December, which Sherwood refused. Ira had come armed with written proposals for a prisoner exchange cartel but had no written authorization "to treat of a union." Sherwood expressed a constant frustration that Ira would not commit himself to anything in writing. Ira would only say that he had been verbally instructed by Governor Chittenden and Ethan Allen to lay the present situation before General Haldimand. Matters were not yet ripe for any permanent proposals. The Vermont leaders were anxious to bring about a neutrality, but dare not make any agreement with Britain until the populace were better prepared for the purpose. Ira wanted a permanent cartel and thereby open a door for further negotiation. It has to be emphasized that right from the first full day of negotiation (May 8), the issues of neutrality and reunion were on the agenda, and they were to have different outcomes as the negotiations proceeded.

At the same time, there was no progress on the prisoner exchange, which led Dundas to conclude that the Vermonters were not really interested in a prisoner exchange at all; rather, they wanted to spin out the negotiations to alarm the Congress and the "particular [claiming] states" for their own ends.[78] Haldimand forbade a partial (limited) exchange of Captain Gideon Brownson for Major Zadock Wright, which was, to Dundas, Ira's prime concern in the proposed exchange. On that first day of May 8, Ira pointed out that the new representatives from the Eastern Union were in the Assembly and the Western delegates would likely be seated by June 15; this will "probably soon enable Vermont to make proposals for a Union with Britain, with more safety than at present." On the 13th, Ira said that the principal men in Vermont are preparing the people for a change in form of government and hoped that General Haldimand would not be impatient: the people have first to turn against Congress before they are invited to a Union with Britain. On the 19th, he said that the Vermont leaders were doing all they could to effect a "union or neutrality."

For Ira's positions, Sherwood's Journal is a good guide, but for the course of the negotiations, we have to rely on the correspondence that passed between Quebec and the Ile-aux-Noix. Sherwood's letters to Mathews of May 7, 11, and 15 all deplore the fact that Ira came without any proposals and was merely prolonging the discussions of "the business" in order for the Vermonters to strengthen themselves.[79] In his letter of May 7, Sherwood said that Ira admitted he was not authorized to treat of the union; the Vermonters could not enter into any agreement until the populace were better molded. Vermont had extended its jurisdiction from Mason's Line to the Hudson, and the western representatives would probably be seated in the Assembly by mid-June.

Later, a series of letters from H.Q. in Quebec arrived at the Ile-aux-Noix. The first was from Haldimand, addressed to Chittenden, dated May 14. Since the subject matter was secret and would be circulated outside Quebec, it was relatively mild, expressing disappointment that six months of deliberations (on the reunion) had led to such little progress, but hoping that proposals would still come from Vermont, to be received under a flag of truce.[80] A second letter from Captain Robert Mathews, Haldimand's Secretary, to Sherwood, was more forthright. Mathews contended that the flag was only to gain time and "unless the intentions of these people are more freely declared," the negotiations are to be curtailed.[81] A further letter from Haldimand to Sherwood on May 17 was even more severe.[82] Haldimand cited his instructions to Sherwood of the previous December; he was told to inform Ira that Haldimand was empowered by His Majesty to offer terms to Vermont, but not a mere Treaty of Neutrality: the State of Vermont must either reunite with Great Britain or "continue at enmity with it." Haldimand deplored the release of Robinson's letters by General Allen to the Congress, and insisted on strict secrecy in his dealings with Vermont. (Ira on the 19th observed to Sherwood that General Allen was obliged, for his own safety, to send Colonel Robinson's letters to the Congress.) Haldimand did not lay down a deadline for a decisive move from Vermont, but suggested that the meeting of the Assembly in June might be the time for "the leading men of Vermont" to come to a decision, in which case there would be a further meeting under a flag.

Justus Sherwood had written on May 12 to Major Lernoult, Haldimand's Adjutant-General, and one of the three British commissioners, the others being himself and Major Dundas. Sherwood told Lernoult that Ira could not fix a time for the exchange. Ira intimated that the designs of the leaders may be communicated to the Assembly at its next session: Haldimand will hear from them on July 20th or sooner.[83] Sherwood said as much to Mathews, writing on May 20 that Ira wanted time to bring the Vermonters into compliance with Haldimand's desires, he thinks by July 21, if they can be permitted to send some prisoners for exchange.[84] Ira warned of the dangers of moving too fast with the Vermonters. Sherwood observed that Haldimand's terms would take much better hold if there were a good army on Vermont's frontiers. It was only after Ira had left that Sherwood got the news that the Western Union had been inaugurated.[85]

In a letter to Mathews of May 23, Sherwood intimated that he had communicated the terms of Haldimand's letter of May 17, which had a "good effect" on Ira, who was now well aware that His Excellency was not to be trifled with; "vigorous measures" were to be used with "these people." Ira, who was of course aware that Sherwood had received Haldimand's instructions in December, was anxious to get a copy of Haldimand's letter to Sherwood, but Sherwood would not oblige.[86] Sherwood also said that the "head and spirit" of Mathews' harsh letter of May 15 would be of service to Allen in the Vermont Council. Vigorous measures must again be used when the opposition to the Allens was offered in other terms, i.e. admission to Congress.[87] In a second letter of May 25, Sherwood reiterated the impact of the letters from HQ on Ira and, in a reversal of his previous skepticism, now thought that Ira was sincere, that he would bring back the Vermont people to Government if he could; but Ira doubted whether he could do more than achieve the position of neutrality.[88]

On May 19, Sherwood had asked Mathews whether Haldimand wanted further negotiations. His own view was that the Vermonters should be given until the conclusion of the June meeting of the Vermont Assembly to respond positively.[89] This was in spite of cynicism expressed the previous day: Ira tried to persuade Sherwood that he was sincere, but Sherwood thought the Vermonters would not be "ripe" until they had despaired of every other interest.[90] Mathews responded on the 28th, saying that Haldimand was satisfied with Sherwood's conduct in the negotiations.[91]

In the end, the negotiators gave Ira until the end of the June session of the Assembly (due on the 24th), and "a reasonable time thereafter," verbally extending the truce in order for Vermont to take concrete, public steps towards reunion.[92] Ira, on the 23rd, was pessimistic: there were difficulties in bringing about a revolution, as a number of the Council and a major part of the Legislature had not yet the least idea of anything further than neutrality, and many of the legislators were ignorant of even that. It looks as though Ira had been rattled by the content of the letters from Quebec, telling him to get a move on, and the clear statement that neutrality was off the agenda. On the 21st, Sherwood recorded that Ira would strive to have commissioners appointed and properly authorized to treat of a union by July 20, but this would likely be conditional on a prisoner exchange, and the General would hear from him before that date. If Haldimand needed to send highly secret messages in the meantime, the messenger must make himself known to Ethan, Ira, Chitttenden or someone on a list comprising one General Officer, Colonel Brownson (not Gideon, for he was still in British custody), Dr (Jonas) Fay, Judge Facit [Fasset] or Corporal [Matthew] Lyons. This group was among those who were then aware of the Negotiations, and all were close to the Arlington Junto. Before Ira left for Vermont on the 25th, Sherwood reiterated Haldimand's offer of a "separate province within the Empire," adding only that a force of three thousand British troops would proceed up Lake Champlain for protection.

Haldimand remained skeptical. In June, he wrote to Sir Henry Clinton about Ira's visit to the Ile-aux-Noix, with his ongoing suspicion of the Vermonters' stance and his determination to ascertain "the real designs of Vermont."[93] Later in the month, Haldimand got word from Vermont that the "friends to Government" were uniting with Mr Allen and were in favor of reconciliation with Great Britain. A vote for neutrality was being held up by some gentlemen of influence on the east side of Connecticut River, something that Haldimand knew already. But the missive did hit on a difficulty that had so concerned Sir Henry Clinton: the Vermonters had unjustly deprived some Yorkers of title to their land, causing turmoil in Vermont. In any treaty, such issues should be settled by Commissioners appointed by Great Britain. In this anonymous paper of intelligence sent to Haldimand on June 3, 1781, and received two weeks later, the author (probably one of the Allens) expressed doubt as to whether a vote for Neutrality could be carried in the Assembly. This was a way of saying that Ira's promises in May could not be fulfilled, since it presumed that the representatives of the Western Union would not be seated to balance the anti-Allen faction from the Sixteen Towns. The letter also referred only to neutrality, which Haldimand had clearly stated he was not empowered to grant. The author hoped that His Excellency would approve "our conduct," presumably referring to that of Ira, and gloomily forecasting an unsatisfactory outcome to the aims of the Allens and the British alike.[94]

For his part, Ira seems to have been forced into a schedule that he was unlikely to be able to meet: the representatives of the Western Union would have to be seated in the Assembly, and the question of reunion broached. In fact, far from increasing support, the June meeting of the Assembly expressed vociferously its discontent with the Allens.

Clandestine negotiations, involving Ethan, continued throughout the winter, spring and summer, with an elaborate system of code names and smoke signals to announce imminent meetings. For instance, David Crowfoot wrote to Sherwood on March 3, 1781.[95] Ethan had refused to meet with him but, through an intermediary, he said he would keep his promises to Sherwood, since he and his people were tired of war. Ethan was clearly worried about the poor impression that Ira had made on the British, first by not showing up, then at the meeting in May, but his attempts to counter this impression were not convincing, as was evidenced by the intelligence that Haldimand received in mid-June.

The situation in Vermont was not quite as bad as Ethan had implied in the unsigned paper. On Saturday, June 16, 1781, the fifteen representatives of the "Western District" were seated in the Assembly, except that two were absent and a third (John Abbot) was reprimanded on the 28th for financial corruption, which resulted in the expulsion of one of its members. On the same day, the Western Union was approved. On the 20th, Samuel Safford was elected commander of the 1st Brigade of Militia (defeating Ira), and Samuel Fletcher the commander of the 2nd; both were in on the secret of the Haldimand Negotiations.[96] On the 28th, Jonas Fay, Ira Allen and Bezaleel Woodward were appointed as delegates to Congress, the last of these oblivious to the fact that he was being set up to fail, that the Allens did not want the delegation to pull off a deal.[97] The question of a rapprochement with the British was not, however, raised, and to that extent, Ethan's fears were confirmed.

Unbeknown to Sherwood and Haldimand, the Allens (with Ira increasingly in the lead) were hatching a plot and strategy that would remove all doubts about their motives and intentions. To anticipate, the Eastern and Western Unions would be declared as part of a Greater Vermont. Armed with this bargaining chip, the three Vermont negotiators would proceed to Philadelphia to obtain an offer from Congress. They would return to Vermont and present the offer to the Assembly, which would reject it, leaving Vermont open to proposals from the British for reunion.

The British were moving in a parallel direction. Germain wrote to Haldimand on April 12, 1781, with hopes of "Ethan Allen and the people of Vermont coming in" and that "our numerous friends at Albany" will join, and the whole district will return to obedience.[98] On May 4, he wrote again, ordering Haldimand to cooperate with Clinton, to use "every means to bring in Vermont," cut off communications between Albany and the Mohawk, and prevent Washington from receiving supplies by the Hudson.[99] Haldimand responded on July 8: the cartel for the exchange of prisoners was "to be made use of for negotiating for the reconciliation of Vermont." He referred to his prime concern, to "prevent the union with Congress they seem bent on." This was in view of the "strength of the country they occupy," thus relating the politics of negotiation with the British military predicament. The letter was written just before Joseph Fay's meeting with Justus Sherwood, and relayed the news that negotiations with Governor Chittenden and Ethan Allen were taking place. He believed that the intention of the "inveterate rebels" was to get better terms from the Continental Congress, but "there may be hope yet of success."[100]

Germain wrote further to Haldimand later in July, telling him that "A considerable force on the frontiers would be the surest means of giving efficacy to negotiations with Vermont; nothing should be omitted to attach that people to His Majesty." Haldimand should be prepared to recognize the Hudson as Vermont's western boundary, as this was in accordance with the policy of cutting off connection between the eastern provinces and Canada by the interposition of the new province and the diminution of the former.[101] To this extent, the strategy of the Allens was succeeding.

The British thought that a success in Cornwallis' campaign "to the southward" would be an inducement for the Vermonters "to declare for us," buttressed by a body of troops from Canada.[102] As the summer wore on, the British became anxious. On August 2, Haldimand wrote two letters to Clinton, only the first of which was sent. In the first, he estimated that Vermont would join the side in the military ascendancy. He said that Ira would not come to the forthcoming meeting since he cannot "stand the test of the interview"; in the second letter, he said that Ira wished "to avoid the test of a discovery"; we will hear what Fay proposes. As for Ethan, "to carry on the deception, Ethan Allen has quitted the service." Haldimand also said that Vermont was arming itself and "in a few months will become an important ally or a formidable enemy."[103] Haldimand's letter crossed with one from Clinton, who wrote on the same day of the importance of a diversion on the northern frontiers and "a speedy decision of Vermont in our favour."[104] To this, Haldimand still counseled delay, on the grounds that the Vermonters were prepared militarily, and to try to force the issue would propel them towards Congress, since they preferred to become the Fourteenth State.

General Robertson wrote to Haldimand from New York, where he was commandant, with the fear that the British would lose Vermont to the Continental Congress, but expressing the hope that Vermont may yet be gained to the King's Government.[105] The British concern was that the Vermonters were using the Haldimand negotiations to lever themselves into the Continental Congress, a move which would likely succeed if the British military situation worsened. Later, on October 2, Clinton wrote to Haldimand, saying that he agreed that Vermont should "declare immediately," as the situation of Lord Cornwallis in Virginia is "become alarming."[106] Haldimand expressed "the advantage of gaining the Vermonters" again in November, in view of the critical position of General Cornwallis.[107]

Justus Sherwood, meanwhile, had been promoted from the position of Commissioner for the Exchange of Prisoners (or Supervisor of Spies and Prisoner Exchanges), which he shared with Dr. George Smyth. He was now to become Head of His Britannic Majesty's Secret Service in the Northern Department, with Smyth as his deputy. Sherwood was now responsible for all scouting and intelligence activities except in the regions of the far western outposts, responsible not to the commandants of the Sorel (Richelieu) forts but directly to Haldimand. He was also given permission to establish the Loyal Blockhouse on what is now North Hero, Vermont, sufficiently remote for spies to pass back and forth unobserved.[108] To have won the trust of Haldimand was a great achievement. The Governor was a stiff, upright, cautious man who had a low opinion of the "Provincial corps," and in some cases, like that of John Peters, he treated them shabbily.

On July 9, 1781, Joseph Fay arrived at the site of the Loyal Blockhouse to meet with Sherwood and Smyth. On the face of it, Fay came empty-handed: he had no written instructions since the issue of reunion had not been raised in the Assembly; but the Governor, Council and leading men (i.e. Ethan) were "bringing about a revolution." Sherwood told Mathews that he and Smyth were "employed with Major Fay on the subject of union."[109] The Vermonters were "anxious to enter on the business." Fay arrived back at Crown Point on July 20, relaying to Sherwood that he had letters from Ira Allen and Thomas Chittenden. The letter addressed to Haldimand from Chittenden of July 15 was of no help; Chittenden acknowledged his letter of May 14 (the mild one) but there was no hint of "the business."[110]

Fay had shown Sherwood the letter from Ira to Haldimand, dated July 10, before it was sent on to Haldimand.[111] Ira recounted his difficulties at the June session of the Assembly, when some members, asking whence the "Reports of Nutrality &c" had come, demanded to see copies of all the correspondence that had passed to and from the Province of Quebec. The Allens had been careful to avoid entering into what Ira described as a "criminal correspondence" with the British.[112] Fortuitously or otherwise, Ira had a convincing alibi. During the May negotiations, the British had kept the commandant at the Ile-aux-Noix, Major Alexander Dundas of the 34th Regiment, as ignorant as possible of the true purpose of the discussions. So far as Dundas was concerned, a man whom Haldimand much later described as "stupid and silly," the negotiations were only about a cartel for the prisoner exchange, not even about a general truce, let alone reunion. So Ira was able to produce a letter to Dundas and Sherwood, protesting with righteous indignation that he had no idea where the proposal of a truce had come from.[113]

In the letter of July 10 to Haldimand, Ira went on to say that three commissioners (himself, Jonas Fay and Bezaleel Woodward) would be sent to Philadelphia, to make an offer which Congress would reject. Those "in favour of Government" would then be able to convince the people that Congress meant only to carve up Vermont between the "claiming states." After the September elections, the new House (with the Allen party strengthened by the representatives from the Western Union) would have a year to "make a Revolution so long wished for by many." Since Ira was still not explicit about his aims and aspirations, his letter, the one reproduced by DePuy, again met with deep skepticism on the part of Sherwood, Smyth and Haldimand, a mistrust that lasted until September. The British agreed to extend the truce in order to give the Vermont leaders more time to prepare the people for a change in government. From his post near Crown Point, Fay wrote to Captain Chambers on July 21, 1781: hostilities would cease on the part of

Vermont and he trusted the same would be true of the King's troops. Chambers confirmed this two days later, saying there would be no hostilities against Vermont without notice.[114]

On September 16, 1781 Ira and Joseph Fay arrived at Skenesborough to receive from Sherwood eighteen American prisoners, the completion of an exchange that had begun early in August, by Joseph Fay, lodged on the *Royal George* near the Loyal Blockhouse.[115] On August 9, Sherwood had reported to Mathews that Major Zadock Wright, the commander of the second company of the Queen's Loyal Rangers, was exchanged for Captain Gideon Brownson of the Regiment of Green Mountain Rangers. So far as "the business" was concerned, the August meeting was no more satisfactory than the one the previous month, since Joseph Fay still had no mandate to negotiate reunion when he arrived for the exchange. The British were convinced that the Vermonters wished to spin out the negotiations until November, when they would know the result of Cornwallis's campaign; meanwhile they could head off invasion by King or Congress.[116] But Ira and Joseph Fay, the two commissioners, wrote to Sherwood and Smyth on September 16, saying that they were empowered by Chittenden "to Negotiate Business with you Relative to a Change of Government."[117] At last, the Allens had come out into the open, confident enough that they could withstand any challenge over "criminal correspondence."

On the 20th, Ira and Fay wrote to Haldimand with a concrete plan. The new legislature would hear the proposals of Congress, made in August, to the effect (merely) that an "indispensable preliminary" for the recognition of independence and admission of Vermont into the union is the dissolution of the Eastern and Western Unions.[118] The Allens took it that the legislature would reject the Congress's proposal. After a few days, there would then be a "Public Litigation of a Change of Government." For that to be done, a Proclamation was requested of His Excellency, setting down the terms that Haldimand was authorized by the "Court of Great Britain" to give to Vermont. (Those Vermonters with knowledge of the secret negotiations assumed that the return to Government would be authorized by the King in Council or by Parliament.) In view of the fact that most Vermonters were emigrants from Connecticut, it was expected that the terms would reflect the privileges of the New England states, of which Connecticut was the most progressive. As soon as the legislature had rejected the Congress's offer, the British would be asked to deliver the Proclamation to Castleton; Brigadier General Roger Enos, the commander of the Vermont militia in place of Ethan, would immediately forward it unopened to the legislature. In the letter to Haldimand of July 10, Ira had intimated that Enos was one of the eight people who was privy to the May negotiations at the Ile-aux-Noix, i.e., with the plan to turn Vermont into a separate government under the Crown.[119]

Haldimand must have known of the Vermonters' proposals even before Ira sent his letter of September 16 and the concrete plan of September 20. On September 13, he wrote to Sir Henry Clinton, saying that the Vermont Assembly would meet on October 1 (later postponed for a week), and that he would send a large detachment to Crown Point, and strong parties to appear on the Mohawk River. He hoped "these steps will produce a favourable effect in the affairs of Vermont."[120] By September 24, Sherwood had apparently arrived at Haldimand's headquarters in Quebec following his meetings at Skenesborough, since Haldimand that day sent a further letter to Clinton, which included the Vermonters' latest demands. He said that the Vermont negotiators had referred to the Congress resolutions of August, making the dissolution of the two unions a precondition of joining the United Colonies, so a union with Great Britain would depend on the British confirmation of the Eastern and Western Unions as part of Vermont. Haldimand then referred to a dilemma which was to recur until the peace treaty of April 1783: he was inclined to meet the Vermonters' demands but not without Clinton's concurrence, something which would take several weeks or more to obtain.

In this letter and subsequent reports of September 27 and 30, Haldimand referred to "the delicacy of handling the troops on the frontiers of Vermont." He had "carefully avoided devastating the country": the protective detachment stationed at Crown Point would provide an incentive for the Vermonters at least to maintain neutrality. In the letter of September 27, Haldimand made it clear that the force would arrive at Crown Point on about the 12th or 14th of October, to coincide with the meeting of the Vermont Assembly.[121]

Sherwood apparently had trouble persuading Haldimand of the utility of a Proclamation, since it was only on September 30 that the Governor wrote to General Robertson in New York, saying that the Vermonters had pressed for the issue of a Proclamation, "promising to confirm the late assumed territory." He confirmed this to Clinton on the following day.[122] Haldimand's dilemma reasserted itself: he told Robertson he could not take responsibility for the confirmation of the two unions but he would consider these territories as belonging to Vermont, and would protect them "until he has received proper authority"; he had sent a runner to Clinton to confirm his promises.

Haldimand's correspondence shows that Sherwood had given him a most exhaustive report.[123] In Haldimand's letter to Clinton of October 1, he told the Commander-in-Chief that the "Leading men in our interest" requested a Proclamation as a "last resource," confirming the Eastern and Western Unions "and other privileges, thinking that from the late refusal of these by Congress the people may be inclined to accept of terms from Government." The leading Vermonters required a protective force to support them and "to awe those in opposition"; "every appearance of hostility will be carefully avoided." This letter reflects the sentiments of the Allens that they had a year to finalize the understanding, since Haldimand said that the situation would be favorable enough for "spring operations."[124] In his letter to Germain of October 23, 1781, Haldimand said that the protective force was to encourage the Vermonters to declare for His Majesty's Government.[125]

In the letter of October 3 to Clinton, Haldimand sketched out the terms of the Proclamation.[126] First, if Vermonters unite under the Crown, they will be recognized as a separate province with charter rights as formerly enjoyed by the Province of Connecticut, except the appointment of the Governor. Haldimand proposed to get clearance for the recognition of Vermont from Mason's Line in New Hampshire to the Hudson, implying that he could only propose the terms of a treaty, not conclude or ratify it. Second, he would confirm "landed property as granted under New Hampshire." Third, Vermont would be accorded "a free trade with Canada." Last, a protective force would be provided by the Crown, and Vermont troops would have the status of the provincials (Loyalist forces) now serving in the King's Army.

In the Proclamation to the inhabitants of the district called Vermont, dated October 5, 1781, Haldimand declared that His Majesty had empowered him to offer terms to Vermont best designed to recall them from opposition. Should Vermont unite with Great Britain, it would be considered by the British government to be a separate province under the Crown, with the charter rights of Connecticut excepting the appointment of the Governor, which was reserved to the Crown. Until His Majesty's pleasure be known (how often had the Vermonters heard that phrase!) or until Haldimand got clearance from the peace commissioners in New York, the New Hampshire titles would be recognized and the Eastern and Western Unions considered to be part of Vermont. Haldimand offered a standing protective force, and the Vermont troops would have the status of Provincials in the King's Army;

but if Vermonters rejected the overture, they alone must be responsible for the "melancholy consequences which must inevitably follow."[127]

In drafting the Proclamation, Haldimand was faced with a dilemma: if it appeared to be an offer conditional for its acceptance on a higher British authority, it would not be convincing. But if it were definitive, Haldimand would be making promises he might not be able to deliver. From the text of the Proclamation, Haldimand erred on the side of the latter horn of the dilemma: he sent a runner to Clinton to get confirmation of the terms offered to the Vermonters—not a conventional mode of diplomacy! So it transpired, for Clinton wrote to Haldimand on November 12, saying that "a change of boundaries may require an Act of Parliament."[128] (It was well after the Proclamation was issued that Haldimand did receive some form of confirmation that the King would approve the boundaries of the new province as extensive as he desired.[129]) From the British point of view, it was perhaps just as well that the Proclamation was not delivered.

On October 10, the Proclamation arrived at St. John's, where Sherwood wrote a covering letter, before it was sent south with the protective force of nearly a thousand men under Brigadier-General Barry St Leger.[130] The Vermont House was supposed to convene in the second week of October and, as soon as Congress's offer was rejected, a messenger was to be sent from Charlestown to pick up the Proclamation at Castleton. By October 18, no message from Ira Allen had arrived.[131] St Leger, fretting at the delay, had by then accepted a crazy plan apparently proposed by Dr Smyth. Instead of waiting for a request, the British would apprehend a patrol of Vermont militia and send the Proclamation down to Enos at Castleton. This they tried to do but succeeded only in capturing five and killing Sergeant Archelaeus Tupper.[132] St Leger sent the prisoners back without the Proclamation, but with a letter of apology to Chittenden.

This letter was conveyed to Charlestown on the 28th by a messenger unfriendly to the conspirators, Simeon Hathaway, who had led one of the two charges against Ethan in the House, the previous October. Hathaway broadcast the news far and wide—that the British, far from attacking, had actually apologized for causing casualties. How could this have come about, but for collusion by the Allens with the British? The Assembly had risen on the 27th but the representatives remaining in Charlestown were in an uproar. The only truce that the representatives knew of was the cartel for the exchange of prisoners and (so far as they were concerned) that had been concluded in September. Once again, Ira calmed things down, as he had done in

June. At the same time as Hathaway conveyed St Leger's apology to Chittenden, General Enos, Colonel Fletcher and Colonel Wallbridge had sent express letters to Chittenden, which contained references to the "private negociations" with the British. Chittenden managed to withhold these letters from the councillors and representatives still in Charlestown. Without a trace of embarrassment, Ira related how the three letters were replaced by forged copies which "contained everything but the existing negociations which prudence and policy dictated to be separated from the other part of said letters."[133] These revised letters were then read to the Council, meeting as the Board of War, "being all in the secret." But permanent damage had been done to the Allens' cause: throughout much of 1782, they exhibited fear and caution over contacts with the British, with anonymous letters and verbal messages, unlike the candor of September.

On October 16, the Assembly rejected the Congress's offer of August 7 and 20; three days later, it upheld Vermont's independence and reaffirmed jurisdiction over the Eastern and Western Unions.[134] On the 20th, Ira conveyed the good tidings to Sherwood[135] that he regarded the motion, carried by all but two votes, as the end of negotiations with Congress. However, the news of Cornwallis's dire predicament indicated that the Proclamation should not be delivered "at this time." The letter reached Sherwood and St Leger at Ticonderoga on the morning of the 24th, followed by news of Cornwall's surrender. Soon after, the protective force departed for Canada. The defeat of Cornwallis meant that the British power was now so weak that Vermonters would have no incentive for reunion. The first phase of the Haldimand Negotiations was over, as Haldimand reported to Germain, "all hope of success with Vermont is abandoned." He told Germain that the critical situation to the southward had prevented the Vermonters from declaring themselves.[136]

The British did not realize at the time what damage had been done by the Tupper affair but they seemed aware that they had made a bad mistake and tried to make light of it. When Smyth wrote to Haldimand's Secretary, he said that St Leger had asked him what should be done about His Excellency's Proclamation.[137] But when St Leger decided to locate a Vermont patrol in the vicinity of Mount Independence, Smyth, clearly embarrassed, reported only (disingenuously) that the patrol was to carry, not the Proclamation, but a letter to the Governor and Council. This was of course what actually happened, though it was not the letter that Smyth had envisaged. The Tupper incident took place on October 23, after Ira Allen had told Sherwood that the Proclamation should not be delivered, but before the

British received his letter. Smyth hoped that his conduct and that of St Leger in burying Tupper and sending letters to Chittenden and Colonel Wallbridge at Castleton would meet with the approval of His Excellency, a neat way of avoiding or distorting the truth that the delivery of the Proclamation had been botched. To the extent that St Leger intended to have the Proclamation delivered and asked Smyth how this should be done, Smyth's explanation of why a letter was sent instead, was dishonest.

Yet Sherwood still believed that the Proclamation could be delivered to Vermont when "its acceptance can be judged of."[138] He wrote again from Castleton on October 29, saying he had met with Brigadier (Ethan) Allen, who was in favor of a cartel; the truce should be kept harmoniously.[139] One reason for optimism was the hope that Vermont would shortly be at war, and the report that Stark had been refused assistance from Vermont.[140] This was a reference to the imminent hostilities between Vermont and New York. So Haldimand soon recovered from his pessimism of November 1781. At the end of the year he wrote to Chittenden, asking for a more permanent cartel, in other words, the continuation of the de facto truce.[141] Germain wrote to Haldimand early in January 1782, asking him to restore the confidence of the Vermonters in the British, in the wake of Cornwallis's defeat.[142]

CHAPTER 11

The Haldimand Negotiations, Phase 2: January 1782 to April 1783

THE SECOND PHASE OF THE Haldimand Negotiations, from the beginning of 1782 until April 1783, found Vermont in a state of turmoil. British agents were abroad, even British troops and their Indian scouts. Continental troops appeared, ostensibly looking for deserters. When a group of recruits for the British army was apprehended, a mob gathered outside the Governor's house in May 1782, demanding to know why they had not been hanged. Ira again calmed things down with a mutual exchange of forty prisoners, including David Crowfoot with his recruits. The Allens continued doggedly to stick to the agenda, in spite of Cornwallis's defeat, then the truce of November 1782, followed by the Peace of Paris in April 1783. After the rebuff by Congress of Vermont's application in February 1782, Ethan openly declared his hostility to Congress, as he contemptuously conveyed to the Guilford rioters in September.[1] Ethan's implication, as many suspected, was that Vermont should rejoin the British Empire. At least, Vermont would not have to pay its share of the Continental debt. From the beginning of 1783, he tried to fill the Onion River lands with Loyalists and continued to pursue the project of free trade with Canada, officially without success. When Vermont became the fourteenth state, it was subjected to the terms of the American constitution of 1787, which gave the Congress power over both interstate and foreign trade, ending the dream of an independent foreign policy and the control of external trade.

Despite the defeat of Cornwallis, the Allens continued to believe that, provided a force was sent to help and protect them, Vermont would declare for Britain in as little as two months.[2] The Allens were putting a brave face on it. On April 19, 1782, Vermont's delegates returned from a futile month at Congress and reported that Congress had no intention of admitting Vermont into the United States.[3] Ethan conveyed to Haldimand that Vermont did not want union with Congress, "heaven forbid it." Vermont was in "critical circumstances," but provided the war terminated in favor of Britain, Vermont would be ready to become a government under the King.[4] Ethan's mood was pessimistic, especially as Washington and other officers of the Continental Congress were making threats against the Vermont legislature, when Vermonters wanted no further part in the war if they could help it. At the same time as the April rejection, Justus Sherwood offered to resume the negotiations. He assured Ethan that Haldimand had full powers to establish a Vermont government and provide for its armed forces.[5] Sherwood reported to Mathews on May 9 that (George) Wright had been sent to Bennington with a verbal message to Ethan.[6]

On May 9, Ira and Fay replied to Sherwood's letter of April 22, reaffirming their commitment but again asking that all communication be verbal only. In this letter and a subsequent one on May 19, Ira acknowledged that there were "popular discontents" in Vermont, but played down their importance, saying that they were exaggerated and on the decline.[7] It was unlikely that the British gave much credence to a report from their agent late in July of a conversation with Ethan: he intimated that with the appearance of an army on the frontiers, Vermont would become a British province in three weeks.[8]

Throughout 1782, the Allens displayed an extreme nervousness and concern for their own safety, limiting most of their communications to anonymous letters, with a marked reluctance to meet personally with the British, understandably so, since their days of hegemony had passed and their own constituency was now almost extinct.[9]

Haldimand pressed continuously for a private meeting with Ethan. Just how apprehensive were the Allens can be seen from the anonymous letters to Haldimand, received early in May 1782. Sherwood's response of May 9 to the two anonymous letters acknowledged the dire circumstances of Vermont, but said that a further chance for reunion would arise.[10] Sherwood was irritated by the Allens' caution. His letter to Mathews on the same day, instructed Wright to ask Ethan "with impatience" to arrange for a confidential person to meet with His Excellency.[11] The pressure on Ethan to meet continued: Haldimand wrote to Clinton in June, saying he was pressing for a meeting with Ethan via his agent, no doubt the same (George) Wright who was working for Sherwood. The time was ripe, since the prospects for reunion were now good; the people of Vermont could now expect very little from Congress and the neighboring provinces.[12] Wright reported that Ethan again procrastinated.[13]

Things did not get better. On June 16, Ethan had written to Haldimand, saying that the latest refusal by Congress had turned the people against Confederacy. However, he could not meet with Haldimand since "it would hazard my Life too much."[14] Though Ethan declared, with an uncharacteristic openness, that "I shall do everything in my power to render this state a British province," the reality was different. Only a very small minority of Vermonters favored the Canadian connection. The Congress and New York seriously contemplated an invasion of Vermont, even Haldimand, after he had been told (again) by Clinton in March that he had no unqualified mandate to negotiate with Vermont.[15]

Desultory contacts with the British produced nothing of substance, no promising line of accommodation, but Haldimand continued to aspire to Vermont's accession. On July 17, he wrote to Lord Shelburne, who had replaced Germain, affirming that he would continue with the attempts to bring in Vermont, but he expressed the first signs of a caution which, in different forms, was to last till the negotiations faded away in the following year. Haldimand said he had orders from Carleton, now the Commander-in-Chief in New York, to act on the defensive; he would do nothing to "embarrass" the peace commissioners sent to negotiate reconciliation with the American rebels. If these peace negotiations failed, a reunion with the Vermonters would be a "strong barrier" (to the invasion of Canada), and their separation from Congress would be followed by that of others.[16]

Haldimand wrote to Carleton on August 11, 1782: the Vermonters were still interested in negotiating, provided "they are not exposed to the rage of the other Colonies." He said that he had written to Chittenden, telling him that the truce was still on, provided the Vermonters did not break it or circumstances changed radically.[17] Haldimand had heard that the Vermonters were alarmed at the presence of General Washington in the region, especially as they had not been informed of the reason for his presence, an ominous sign of the Congress's intentions.[18] In October, Haldimand noted the "despondency of Vermont with the rebel success" in forcing the evacuation of Savannah. Haldimand undertook to keep alive the Vermonters' discontent with Congress and to try to remove their doubts about protection on the part of Great Britain.[19] In the background was Haldimand's fear that a secret treaty with Vermont would expose the state to American intervention at a time when the British could not jeopardize the truce of November 1782. He did, however, assure the British Ministry early in November that he was continuing to negotiate with Vermont.[20]

The difficulties of the negotiations were becoming apparent. Haldimand wrote again to Townshend on February 14, 1783: it would be embarrassing (the General's favorite word) if Vermont were attacked and applied for help, since he was not authorized to intervene on their behalf; he had negotiated in good faith with the Vermonters and was now uncertain of the steps that should be taken to secure that province to Britain. He supposed that the reports of preparations to attack the British forts on Lake Champlain from Albany were, if true, really aimed at subduing Vermont. Far from expressing his usual contempt for the Allens, he now sympathized with the Vermonters who had sincerely attempted accommodation and were now being left in the lurch.[21] Haldimand reiterated his resolution not to intervene in a letter to Lord North in the following October, since he had orders to conciliate the subjects of the United States.[22]

From the last months of 1782 to the Peace Treaty of April 1783, all hopes of a reunion with Britain faded away to extinction. The peace negotiations made Vermont vulnerable to the Continental Army, and therefore open to reunion with Great Britain for its own protection but, by the same token, Britain could not aid Vermont without jeopardizing, then violating, the Treaty. This made it clear that since the northern boundary of the United States was the latitude 45 degrees, Vermont was within its sphere of influence.

Ethan's anonymous letter of December 20, 1782, warned that Washington was preparing an army to attack Vermont, under suspicion of an illicit trade with the enemy. This followed the resolution of the Congress on the 5th to take "effectual measures" against Vermont. In February 1783, Congress resolved to invade Vermont, and though this was rejected by Washington, the threat from the United States was real.[23] On March 25, Sherwood wrote to "A" (EA). He told Ethan that with the fate of Britain and the US in the air, His Excellency (Haldimand) does not see how he can help the "unfortunate inhabitants of Vermont, whose fate will be determined in a very short time."[24] From the other side, there were repeated assurances that Vermont would not unite with Congress.[25]

The game was changing from one of negotiation to the unilateral annexation of Vermont to Canada. On April 10, 1783, an anonymous letter was sent to Haldimand from Arlington, saying that the legislature was determined to have Vermont annexed to Canada and become a royal government. On the same day, Sherwood wrote to Ethan, saying that the boundary negotiated in the peace treaty had put Vermont within the sphere of the United States, and a British claim to Vermont would violate the treaty.[26] The Vermonters' predicament was worse than that: in view of the peace treaty, American independence would mean that Vermont would "engross the attention of Congress."[27] With the peace treaty, Ethan could only speculate on the future of Vermont, saying to Sherwood that, in view of the Continental debt and the fact that good people were "flocking into the State," Vermonters were determined not to join Congress.[28] This was likely a response to Sherwood's letter to "A" of March 25. Additionally, Ethan got a verbal message to Sherwood, saying that the time would soon be ripe for "a revolution in favour of Vermont uniting with Canada and becoming a British government."[29] (In his anonymous letter of December 20, 1782, Ethan had even referred to Vermont becoming a British Colony.)

This exchange was at a time when most of the communications between Vermonters and the British involved questions of trading, free trade and the settlement of Americans, including Loyalists, on both sides of the northern border. If the Peace Treaty meant the decline in negotiations, it also took annexation off the agenda. Lord North formally shut down the negotiations in August 1783, when he wrote to Haldimand, telling him that no assistance can be given to the people of Vermont "to enable them to act against the Americans."[30]

Because of the slowness of communications, Haldimand had not always been certain of British policy since the signing of the Provisional Articles of Peace in November 1782. Haldimand wrote to Lord North in October 1783, saying he had been told that "Vermont must either be annexed to Canada or mistress of it [Lake Champlain], as it is the only channel by which the produce of their country can be conveyed to a market, but they assured me that they rather wished the former." This echoed Ethan's sentiments in his anonymous letter to Haldimand in April. The Vermonters saw annexation as the only option left: the alternatives were to defend the state against attack by the Americans, or joining the Congress on the assumption of a share of the continental debt, which they would not do. But by now, the British had ruled out annexation altogether, "a hardy, enterprising people" though the Vermonters were![31]

Ethan's subsequent attempts to revive the negotiations were met with formal courtesy and private ridicule. Lord Sydney still held out a faint hope of offering the Vermonters protection, but warned Haldimand that he must first get clearance from Whitehall before making any final decision.[32] On June 29, 1784, Haldimand wrote to Lord Sydney, saying that Vermonters realized it would be a catastrophe to declare for Great Britain; they desired only close relations with Canada. He still thought that, by "proper management," the Vermonters would be a useful barrier" (to free military communication between New England and the other American states).[33]

Critique of the Haldimand Negotiations

The attitude of Haldimand and Sherwood towards the Allens lurched back and forth from mistrust to sincerity of motive, from a cynical pessimism to optimism about the prospects of success. Despite his reservations, Haldimand tried persistently to bring about a reunion of Vermont with the British Empire because he feared the alternative: the admission of Vermont to the Continental Congress.[34] Haldimand's reasoning was entirely defensive. He was well aware that the French population of Quebec was in a state of potential revolt: a rebel army, especially with the European French at their head, would lead at least to a total non-cooperation and probably to active support for the invaders. He was even afraid that by encouraging Ethan Allen, the four thousand troops he promised (a gross exaggeration) would invade Canada, as he had tried to do in 1775.[35] At the same time, the return of Vermont would bar the Continental Army from invading Quebec via the Bayley-Hazen Road, and the route to the disaffected Abenaki in St Francis (Odanak). It would also, as Germain was aware, help to separate New England from the other revolted colonies.

Beyond that, there were great obstacles to a rapprochement with Vermont, which were only avoided because the events of October 1781 did not result in a concrete, public offer to the leaders of the conspiracy. Germain had given a direct mandate to both Clinton and Haldimand to pursue negotiations with Vermont in his letters of March 3, 1779, but the two had different ideas as to their powers. To Haldimand's observations of October 3, 1781, as to what he proposed to offer the Vermont leaders, Clinton replied on November 12 that an Act of Parliament would likely be needed to authorize a separate government for Vermont. Further, the negotiating arm of the Commander-in-Chief was the Peace Commission of 1778[36] and the Commissioners had no powers to settle land titles and disputes.[37] Haldimand for his part also doubted whether he had the power to rule on property disputes, since questions of property were in law different from questions of jurisdiction.[38] Nor was Haldimand even sure whether he could allow Vermont to claim the territory of the former royal provinces of New Hampshire and New York, though they were actually offered to Vermont in the Proclamation. Haldimand, following Sherwood, with his personal experience of the pre-revolutionary disputes in the Grants, thought that the only property issue was that of the New Hampshire titles. But Clinton was more cautious, because the separation of Vermont and the confirmation of New Hampshire titles would alienate the powerful New York Loyalists and crypto-Loyalists with New York patents. All told, only a conditional offer could be made to the Vermonters and this could be overturned, wholly or in part, by Whitehall, making the Vermonters' stance vis-à-vis Britain and the Continental Congress even worse than before a public offer had been made.

The Vermont leaders had difficulties which were somewhat analogous, for they had to win over both the legislators and the public at large, but they could not prepare the ground by revealing the circumstances, such as the secret negotiations, the general truce of 1781, and the forthcoming Proclamation. When we recall the revolts among the representatives of October 1780 and October 1781, and the embarrassments of the previous June, it is unlikely that a British offer would have been received as a subject of calm debate. On the contrary, there is every reason to believe that Haldimand's Proclamation would have led at least to the Allens being driven from office, and at most a civil war; in other words, that the Allens' plan in the autumn of 1781 was a monstrous miscalculation. The only way that the Proclamation could have been delivered was through a mistake of the sort that St Leger made in trying to deliver it without a request, or through bad communication, as when Haldimand made the offer to confirm the New Hampshire titles in his Proclamation, before Clinton told him that neither the Governor nor the Peace Commissioners had the power to do so (Clinton was by then the sole Peace Commissioner). Even in March 1782, Clinton informed Haldimand that he had received no statement of powers adequate to the accomplishment of the wishes of the people of Vermont, "because as to some of them, the Executive will want the legislative aid." Clinton had been advised to continue the dialogue with the Vermonters, so that they should expect that if there were a reunion, their interests would be properly attended to.[39] The following month, Haldimand complained that his negotiating mandate was "so differently expressed" (i.e. contradictory) that, if he were successful, he would get the blame for betraying that mandate, when at the same time he had no instructions for the "ensuing campaign."[40] All told, it was unlikely that the return of Vermont to the British Empire would ever have taken place.

Like Sherwood, Haldimand mistrusted the Allens. The Governor had a more or less constant suspicion that the Allens were using the negotiations to delay, and to wring the best terms possible from the Continental Congress or, at least, they would gravitate to the side that offered the best deal, which in turned depended on the military situation. Despite his contempt for the Allens, he had the greatest respect for the Vermonters; their military power was formidable and they were most determined in their political aspirations.[41] All the more reason why they must be prevented from joining the Continental Congress. He tried consistently to bring in the Vermonters, wholeheartedly, until the British truce with the Americans at the end of November 1782

On the Vermont side, all the available evidence now points to the fact that, from the beginning of July 1780, the Allens hoped and preferred to join with the British rather than the Congress. Professor T. H. Breen, supporting the views of Willard Sterne Randall, says:

> During the closing months of the Revolutionary War, he [Ethan] and a tight-knit circle of political allies entered into secret negotiations with the British governor-general of Canada. . . . It seems extremely unlikely that Allen was serious about withdrawing from the United States.[42]

On the contrary, the negotiations began nearly three years before the end of the Revolutionary War, and were conducted with a determination to have Vermont become a separate province under the British Crown. Had Haldimand's Proclamation of October 5, 1781 been delivered and publicized, the Allens would have burned their boats and committed themselves unequivocally to the British cause.

One of the first clear statements that the Allens had the sincere intention of Vermont becoming a British province came from Henry Steele Wardner in 1931:

> I think that as the Revolutionary War progressed, several of Vermont's leaders, when prospects of recognition of Vermont's statehood by Congress were discouraging, had serious intentions of the State's becoming a British province. I think generally that they kept

> faith with the British. They did, no doubt, frequently predict too strongly the ease or speed with which the result could be accomplished and no doubt they waited at times to see which way a cat would jump; but generally in their intercourse with General Haldimand's agents, they conducted themselves without deception or duplicity and with the frankness which General Haldimand's candor and courtesy deserved.[43]

This followed Walter H. Crockett's solemn statement, echoing Samuel Williams and Jared Sparks, that "there never was any thought of disloyalty on the part of the Vermont leaders"; contact with the British was only to protect Vermont in a desperate situation, which succeeded.[44] Wardner was not the first to presume that the Allens were serious in their conspiracy to join the British, but previous contentions came from pro-Yorkers who were all too willing to believe the worst about Ethan.[45] Though Wardner underestimates Ethan's wiliness as a negotiator, and Haldimand was only courteous when he knew that his less than candid letters would be made public, this author shares Wardner's stance in gauging Ethan's aspirations over a reunion with the British. John Pell (1929) was well aware that Wardner had discovered Sherwood's Journal of October 1780, and seems in general to have supported its implications. For instance, he says the cartel for the prisoner exchange was "only an excuse for some mysterious negotiation—as, in fact, it was."[46] Pell also says that the plan for the Proclamation and the protective force was concocted by Ira and Joseph Fay, and that Ira was serious about reading the Proclamation to the Assembly.[47] He gives Ethan credit for "repelling a British fleet with words," as if St Leger intended to invade Vermont; but this may be ironical, one of the many things that makes his biography so entertaining. Charles Jellison (1969) takes it that Ethan's position evolved from a possibility to one of active support for reunion, in the late spring of 1781;[48] whereas this author holds that Ethan from the beginning wanted reunion; only his negotiating stance changed. But Jellison also says (correctly in this author's view) that the betrayal of the Vermonters, as he characterizes the Allens' conduct, began sometime in the summer of 1780.[49]

Since then things have gone backwards, for instance, in Randall (2011), whose treatment of the Negotiations is slight and cursory. A more formidable treatment is by Michael A. Bellesiles (1993). His first contention is that the British lacked a coherent policy.[50] But so far as Ethan is concerned, British policy from 1779 to 1783 was consistent, coherent and utterly sound: to have

Ethan bring Vermont back into the British Empire. Clinton and Haldimand did have different conceptions of their mandate to negotiate, and Clinton was far more optimistic than Haldimand; but it did not mean that the British policy was incoherent. Since the negotiations were only about a prisoner exchange, Bellesiles is then able to say that they were not even secret.[51]

According to Bellesiles, Ethan's first direct contact with Sherwood was over a prisoner exchange, when Sherwood became convinced that Vermont could be won over by the British. But the source cited is Sherwood's Journal, which records events after, not before or during, the contact that Sherwood allegedly made with Ethan, a contact that Pell had suggested, with an impossible chronology.[52] The next event was the raid in October 1780 by Major Charles Carleton (Bellesiles surely means Christopher), where he says that Ethan preferred to avoid battle and (without any evidence) that Ethan shadowed Carleton with three hundred men as he moved into Upper New York. Bellesiles depicts a series of contingencies, of Carleton avoiding Vermont, then sending Sherwood to meet with Ethan (who was at Castleton, not in the Green Mountains, and always had been). According to Bellesiles, Carleton's motive in sending Sherwood to meet Ethan was "to avoid the harassment which so damaged Burgoyne's army," a contention which bears no relation to the military situation of the time and finds no support in the documentation. The truth was that Carleton had been ordered not to attack Vermont, only to give the Vermonters reason for accommodating the British. And the meeting had been planned in September, not on a whim by Carleton. Bellesiles contends that Ethan had out-generaled Carleton, when Carleton had no intention of attacking Vermont.[53] All this time, Washington was supposed to have withdrawn Warner's regiment from the northern frontiers, when in fact it had been returned there from Albany, only to be effectively wiped out in Carleton's raid.[54]

Bellesiles (following the early account of Samuel Williams in 1794) says that Ethan's negotiations with Sherwood were "a study in contradictions and evasively non-committal."[55] This is a way of claiming that the negotiations were really only about a prisoner exchange. Ethan did not know at the time how serious Haldimand was about negotiations, nor could he predict the course of coming events. Throwing out possibilities and showing his inclinations was quite normal for the start of a dialogue; there was nothing evasive, contradictory or non-committal about it. Apart from endorsing the truce and the prisoner exchange, Ethan made two suppositions: (i) the neutrality of Vermont if Congress rejected affiliation; and (ii) joining the British Empire if he found that Congress was preparing to raise a force against him. When Ira met with Sherwood in the following May, he immediately raised the issue of neutrality when affiliation to Congress was still in the air, and on the very first day he brought up the issue of reunion, but without Vermont having been threatened by Congress. Of course he did: to raise these issues was the whole point of his meeting on the Ile-aux-Noix, and both issues had been raised by Ethan with Sherwood in October, the latter of which Bellesiles distorts, then glosses over.

On Ira's mission in May, Bellesiles says only, "In spring 1781 Ira Allen persuaded the British of the wisdom of not fighting on Vermont's territory, agreeing to another truce and prisoner exchange with Haldimand." Thus Bellesiles gives the impression that all Ira did in his eighteen days at the Ile-aux-Noix was to resume the truce and negotiate a prisoner exchange. To see the May meeting as an isolated episode without any negotiation over reunion, unrelated to the meeting of the previous October and divorced from the events of the following summer, is frankly perplexing, when the documentation is staring us in the face. Bellesiles makes no attempt to reconstruct a narrative from the points of view of the British and the Vermonters. There is no discussion of what led up to Sherwood's meeting with Ethan; Bellesiles cites the key letter of Sherwood to Powell of August 24, 1780, but only as a source for a Loyalist proposal to kidnap Ethan, when the letter contains nothing of the sort.[56] There is then an immediate leap from October to the single sentence about Ira in May, then nothing happening until Haldimand and Sherwood concluded in the autumn of 1781 that the negotiations were dead. In the meantime, Bellesiles reverses the significance of the Western and Eastern Unions, stating that the Eastern followed the Western, when in fact the Allens put forward the Western to counter the Eastern, in order to restore their control of the Assembly with allies sympathetic to the Negotiations.

The account of the events of October 1781 is a travesty. Bellesiles has Haldimand offering the Proclamation and St Leger's protective force, one last try, when it was Ira who put forward the proposal for the Proclamation, which Haldimand accepted. Even in 1931, Henry Steele Wardner could write that the assertion that Haldimand had suggested the Proclamation was "an amazing misstatement," a distortion in Ira's *History*. Bellesiles has Sherwood responsible for killing Tupper, when in fact it was Smyth and St Leger. Then he has the Assembly in an uproar; in reality the Assembly had risen.

Why is Bellesiles so insistent that the Allens were only engaging in a prisoner exchange ? The reason is that the Allens were supposed to be equalitarian democrats. That Vermont's Constitution and the governance of the Republic were radically democratic and equalitarian, there is no doubt. But this was in spite of the Allens, who had the Assembly under their control for the first three years of its existence and who packed it with representatives of the "Western District" in order to push the Negotiations through. The Assembly was not to drive policy; it was only there to be managed, while Ira's strategy was to work for the rejection by the Assembly of affiliation to the Congress in favor of reunion with Great Britain. Any faction that deceived the Assembly for a year between October 1780 and October 1781 cannot possibly be regarded as democratic.

Whether or not the Allens ever had the motive of putting pressure for recognition on the Continental Congress, the Haldimand Negotiations clearly had that effect. On August 14, 1781, when the beginnings of a Congressional offer were being made to Vermont, James Madison wrote that several factors would lead to the establishment of Vermont into a "separate and federal state." Among these factors was "the just apprehension that their rulers were engaging in clandestine negotiations with the enemy."[57] When New York began moves to recognize Vermont's independence through a Bill of March 28, 1787, Alexander Hamilton argued in Assembly that Vermont's dealings with the British were a danger to the United States. Vermont's leaders were still, he contended, colluding with the British, as they had been ever since the Haldimand Negotiations, which meant that it was in the interests of both New York and the United States to recognize Vermont.[58] In the event, New York bypassed the stage of recognition and dealt directly with Vermont over the future of New York land titles in return for consent to Vermont's admission to the union, which took place on February 18, 1791.[59]

How are we to evaluate the performance of each side? Right from 1779, the British had a consistent and coherent policy of bringing Ethan Allen over to the British side. The whole hierarchy was a credit to the British, from Sherwood up through Haldimand's efficient and judicious secretary, Robert Mathews, to His Excellency, then behind him the towering figures of the two successive Commanders-in-Chief, Sir Henry Clinton and Sir Guy Carleton. Justus Sherwood handled the actual negotiations with the Allens in a professional manner, combining skepticism about their motives with a determination to see the negotiations through, if it were at all possible. He came close in October 1781 to implementing the plan which he had persuaded Haldimand to adopt. For his intelligence, Sherwood relied on publicly available information, on his network of spies and on documents leaked to him by the Vermonters, even the British letters sent from New York by Beverly Robinson. The intelligence service that Sherwood ran was highly efficient, despite being in receipt of wild rumors, such as the report that Vermont had become the Fourteenth State or that Ira Allen had been clapped in irons on account of the exposure of his dealings with the British. The blunder that led to the killing of Sergeant Tupper was possibly due to the fact that St Leger did not know how secret and delicate the negotiations were, since it was only in November that Haldimand authorized the disclosure to St Leger of the substance of the negotiations and the inclusion of St Leger in the loop.[60] That Dr Smyth was incompetent can be conceded.

For all that, it was unlikely that the negotiations could ever succeed in their purpose. Even in 1781, there were doubts as to whether Haldimand had the power to conclude a treaty; any offer taken up by the Vermonters would unravel if Whitehall modified the agreement and cast the whole project into radical uncertainty. In the second phase of the negotiations, there were so many caveats that the project was very unlikely to resume, let alone come to a conclusion. Haldimand complained that Germain had given both him and Clinton a direct mandate to negotiate, but they had different ideas as to what the mandate entailed, so the doubts about the feasibility of the negotiations continued.

Despite having assured the Allens in April 1782 that he had full powers to negotiate, Haldimand repeatedly observed that he was "embarrassed" by the lack of instructions from Whitehall.[61] Haldimand also pointed out to Clinton the difficulties occasioned by the "divergent instructions" given to him and the Commander-in-Chief. Further, from August 1782, Haldimand could not jeopardize the peace negotiations by dealing with Vermont, even though the enemy seemed inclined to continue the war and a Vermont alliance would be valuable in case of an American attack on Canada.[62] At the same time, Haldimand assured Chittenden that he would honor the truce with Vermont, unless the other party broke it or circumstances radically changed.[63] After the truce with the Americans crystallized at the end of November 1782, Vermont fell within the sphere of the Americans, and an alliance with Vermont would have been far more trouble than it was worth.

Ethan Allen openly expressed a hostility to Congress after it again rejected Vermont's admission, and the Republic repudiated the Eastern and Western Unions in February 1782. Only his contacts with the British remained, officially, a secret. Haldimand kept getting assurances from the Allens that the final rejection by Congress in February had turned the people against the Confederacy and in favor of reunion with the British Empire. In fact, the Allens had lost their power to drive Vermont's foreign policy and to engender public support for reunion with Britain. By the end of October 1781, reunion was a lost cause, concealed from the public because the failure to deliver the Proclamation had, paradoxically, prevented the Allens from being driven from office—or worse. Ira Allen could at least celebrate. "Thus [the departure of St Leger's force] ended the campaign of 1781, with the accidental loss of only one man, on the extensive frontiers of Vermont, exposed to an army of ten thousand men [actually, fewer than one thousand]; yet she did not incur any considerable debt.—Such were the happy effects of these negociations."[64] Another way of putting it was that with the truce of October 1780 and the destruction of Warner's regiment in the same month, Vermont was effectively out of the Revolutionary War. Ethan freely admitted that "hostilities ceased between Great Britain and Vermont the last three years of the late war, which answered all the purposes of an alliance of neutrality, and at the same time prevented the United States from taking any advantage of it."[65]

Yet the project of reunion was not to sell out Vermont to the British. Bellesiles uses the term "sincere Loyalists" as the designation of those historians who (following the work of Chilton Williamson) believe that the Allens wanted to go over to the British. This author does not take such a view: Levi apart, the Allens were never Loyalists, nor is there any claim that they were. In a remarkably early statement (1927), the Canadian W.A. Mackintosh took it for granted that the Allens were serious about rejoining the British Empire, doubting only that their motive was loyalty to the Crown.[66]

What Haldimand referred to as the Allens' God, independence, meant only freedom from New York or the partition of Vermont among the "claiming states." For Ethan, neither union with Congress nor with the British meant the loss of independence, though he conceded, when the Negotiations and his part in them were long gone, that a separate government meant yielding up "independency." What Ethan did want, as a consequence of independence, was a free trade with Canada, which was one reason why reunion with Great Britain was preferable; this hope of an independent commercial policy disappeared with the American Constitution of 1787. The attempt to maintain Vermont's independence via the Canadian connection was not in itself a shameful one, however much the Allens betrayed the Assembly and, through the Assembly, the citizens of Vermont. The only question still to be addressed is whether the Allens pursued independence merely to protect their own narrow interests in the Onion River investments or whether this was only one motive among many others.[67]

Those who contend that the Haldimand Negotiations were just one gigantic bluff ask us to believe that the Allens conducted an elaborate charade for over a year. Ira's request for Haldimand's Proclamation then becomes an exercise in brinkmanship, enticing the British with repeated promises of delivery and risking exposure of the whole project. To make these contentions in the face of a large body of contrary evidence is a perverse pursuit of historical study which, if generalized as a method of enquiry, would lead to a total breakdown in the quest for historical truth. The contentions rely, too, on some blatant distortions of historical fact and narrative in order for the bluff theory to gain any purchase at all.

CHAPTER 12

The Political Philosophy of Ethan Allen

THE POLITICAL PHILOSOPHY of the American revolutionaries owed much to the European philosophers of the Enlightenment and earlier writers, but the basic position of the Allen family derives more from the seventeenth century theories of Thomas Hobbes (1588–1679). Apart from John Locke, the Allens were not much influenced by other writers; they harked back directly to Hobbes. There is no evidence that Ethan Allen read any of the works of Hobbes, though it is likely enough that he discussed the author of *Leviathan* with Dr. Thomas Young. Had Ethan read Hobbes' diatribes against religious pretensions and superstition in the second half of *Leviathan*, he would have been even more enamored of the writings of this influential thinker.

In the schema of Hobbes, the people are in a "state of nature" until they "covenant together" to authorize a sovereign, in the form of a king or a republic, to rule over them, who then undertakes protection in return for submission and obedience. For Hobbes, the obligation of subjects to sovereign lasts only so long as he has the power to protect them.[1] Some of the American revolutionaries put it rather differently: when the sovereign "withdraws his protection" of the people from the "Despotick Ministry," the people revert to the state of nature and are free to enter into a new compact and turn to another sovereign.

The Allens frequently referred to the Grants as being in a "state of nature and anarchy,"[2] not always because the King had withdrawn his protection: the Declaration of Independence in 1776 had "annihilated the British government in America" and had thus extinguished the claims of New Hampshire and New York alike. To the Allens, the Hobbesian schema was only a crude framework in which the content was different. For Hobbes, there were neither political rights nor liberties in the state of nature; the liberty in the sovereign state is then only "corporal," an absence of physical constraint (which fits neatly but coincidentally in Vermont's phasing out of slavery). Sovereignty derives from the people, not from God.

When it comes to the defense of property, Ethan relied (as did many of the revolutionaries) on the arguments of John Locke rather than Hobbes. The right to property, which was claimed explicitly in Vermont's Declaration of Independence, turned not on ownership as such but on the value that the owner had added to it through "improvement." Wild lands were of "little value, exclusive of their Toil and Cultivation."[3] As Locke himself put it:

> Though the earth and all inferior creatures be common to all men, yet every man has a *property* in his own *person*. This nobody has a right to but himself. The *labour* of his body and the *work* of his hands, we may say, *are properly* his. Whatsoever, then, he removes out of the state that nature hath provided and left it in, he hath mixed his labour with it, and joined to it something that is his own, and thereby makes it his property.[4]

The "Right of Soil" rested not just on philosophical arguments but on legal reasoning, concerning the notion of possession, reflecting the medieval maxim, "possession is nine tenths the law": "a meer Possession is of itself abundantly sufficient to maintain the Right in the Possessor, and on a judicious Tryal at common Law, (cou'd such a One be had) would be judged Paramount to it [the least Conception of Title whatever]."[5]

Ethan's *Reason, the Only Oracle of Man* was published in 1784 and is thus a mature statement of his views (and those of its unacknowledged co-author, the late Dr Thomas Young). It should not be assumed that Ethan's past actions and opinions can always be framed in the light of the perspective articulated in the *Oracle*. There is, however, little in it that would correct the political opinions that he expressed from 1774 onwards. The work is one of Deistic theology but it also contains the foundations of Ethan's philosophy and hence his political thought. For Ethan, the universe comprised two worlds, the natural and the moral, both governed by the fitness ordained by God the creator. The former "operates according to the laws of nature" which, like creation itself, are eternal and immutable.[6] There is nothing arbitrary in nature, which is a system of "causes and consequences"; God does not intervene in the natural world, for instance through miracles or answering prayers.

The moral world is the world of human agency, which admits of variation, because human choices have different outcomes. Our liberty, he says, "consists in the power of agency," for liberty is agency itself. The mental faculties with which the creator has endowed humankind enable us "to investigate the knowledge of moral good and evil, from which, together with the power of agency, results the human conscience." Ethan advanced arguments to protect morality from arbitrariness (or, as we would now say, from relativism) so that it had all of the certainty of the laws of nature. The divine law of virtue is as immutable in its nature as the divine will: "the moral law of virtue is in its nature eternal and of universal obligation"; Ethan refers to "the obligatory nature of the natural law." The result is that, while human beings have freedom of choice, moral laws are laws of nature, as eternal as the laws of the natural world. "Right reason" enables man to live in harmony with nature.

The most prominent of all laws is the law of self-preservation, which is moral because it is the product of human agency, but it is also a natural law. This law is frequently invoked by Ethan among the other revolutionaries. For instance, when the Continental Congress wrote to "the Oppressed Inhabitants of Canada," it claimed that the taking of Ticonderoga and Crown Point "was dictated by the great law of self-preservation."[7] However, since it lies beyond Deistic theology, Ethan does not mention the "overriding law" in the *Oracle*. He refers elsewhere to the "Law of Self-Preservation, which the Law of GOD and Nature enjoyns on every intelligent, wise and understanding Being."[8] The law of self-preservation was the common currency of the Enlightenment, but since it can be traced at least as far back as the medieval tradition of natural law, it is not surprising to find it in Hobbes, for whom it is the second law of nature, the first being the duty to strive for peace. For Jean-Jacques Rousseau, self-preservation was both a need and a law, to save humanity from peril and uncertainty.[9] Ethan's language also reflects that of John Locke when he refers to "the law of God and nature," which confers a trust on legislators, setting a limit to their powers.[10] Similarly, the American Declaration of Independence talks of the "Laws of Nature and Nature's God." However, the contention that civil society preserved natural rights and liberties was a departure from the tenets of Hobbes, for whom there were no rights and liberties in the sovereign state, only such terms and conditions of social being that the sovereign "praetermitted."[11] As Ira Allen put it:

> The Representatives from the several towns on both sides of the mountain, met in January [1777], at Westminster, and deliberately debated, for and against the formation of a new state. After mature deliberation, the members were of opinion, that the interest and safety of the people required the district of the New Hampshire Grants, to be a free state. That the power of Government was vested in the people by the supreme arbiter of rights. That the people had not delegated their natural right of chusing what form of government they should be governed by, to any King, State or Potentate on earth; and that they therefore had the right and power, and would henceforth use and exercise the right and power of government vested in them by the beneficent Creator.[12]

In another late statement of 1786, Ethan and his associates wrote:

> The original design and ultimate end of law is to secure the lives, liberty and property of the subjects. But when government and law are degenerated in the administration, and subverted to answer the over-bearing, unjust and monopolizing purposes of cruel men, or to dispossess and ruin a large settlement of industrious yeomanry (the supporters of the world of mankind) in such cases the oppressed have a just and natural right to make a bold and manly resistance, agreeably to the greatest of all laws, to wit, that of self-preservation. Nor is it, in the nature of things, possible, that the human species should be under any obligation of allegiance to a government that does not and will not protect them in their property. In all such instances as these, the subjects are thrown into a condition, commonly called, a state of nature, and from the sanctions of the eternal law of self-preservation, and have a right to defend their persons and property against all manner of usurpation.[13]

Though this reasoning was applied to the settlers of the Susquehannah Valley in Pennsylvania, it could equally well have applied to Vermont. In that context, the law of self-preservation was invoked in two distinct phases. In the first phase, against New York, the dissenters did not claim that the Grants were in a state of nature. Neither did they deny New York its jurisdiction, claiming only that the law of self-preservation forced them to carve out, as it were, the areas of land disputes and riots (outlawry) from the purview of

Yorker authority. In this phase, the flexible notion of self-preservation is invoked within the confines of a recognized civil government. The Vermonters entered the second phase when they claimed that the extinction of royal authority had put the Grants in a state of nature, so that the law of self-preservation obliged them to "compact together" to form the free state of Vermont. Thus the Address quoted above refers more appropriately to the second phase than the first.

We have seen how Ethan Allen is not to be categorized among the revolutionaries who founded the United States. His republican convictions were not strong; his rebellion was directed against New York and the other "claiming states," so that he was primarily a Vermont nationalist. Despite his claim to have a long-standing and sincere passion for liberty, Ethan had no revolutionary philosophy or program to interpret events and guide action, as did the Russian Bolsheviks. Nor was he like John Brown, who certainly had a passion for liberty, but without, it seems, any idea as to where liberation from the British would lead. Ethan's political thinking was the product of the various predicaments in which he found himself, being used as arguments and vindications of the positions he took. These arguments are not to be found primarily in the two longer works, the *Brief Narrative* and the *Oracle,* but rather in the series of tracts, broadsides, submissions, polemics and pamphlets, which he published between 1774 and 1780, with a gap when he was in captivity, and a further broadside in the Wyoming Address of 1786. The challenges that Ethan faced, in which political reasoning was introduced, were essentially threefold:

> *1. The Defense of the New Hampshire Titles*
> The campaign to defend the New Hampshire titles from the claims of New York began in 1770 and was characterized by legal and historical arguments, along with resistance to Yorker authority. The different solutions proposed were an appeal to the King to bring New York to its duty; reannexation to New Hampshire or a separate government for the district of land known as the New Hampshire Grants. The law of self-preservation was only invoked to justify the actions of the Green Mountain Boys and to defy the authority of New York over land disputes and outlawry. After the Revolution, recognition of the independence of Vermont would at the same time guarantee the New Hampshire titles.

2. The Defense of the Rights of Settlers under New Hampshire Titles
The focus of the defense of New Hampshire titles shifted from proprietors to settlers, because the prime subjects of Yorker intrusion were the actual settlers and conflict was precipitated in the Ejectment Trials. Again, the Grantees used legal and historical arguments to buttress their case, for instance the contention that the common law of property was not changed by the transfer of jurisdiction from New Hampshire to New York. But behind these arguments lay the Lockean philosophy of persons, property and labor.

3. The Defense of the Republic
The defense of the Grants against New York, then the Republic against the claims of New York, New Hampshire and Massachusetts continued from the Revolution of 1775 to the admission of Vermont as the fourteenth state in 1791, though it died down in practical terms when the threats from New York and the Congress diminished from 1784 onwards. Arguments from the state of nature were raised primarily in the move to independence and were directed against New York, rather than the royal authority of the British.

These challenges give rise to two important historical questions: how far was Ethan the leader of the settlers rather than the New Hampshire proprietors; and how far were the aspirations of the Allens to rejoin the British Empire motivated by the desire to protect and develop their extensive holdings under New Hampshire titles? As to the first, Ethan acquired the reputation of a Robin Hood, coming to the aid of the oppressed. As to the second, it is quite clear that a free trade with Canada was to be an essential feature of the separate government under the Crown.

The key to answering both questions lay in the pattern of the Allens' land holdings in Vermont. Ethan owned no land or rights in the Grants when he took up the cause of the Connecticut proprietors in January 1770. Before the Ejectment Trials, he bought three rights in the Grants, about a thousand acres, but he never settled in the Grants or in Vermont until two years before he died in 1789.[14] The major emigration of the Allen clan to the Grants took place in 1770 and 1771. When Ethan agreed to represent the proprietors in the Ejectment Trials, he did not do so as the first episode in a strategic plan to vanquish New York and restore the jurisdiction of New

Hampshire, thus protecting the New Hampshire titles. Ethan's motives were more prosaic. The protection of the settlers' right of soil was, initially, only a way of securing New Hampshire titles. From the time of the failure in the Ejectment Trials, the issue turned from the protection of title to the defense of the rights of settlers, including the Allen clan, against the pretensions of New York.

At the same time, Ethan's land purchases were evidence that he thought that the New Hampshire titles could be protected: the success of the Green Mountain Boys, then the Republic of Vermont, was also the successful protection of New Hampshire title. The American Revolution suspended in practice the aspirations of New York. So far as New Hampshire titles were concerned, the Allens had to defend the Republic against invasion by New York, the British and the Continental Congress. In this way, the defense of land acquisitions shifted back from settlers to the proprietors.

The Onion River purchases began in 1773 and sales started in the following year. By the Revolution, Ethan held a one-fifth share of the Onion River holdings, roughly 27,000 acres. The huge Onion River purchases were made in 1778, after Ethan had returned from captivity. When the Onion River holdings were broken up in 1782, Ethan acquired 2,000 acres in Burlington as part of his stake, and became a settler for the first time in 1787 and, apart from a brief, early period on the family farm in Connecticut, the first time that he had ever farmed.

In terms of Ethan's whole career, land speculation in rights was one of the many ways in which this restless man tried to make a living. It certainly became his preoccupation after the return from captivity in 1778, taking up at least as much time as his politics. Whatever else his motives, one thing seems to be ruled out: Ethan had no desire to accumulate wealth to live in regal splendor, like Governor John Wentworth of New Hampshire or the New York grandees of the Hudson Valley. His motives were more practical: to be able to finance the development of the Onion River resources. Geography, communications, and the hostility of New York, along with the Continental Congress, ruled out the shipping of the Onion River products from Lake Champlain, down the Hudson to the port of New York. The only feasible outlet was to ship the goods—primarily timber, potash, hogs and cattle (or their dressed meat)—down the Lake and the Sorel, over or around the Richelieu Rapids to Montreal and the St. Lawrence River. This would require not only a cessation of hostilities with the British, which Ethan achieved, but a free trade agreement, which he did not. Was this an all-consuming economic motive on Ethan's part? Again, it seems unlikely, since it was not just the northern regions of Vermont that needed Lake Champlain as a channel for conveying its goods to a market, as Haldimand pointed out to Lord North in his letter of October 24, 1783. Again, the independence of Vermont, which included confirmation of the New Hampshire titles, required addressing a whole series of political issues of which the exploitation of the Onion River holdings was only one; there was little development on Onion River holdings prior to the peace of 1783.

Ethan was a charismatic leader who won the loyalty of settlers, and from this phase of Ethan's activism he got the reputation of a Robin Hood, coming to their rescue with the Green Mountain Boys. His prestige in these endeavors and from the capture of Ticonderoga turned him into a popular, if unofficial, leader after his return from captivity, a reputation which declined rapidly after the early months of 1782. He cannot be regarded as a great populist leader in this period. The Arlington Junto was not a popular body and did not govern through the people, nor in their name.

In August 1785, Ethan was hired to take up the cause of the Connecticut proprietors of the Susquehanna Company in the Wyoming Valley of Pennsylvania, undoubtedly because of his reputation as the defender of settlers' rights. The company held a charter from Connecticut, and though that state had given up its claim to the territory in 1783, the proprietors were anxious to retain what Ethan himself referred to as "legal title."[15] Thus the scenario was comparable to that of the New Hampshire Grantees, where Ethan was hired by the proprietors, not the settlers,[16] though in the case of the Susquehanna Company, Ethan tried to collapse the distinction by referring to the "right of soil of those proprietors to that territory."[17] In addition to a meeting with the proprietors in Hartford, Ethan made two visits to Wyoming in April and August 1786, though without "the small detachment of Green Mountain Boys"[18] which he had offered. These visits boosted the morale of the settlers, whose militancy the proprietors relied on to protect their titles. Though Ethan abandoned the project, his involvement was one factor in Pennsylvania's passage of the Confirming Act in March 1787, which entrenched the settlers in their holdings (in marked contrast to the policy of New York in the Grants). The proprietors, however, lost their titles. At the same time, Shay's Rebellion in Massachusetts broke out, in which the settlers had grievances similar to the Grantees of the 1770s and the Green Mountain eastsiders in the same decade. When Ethan was offered the command of Shay's "revolutionary army," he "contemptuously refused" and ordered Daniel Shays' commanders out of Vermont.[19] He referred to Shay's followers as malcontents and "a damned bunch of rascals"; he "heartily despised both them and their cause,"[20] hardly the language of a Robin Hood.

If we look at Ethan's whole career, his reputation as a Robin Hood is largely undeserved.

Ethan was a first class political operator and, despite his deceptions, his moves can invariably be construed as in the interests of Vermont. There was more than one way to secure Vermont's independence, and Ethan's was one of them. He did not treat the New Hampshire settlers in the Grants merely as objects to be manipulated; but neither did his ruling passions include justice for the peasants and yeomanry of Vermont.

CHAPTER 13

Ethan Allen: Endgame and Assessment

After his release in 1778, Ethan resumed his military career intermittently, in a number of police actions on behalf of Vermont and against Yorkers in the south-east of the state. Though he held no military command, he was called upon to lead a military expedition in orders from Governor Chittenden that he received on May 3, 1779, the anniversary of his release from British captivity.[1] Cumberland County in the south-east of the state was full of Yorker sympathizers, resisting the military recruiters of Vermont and appealing to revolutionary New York to bring them back under their rightful jurisdiction. The Governor and Council in Arlington had received word of an insurrection which was in fact merely a series of riotous protests in the towns of Putney, Hinsdale, Guilford, Westminster and Brattleborough. Ethan was ordered to raise a hundred volunteers to assist the sheriff of Cumberland County "to execute such orders as he has or may receive from the civil authorities of this State." Ethan moved with a speed that recalled the Ticonderoga expedition from Castleton to Hand's Cove. He set out from Bennington with over a hundred men, many of them former Green Mountain Boys, and recruited about a hundred and fifty more en route to Cumberland County. On the way to Westminster, Ethan and his troops intimidated and assaulted the dissidents in the manner of the Green Mountain Boys up to the Revolution. About three dozen were arrested and confined to the county jail in Westminster.[2] Ethan intervened quite improperly in the subsequent trial, in which the punishments were not draconian; militarily, the expedition finished when the Yorkers were consigned to jail.

As a result of the success of the expedition against the Cumberland County "insurrection," Ethan accepted the appointment of Brigadier-General "to command the militia of this state" on June 3, 1779. When he resigned on November 4, 1780, he said that if he were offered the command, he "would endeavor to serve the State to the best of his ability." This he did on two subsequent occasions, despite the fact that he declined to lead the 1st Brigade of Vermont militia on June 20, 1781.

In the summer of 1782, there was a operation comparable to that against the Cumberland County rioters of 1779. On August 29, the Assembly authorized Governor and Captain General Chittenden to raise a force of 250 men to assist the Sheriff in opposing the activities of Col. Timothy Church, the commander of the New York battalion of militia, and to enforce the laws (over taxation) in what was now called Windham County. Church had been ordered by Governor Clinton to move against Vermont. On September 2, Ethan was commissioned as Brigadier-General and instructed to raise a posse comitatus of 250 men, some of whom were mounted.[3] He executed the commission between the 8th and the 10th of September.[4] Ethan marched on Guilford. En route, his advance guard bolted on being fired upon by a party of Yorkers, whereupon Ethan rallied his troops and threatened to destroy the town if the residents did not submit to the authority of Vermont.[5] He arrived in Guilford, unopposed, on September 9; on the following day, the principal offenders were arrested in Brattleborough and the expedition concluded.

Ethan's final police action was really a non-event. On January 18, 1784, Stephen R. Bradley led a party of a hundred men to Guilford, again to enforce Vermont law and authority. Ethan followed with three companies of Bennington militia, reaching Guilford on January 22. By then, the Yorkers had taken refuge in Massachusetts, so the posse returned to Brattleborough and was dismissed on January 23.[6]

The period 1777–1784 had seen Yorker defiance of Vermont's authority in the south-east of the state: the recruitment of militia, representation in the New York Assembly, and appeals to New York for military intervention to support local governments. By the end of 1784, all this was extinct: Yorkers had either taken the oath of allegiance to Vermont or emigrated, mostly to New York, where some were compensated for their confiscated lands. New York could continue to block Vermont's admission to Congress but it could no longer challenge Vermont's independence. Ethan continued to dream of reunion with Great Britain,[7] but since that was impossible and since he opposed the admission of Vermont to Congress, there was really nothing more for him to do. He held no office of state, so he went into retirement, with the continuation of his pursuit of philosophy and his writing career.

Ethan continued so speculate in property, combining wealth in land with an acute shortage of cash for day to day living. He did occasionally venture back into politics, for instance the Susquehanna Company venture in 1785–1786 and a journey to Quebec in 1788 to lobby Governor Carleton, now Lord Dorchester, in securing free trade for Vermont. Yet all the indications are that he was an aging man, content in retirement with farming and his philosophical writings. On February 9, 1784, less than a year after Mary's death, he married Fanny Buchanan, on an instant, without any courtship worth the name. Fanny was a young, vivacious widow, the step daughter of the wealthy Yorker and Loyalist, Crean Brush. She was also the daughter of Major John Montresor, Carleton's Commanding Engineer, who had surveyed the fortifications of Boston, Quebec, Crown Point and Ticonderoga and found them all wanting. Ethan, it can safely be assumed, had no reservations at all about Fanny's pedigree. In October 1787, he finally moved to a fourteen-hundred acre farm at Burlington, which had been extracted from the Onion River holdings, with Ira as his neighbor. He died, apparently of a stroke, on February 17, 1789.

In estimating Ethan Allen's politics, it seems possible to place him on a spectrum of two parameters, the democratic-autocratic and the radical-conservative. On the first of these, Ethan of course held no major office of state and his political role was informal, influential and forceful. Comparably, the Arlington Junto was also an informal organization, including some members of the Council and the executive officers of state, as well as a few Assembly members. Those military officers privy to the Haldimand Negotiations could also be regarded as an arm of the Junto in that they colluded in a de facto national policy that had no democratic underpinnings. In all of this, the informal mode of government of the Junto was oligarchy: Ethan was an oligarch, not a democrat.

On the radical-conservative spectrum, the picture is more complex. It has been seen how Ethan's part in the revolution of 1775 was really, in his eyes, an attack on a Yorker power backed by the royal authority. Up to that time, Ethan had supported various solutions to the problem of the Grants: reliance on the King to return New York to its duty; reannexation to New Hampshire or a new state, recognized by the Crown. When he returned from captivity, Vermont had already become independent and Ethan's role was not only to defend Vermont from the Yorkers in the period 1778–1784, but also from the British, the Continental Congress, at times with New Hampshire and, in a smaller way, from Massachusetts.

The response of critics has been to label Ethan as a rebel or a revolutionary—Jellison's "Frontier Rebel" or Bellesiles' "Revolutionary Outlaw." A rebel against New York Ethan certainly was, yet even here the picture is not entirely persuasive. When we speak of "rebels" we usually mean a revolt against an established government; but there was nothing established about Yorker government in the Grants; it was uneven and partially effective only in selected regions. Ethan and his kind (only a few of whom were declared outlaws) had only the limited aim of driving out Yorker officials, tenants, and surveyors. Had they been completely successful prior to the revolution, the problem of the status of the Grants would have remained, not to be solved by the para-military force of the Green Mountain Boys.

How far, then, were the fathers of the Vermont Constitution revolutionaries? Here again, there is more than one perspective. On one view, the Vermonters had declared independence from New York as a revolutionary act, and the Junto worked to consolidate the revolution during 1777; they were to that extent revolutionaries. There was no great, singular, dramatic act of revolution, violent or otherwise and, if there had been, the captive Ethan could not have been part of it. If there are difficulties about seeing Ethan as a rebel, they are even bigger about categorizing him as a revolutionary. There are yet greater problems when we consider that the Allens did not even construe Vermont's declaration as a revolutionary act.

On this perspective, there was no government in the Grants to overthrow. The King had "withdrawn his protection": in Hobbesian terms, he no longer had the power to protect his subjects. Royal government was extinguished. So the Grants were in a state of nature, free to compact together to institute a new sovereign, in this case the Governor, his Council, the Assembly and the Council of Safety. This is what Ira Allen wrote and, as with many of the theoretical positions taken by the Allens, they were the products of circumstance, not the intellectual underpinnings of political action. Alternatively, Vermont's Declaration of Independence held that the American Declaration had totally dissolved the jurisdiction of New York. So the Grants were in a state of nature, without law or government, and free to erect their own government to secure property, well-being and happiness. Thus the creation of Vermont was a bold and radical move, but it did not constitute a revolution but was, rather, one political consequence of the American Revolution, which the American revolutionaries were reluctant to acknowledge!

Ethan Allen was the leader of a move to bring Vermont back into the British Empire. He was not a monarchist or a Loyalist, and his movement failed or, rather, faded away. But when we consider that Ethan actually took Vermont out of the Revolutionary War, which was what "cessation of hostilities" really meant, he appears as a conservative, rather than a rebel or revolutionary. The moral of the story is that a priori political categorizations of Ethan are ill-advised because they lead to a false overarching perspective on his actions and to gross distortions of the historical record in order to fit the preconceived perspective—Ethan as an equalitarian democrat, Ethan as a republican revolutionary, Ethan deceiving and outmaneuvering the British at every turn etc, etc. Even worse, such history or "history" underestimates Ethan's enormous achievement in maintaining Vermont's independence, leading to Vermont as a State of the Union in 1791. For this we have, as this author has tried to do, to look at the individual, his actions, writings, thoughts and achievements—and only then proceed to an evaluation.

And what a character he was! A Renaissance man, in the wrong time and place, with a truly staggering range of talents. He was a huge, strong man of the "wild frontier," intellectual as well as practical, writer, thinker, orator, soldier, politician, business man and speculator, charismatic, a natural leader of men. He was also vain, ostentatious, self-promoting, self-dramatizing, "the philosopher" as he pretentiously described himself, wishing to be regarded as a gentleman when his peers were peasants or yeomen. He was frequently drunk, dedicated to the "flowing bowl" and the rum ration, given the least opportunity. Yet there is no evidence that heavy drinking distorted his judgment; only one uncharacteristically vague and pessimistic letter, written "half-overseas," that is, more than half drunk, though this has been interpreted as a ruse.[8]

A fellow prisoner in New York, Alexander Graydon, wrote of Ethan:

> I have seldom met with a man, possessing, in my opinion, a stronger mind, or whose mode of expression was more vehement and oratorical. His style was a singular compound of local barbarisms, scriptural phrases, and oriental wildness; and though unclassic and sometimes ungrammatical, it was highly animated and forcible . . .[9]

There is something suspect in this description. We know that Ethan was a competent writer, no Burke, Hume or Gibbon certainly, with eccentric spelling, punctuation and capitalization, but usually grammatical, full of jokes and irony. No "local barbarisms." Then again, he despised and pilloried the scriptures, which were quoted only for their impact on the listener. His self-dramatizing was for effect, so much so that he has been regarded as an actor,[10] when the truth may be more that his character was many-faceted, with a display of self according to company and circumstance.

The best explanation of Ethan's character is that he had a mind overflowing with thoughts and ideas, a "teeming brain" that constantly sought expression in action, debate or in writing. This would account for his restlessness and impulsiveness, already noted, which makes it even more remarkable that the salient fact about Ethan's career should be the utterly consistent opposition to the power of New York from 1770 to 1784. It was this opposition, as forceful in practice as it was in the speech that Graydon noted, that ensured that the Republic maintained its independence amid all the threats to its existence. And it is for this reason that Ethan is rightly celebrated as the principal founder of the State of Vermont.

APPENDIX

Seth Warner's Letter to General Montgomery, September 27, 1775.

Lesponany, the 27th September, 1775

May it please your honor,
I have the disagreeable news to write to you that Colonel Allen hath met with a defeat by a stronger force which sallied out from the town of Montreal after he had crost the river about a mile below the town. I have no certain knowledge of Allen yet whether he is killed, taken, or fled. But this defeat hath put the French people into great consternation, they are much concerned for fear of a company coming over against us [.] furthermore the Indian Chiefs were at Montreal at the time of Allen's Battle, and there were a number of Coachnewago Indians in the battle against Allen, and the people are very fearful of the Indians. There were six in here last night. I suppose, as spies. I asked the Indians concerning their appearing against us in every battle. Their response to me was that Carlton made them drunk and drove them to it. But they say they would do so no more. I should think it proper to keep a party at Longuil and my party is not big enough to divide. If I must tarry here, I should be glad of my regiment for my party is made up of different companies and different regiments and my reputation is not as good as I could wish for.

Subordination to your orders is my pleasure
I am . . . with submission,
Your Humble Servant,
Seth Warner

This morning arrived from Col Allens defeat Capt Duggan with the following intelligence. Col Allen is absolutely taken Captive into Montreal, with a few more and about two or three killed and about as many wounded.

The living is not all come in. Something of a slaughter made among the Kings Troops.

From yours to serve,
Seth Warner

Source: VSA, *Stevens Papers,* Vol. 1 (2), 1775, 467; Force, Series IV, 953

NOTES & REFERENCES

KEY TO THE REFERENCES:

Assembly Journals: Journals and Proceedings of the General Assembly of Vermont
B Series: Haldimand Papers or Haldimand Collection
CHS: Connecticut Historical Society
CSA: Connecticut State Archives
CO: British Colonial Office documents
Copies: *Copies of Letters and Messages etc which passed between Lieutenant General Sir Henry Clinton and Lieutenant General Burgoyne between the 10th of September and the 23rd of October, 1777*
Documentary History: Documentary History of the State of New York
EA: Ethan Allen
EA ***Brief Narrative***: *A Brief Narrative of the Government of New York, Relative to Their Obtaining Jurisdiction of That Large District of Land, to the Westward from Connecticut River* (Ethan Allen, 1774)
EA ***Concise Refutation:*** *A Concise Refutation of the Claims of New Hampshire and Massachusetts Bay to the Territory of Vermont* (Ethan Allen, 1780)
EA ***Narrative:*** *A Narrative of Colonel Ethan Allen's Captivity* (Ethan Allen, 1779)
EA ***Oracle:*** *Reason the Only Oracle of Man* (Ethan Allen, 1784)
EA ***Vindication:*** *A Vindication of the Opposition of the Inhabitants of Vermont to the Government of New York, and of Their Right to Form an Independent State* (Ethan Allen, 1779)
EA-IA: *Ethan and Ira Allen, Collected Works*
IA: Ira Allen
IA History: *The Natural and Political History of the State of Vermont* (Ira Allen, 1793)
JCC: *Journals of the Continental Congress*
LAC: Library and Archives Canada
Records: *Records of the Council of Safety and the Governor and Council of the State of Vermont*
UVM: University of Vermont
VHS: Vermont Historical Society
VSA: Vermont State Archives
WLC: William L. Clements Library

INTRODUCTION

1 Harvey, 172–3, 180
2 Fryer, 49
3 Fryer, 110
4 Reuter, 50
5 Williamson (1), 51
6 H. Nicholas Muller III, entry on *The Arlington Junto* in the Vermont Encyclopedia, 42
7 Chapters 10 and 11 below

CHAPTER 1: *The Fronter*

1 Bellesiles, 17–19
2 Jellison, 15
3 EA *Brief Narrative,* EA-IA I, 1
4 Pell, 22; Bellesiles, 22
5 Pell 24–25; Bellesiles, 23
6 Pell, 41

CHAPTER 2: *Controversy: The New Hampshire Grants*

1 EA *Brief Narrative*, EA-IA I, 102
2 EA *Brief Narrative*, EA-IA I, 70
3 EA *Brief Narrative*, EA-IA I, 44
4 Jones, 40–66
5 Jellison, 20; EA-IA I, viii
6 UVM, EA Family Papers, Box 2, Folder 205
7 cited in Samuel Robinson's petition: Jones, Appendix B, 405–409, n.d.
8 UVM, EA Family Papers, Box 1, Folder 6; EA *Brief Narrative*, EA-IA I, 91–93
9 Jones, Appendix A, 397
10 *Documentary History* IV, 574–575, italics added
11 EA *Brief Narrative,* EA-IA I, 33
12 IA *History,* EA-IA III, 12–13
13 quoted in Williamson (2), 8
14 Jellison, 22
15 Jones, 79; 88
16 Jones, Appendix B, 404–407, n.d., actually prepared on March 16, 1767
17 VHS *Collections,* 1, 279; Jones, 86, 130
18 *Reference of the petitions of the Grants settlers and of the Society for the Propagation of the Gospel to the Lords of the Committee of Council for Plantations for their opinion,* March 31, 1767, UVM, EA Family Papers, Box 1, 21
19 reproduced in Jones, Appendix B, 408–409, n.d., but delivered to the King in Council, March 23, 1767
20 UVM, EA Family Papers, Box 1, Folder 23; see also the *Representation to the Privy Council for Plantation Affairs* in Jones, Appendix C, 410–11 n.d.
21 Decree issued at "a Court at St James's, the 24th Day of July, 1767," eg in EA-IA I, 93 and in UVM, EA Family Papers, Box 1, Folder 25; Shelburne on behalf of King

George II, quoted in Petersen, 21
22 UVM, EA Family Papers, Box 1, Folder 62
23 EA *Brief Narrative*, EA-IA I, 70–71
24 John Munro to James Duane, December 5, 1770, UVM, EA Family Papers, Box 1, Folder 72
25 Petitions of October 18 and 24, 1769, UVM, EA Family Papers, Box l, Folders 51 and 52
26 quoted in Ketchum (2), 281
27 EA *Brief Narrative*, EA-IA I, 10
28 IA 1777, EA-IA I, 124
29 See EA *Brief Narrative*, EA-IA I, 94–96; Jones, 241
30 Jones, 280–281
31 IA *History,* EA-IA III, 27
32 Robert Yates to James Duane, July 20, 1771, UVM, EA Family Papers, Box 1, Folder 91
33 Munro to Duane, March 20, 1772, UVM, EA Papers, Box 2, Folder 32; letter of Peter W.Yates to Duane, concerning Ethan's Allen's offer of a reward for Duane and Kempe, UVM, EA Family Papers, 2, Folder 36
34 EA *Brief Narrative*, EA-IA I, 31–33
35 *Documentary History* IV, 777
36 EA *Brief Narrative*, EA-IA I, 27
37 EA *Brief Narrative*, EA-IA I, 31
38 Jones, Appendix F, the Fays' Journal, June 27, 1772, 426
39 EA *Brief Narrative*, EA-IA I, 37
40 EA *Brief Narrative*, EA-IA I, 38
41 EA *Brief Narrative*, EA-IA I, 94–96
42 *Documentary History* IV, 827; EA 1774, *Brief Narrative* I, 94–96; Jones 244
43 *Documentary History* IV, 831
44 Dartmouth to Haldimand, October 14, 1773 and December 1, 1773, LAC B35, 42, 52; *Documentary History* IV, 856
45 Haldimand to Dartmouth, September 1, 1773 and October 6, 1773, LAC B35, 36, 38; *Documentary History* IV, 843, 844
46 Dartmouth to Haldimand, April 15, 1775, LAC B35, 134; Haldimand to Dartmouth, May 15, 1774, LAC B35, 115; Germain to Carleton, September 19, 1777, LAC CO42/37, 1
47 *Documentary History* IV, 800; 843
48 EA *Brief Narrative*, EA-IA I, 11
49 Jellison, 88
50 EA *Brief Narrative*, EA-IA I, 12
51 Duffy ed.1, 12, n. 3
52 quoted in Williamson (1), 47
53 Meeting of the Commities for the New-Hampshire Grants, April 11, 1775, Force IV, v2, 315, quoted in IA *History*, EA-IA III, 32
54 EA to Oliver Wolcott, Duffy ed. 1, 18

55 Jones, 350–352; 378
56 Jacob Bayley to the New York Convention, June 14, 1777, *Records* 1, 375 n.
57 Bayley, 67
58 Jones, Appendices J and L
59 Bayley, 73
60 Jacob Bayley to the New York Congress, June 29, 1775, *Records* 1, 371; Jacob Bayley to the New York Congress, October 20, 1775, *Records* 1, 373 and Force IV, v3, 1124
61 Jones, 372, n. 66
62 Bayley, 73
63 eg Jacob Bayley to George Clinton, September 30, 1782 and Bayley to Washington, May 24, 1781, UVM, EA Family Papers, Box 5, Folders 87, 48
64 Bayley, 76, 77
65 Bayley to Weare, November 22, 1781, VHS *Collections* II, 81; Bayley, 80
66 Jacob Bayley to George Clinton, September 30, 1782, op. cit. at note 63 above
67 Jellison, 85
68 VHS *Collections* I, 147 f.
69 Duffy ed. 1, 12, n.3
70 EA *Brief Narratve*, EA-IA I, 1–113
71 EA *Brief Narrative*, EA-IA I, 42
72 EA *Brief Narrative*, EA-IA I, 59
73 EA *Brief Narrative*, Appendix, EA-IA I, 102
74 EA *Brief Narrative*, EA-IA I, 51; 71
75 EA *Brief Narrative*, EA-IA I, 57
76 T.H. Breen, review of Willard Sterne Randall's *Ethan Allen: His Life and Times,* New York Review of Books, April 5, 2012, 64, 65
77 Jones, Preface, vii
78 Jones, Preface ix, x; 96–7; 317
79 Jones, 75
80 Jones, 92, 96
81 Proclamation of April 10, 1765 at New York, UVM, EA Family Papers, Box 1, 10
82 State of Vermont v. State of New Hampshire, 289 U.S. 593, decided May 29, 1933
83 Bellesiles, 266

CHAPTER 3: *Ethan Allen and the Assault on Ticonderoga, May 10, 1775*
1 Haldimand to Dartmouth, May 15, 1774, LAC B35, 115, quoted in Smith, 32
2 Skene's Petition, *Documentary History* IV, 843
3 October 27, 1772, quoted by Pell, 54
4 A Committee of the Continental Congress appointed to examine the papers of Major Skene, Force IV, v2, 1844
5 IA *History,* EA-IA III, 30–1
6 Carleton to Dartmouth, May 15, 1775, LAC CO42/34, 123
7 Carleton to Dartmouth, August 14, 1775, LAC CO42/34, 274
8 Carleton to Dartmouth, April 6, 1775, LAC CO42/34, 127
9 Carleton to Dartmouth, April 7, 1775, LAC CO42/34, 128

10 Paper of Intelligence from Montreal, April 3, 1775, LAC CO42/34, 125
11 Thomas Walker, John Welles, James Price and William Heywood to the Boston Committee, April 8, 1775, VSA Stevens Papers I, 55–57
12 Brown to Adams and Warren, March 29, 1775, VSA Stevens Papers 1, 51–54
13 Brown to Adams and Warren, March 29, 1775, op. cit. at note 12 above
14 EA 1779 in EA-IA, I, 166
15 Samuel Parsons to Joseph Trumbull, June 2, 1775, CHS Collections Vol. 1, Papers Relating to the Ticonderoga Expedition, 181
16 CHS Collections, Vol. 1, Papers Relating to the Ticonderoga Expedition, April and May, 1775, Journal of Captain Edward Mott, 163–172, Introductory Note, 163
17 Edward Mott to the Massachusetts Congress, May 11, 1775; *Authentick Account of the Taking of Fortresses at Ticonderoga and Crown Point* (Anonymous), Force IV, v2, 557, 638
18 Smith, 51
19 Edward Mott to the Massachusetts Congress, May 11, 1775, Force IV, v2, 557
20 Mott Journal, CHS Collections Vol. 1, 169; Captain Elisha Phelps to the General Assembly of the Colony of Connecticut, May 16, 1775, CHS Collections Vol. 1, 174
21 CSA, Revolutionary War Series 1 (1763–1789), v. 3, 25, 26a; CHS Collections Vol. 1, 173
22 Captain Benedict Arnold's Report to the Massachusetts Committee of Safety on the Quantity of Cannon at Ticonderoga, April 30, 1775, Force IV v2, 748; Committee of the Massachusetts Committee of Safety on the Proposal of Colonel Arnold for the Attempt Upon Ticonderoga, May 2, 1775, Force IV v2, 750; Edward Mott to Colonel Ethan Allen, CHS Collections Vol. 1, 172; Mott to the Massachusetts Congress, May 11, 1775, Force IV v2, 559
23 Benedict Arnold to the Massachusetts Committee of Safety, May 19, 1775, Force IV, v2, 654; Massachusetts Congress to Benedict Arnold, May 22, 1775, CHS Collections Vol. I, 179 and Force IV, v2, 676
24 EA *Narrative* 6; Easton to the Massachusetts Provincial Congress, May 18, 1775, Force IV, v2, 624
25 EA to the Massachusetts Congress, May 11, 1775, Force IV v2, 556; Duffy ed. 1, 21
Edward Mott to the Massachusetts Congress, op. cit., 558; *John Brown arrived at Philadelphia from Ticonderoga*, Anonymous, Force IV, v2, 623
26 Crockett, 428
27 EA *Narrative,* 6
28 Benedict Arnold to the Massachusetts Committee of Safety, May 19, 1775 and Benedict Arnold to the Albany Committee, May 22, 1775. Force IV v2, 654, 839
29 Benedict Arnold to the Massachusetts Committee of Safety, May 19, 1775, op. cit., at note 23 above
30 EA to James Morrison, May 18, 1775, Duffy ed. 1, 25; LAC CO42/34, 146
31 Arnold to Walker, May 20 and 24, 1775 and EA to the Caughnawagas, May 24, 1775, LAC CO42/34, 148–151
32 EA to the Caughnawagas, op. cit., at note 31 above, 149
33 EA to the Canadians, June 4, 1775, Duffy ed. 1, 36

34 Carleton to Lord Dartmouth, June 7, 1775, LAC CO42/34, 142
35 Carleton to Dartmouth, June 7, 1775, LAC CO42/34, 142
36 Record of the Continental Congress, May 18, 1775, Force IV v2, 1833
37 EA to the Continental Congress, May 29, 1775, Duffy ed. 1, 31
38 Elisha Phelps, Commissary, to the General Assembly of Connecticut, Skenesborough, May 16, 1775, CHS Collections Vol. 1, 174
39 LAC CO 42/34, 179; English translation: Force IV v2, 1838
40 Report of a Congress Committee, June 1, 1775, Force IV v2, 1841
41 Philip Livingston to the Canadians, June 2, 1775, LAC CO42/34, 183
42 EA to the New York Congress, June 2, 1775, Duffy ed. 1, 33
43 EA to the Massachusetts Congress, June 9, 1775, Duffy ed. 1, 38
44 Instructions of the Continental Congress to General Schuyler, June 27, 1775, Force IV v2, 1855
45 Letter of June 10 from the officer at Crown Point and Record of the Continental Congress, June 23, 1775, Force IV v2, 1853
46 EA to the New York Congress, July 20, 1775, Duffy ed. 1, 45
47 July 4, 1775, *Records* 2, 112n
48 *Records* 1, 6
49 UVM, EA Family Papers, Box 4, Folder 34
50 UVM, EA Family Papers, Box 4, Folder 35
51 discussion: Jellison, 143–45
52 e.g. Remember Baker and Zimri Allen to the *Connecticut Courant,* June 1, 1773, Duffy ed. 1, 10
53 Meeting of the Commities for the New-Hampshire Grants, April 11, 1775, Force IV, v2, 315; EA to Jonathan Trumbull, August 3, 1775, Duffy ed. 1, 46
54 EA *Narrative,* 5, quoted by Pell 77; Jellison 103; Smith, 52
55 Duffy ed.1, 18–19, quoted by Smith, 31
56 EA *Narrative,* 6–7
57 EA *Narrative,* 6–7
58 discussion: Jellison, 102–105
59 EA *Vindication*, EA-IA 1, 187, quoted in Bellesiles, 114
60 EA *Narrative,* 8
61 Pell, 291
62 DePuy, 209
63 Massachusetts to the Continental Congress, May 16, 1775, Force IV v2, 620
64 EA *Vindication,* EA-IA I, 187
65 EA to the Albany Committee of Correspondence, May 11, 1775, Duffy ed.1, 20
66 Randall, 300
67 Randall, 24–25
68 EA to the Continental Congress, May 29, 1775, Duffy ed., 1, 31

CHAPTER 4: *The Capture of Ethan Allen at Montreal, September 25, 1775*
1 Schuyler to the Continental Congress, October 26, 1775, Fenton, 332
2 EA *Narrative,* 12–13

3 Force IV v3, 953, quoted by Pell, 114
4 Brown to Walker and Price, Chambly, August 1, 1775, LAC CO42/34,185
5 Carleton to Dartmouth, August 14, 1775, LAC CO42/34, 174
6 Baker to Schuyler, UVM, EA Family Papers, Box 4, 37
7 Schuyler to Washington, August 31, 1775, Sparks ed. I, 28
8 Carleton to Dartmouth, April 6, 1775, the Cramahé-Dartmouth letter of September 30, 1775 attached, LAC CO42/34, 206
9 Schuyler to Washington, September 20, 1775, Sparks ed. I, 40
10 op. cit. at note 8 above
11 EA to Philip Schuyler, September 14, 1775, Duffy ed. 1, 50
12 Schuyler to Washington, September 20, 1775, Sparks ed. I, 43
13 Cramahé to Dartmouth, September 24, 1775, LAC CO42/34, 202
14 EA *Narrative*, 13
15 Force IV v3, 797
16 EA *Narrative*, 14, 16
17 Return of August 10, 1776, Recapitulation of Rebel Prisoners Taken to August 10, 1776, LAC CO42/35, 147 ; UVM, EA Family Papers, Box 4, Folder 40.
18 Force V v1, 498
19 Livingston to Montgomery, n.d., Force IV v3, 744
20 Schuyler to Washington, September 20, 1775, Sparks ed. I, 39; Abbot W.W., ed. v2, 17–21
21 Fasset Diary, 217
22 Schuyler to Washington, September 20, 1775, Sparks ed. I, 39
23 Hector Cramahé to Lord Dartmouth, September 24, 1775, op. cit. at note 13 above Cramahé to Dartmouth, November 9, 1775, LAC CO42/34, 229
24 EA *Narrative*, 15
25 EA to Richard Montgomery, September 20, 1775, Duffy ed. 1, 51–52
26 EA *Narrative*, 14
27 Montgomery to Schuyler, No. 1 of September 28, 1775, Force IV v3, 954; Pell, 116–117
28 EA *Narrative*, 14
29 *Journal Kept in Quebec in 1775* by James Jeffry, Historical Collections of the Essex Institute, Vol. L, April 1914, para 149 (UVM)
30 EA *Narrative*, 14–15
31 EA *Narrative*, 21
32 Recapitulation op. cit. at note 17 above
33 List of the Rebel Prisoners put on board the Ship *Adamant*, Quebec, 9th November, 1775, LAC CO 42/34, 255
34 Recapitulation op. cit. at note 17 above
35 EA to the Connecticut Assembly, Duffy ed. 1, 59
36 List of Prisoners Taken with Ethan Allen at Montreal, September 25, 1775, CSA, Revolutionary War Series I, 4, Document 396
37 Brooke Hindle, Introduction to EA's *Narrative* vii; see also Murray N. Rothbard, Conceived in Liberty, The Revolutionary War 1775–1784, Arlington, New Rochelle,

New York, 1979, Vol. IV, 48; Petersen, 149
38 Willard Sterne Randall, Ethan Allen, His Life and Times, W.W. Norton, New York 2011, 370, 454; "Ethan Allen's Big Misadventure," in American Heritage, Fall 2010, 75; **39** DePuy, 302; Crockett, 508
40 George Clinton's report on Brown's death: Clinton to Washington, October 30, 1780, Sparks ed. III, 130
41 EA *Narrative,* 15, 22; Cramahé to Dartmouth, September 30, 1775, LAC CO42/34, 206; unsigned letter of October 20, 1775, VSA Stevens Papers Vol. 2, 193; Carleton's report of October 25 (three miles), op. cit, at note 42 below
42 Carleton to Dartmouth, October 25, 1775, LAC CO42/34, 216
43 Force IV v.3, 954, Letter No.1 to Schuyler, italics added.
44 Force IV v.3, 951–952, as letter No.2
45 Force IV v.3, 954, letter No.4 of September 28, enclosed by Montgomery to Schuyler the same day
46 Force IV v. 3, Schuyler to the Continental Congress, September 19, 1775; Sparks ed. I, 39
47 letter No.7 from Montgomery to Schuyler, circa September 27/28, Force IV v3, 955
48 quoted in Petersen, 51
49 IA *History,* EA-IA III, 35–36
50 Warner to Montgomery, September 27, 1775, VSA, *Stevens Papers,* Vol. 1 (2), 1775, 467, reproduced below as the Appendix
51 Force IV v3, 800
52 Washington to Schuyler, October 26, 1775, VHS *Proceedings*, New Series, Vol. VIII, No. 4, December 1940, 335
53 Thompson, 35
54 EA to Steven R. Bradley, June 8, 1779, Duffy ed.1, 93; Ethan Allen Papers, Box 1, Folder 1
55 EA *Narrative*, 25
56 Duffy ed. 1,101 n.2; Randall, 373
57 Fasset Diary, 234; General Charles Lee to the Governor of revolutionary New York, Major General George Clinton, July 11, 1776, Sparks ed. III, 505
58 below, Chapter 7
59 quoted in Mathews, 3

CHAPTER 5: *Carleton's Campaign of 1775–1776*
1 Carleton to Dartmouth, September 20, 1774 and Carleton to Gage, September 24, 1774, LAC CO/33, 78–83; Shorrt and Doughty, ed. 410–11
2 Carleton to Dartmouth, June 7, 1775, LAC CO42/34, 142
3 Cramahé to Dartmouth, September 21, 1775, 198 and Carleton to Dartmouth, November 5, 1775, LAC CO42/34, 222
4 Carleton to Dartmouth, August 14, 1775, LAC CO42/34
5 Carleton to Dartmouth, November 5, 1775, op. cit., at Note 3 above
6 Force IV v3, 1426
7 Ainslie, 24

8 Carleton to Dartmouth, Montreal, October 25, 1775, LAC CO42/34, 216
9 Historical Collections of the Essex Institute, Vol. L, April 1914, 189
10 Thompson, 36; Chipman, 37
11 IA *History,* EA-IA III, 37–38; Crockett, 511; Petersen, 55
12 Diary of Cephas Kent, quoted in Mary A. Mettler, *The Military Service of Cephas Kent Jr., and the New Hampshire Grants/Vermont,* Walloomsack Review, Vol. 9, September 2012, 14; Fasset Diary, 238
13 Carleton to Dartmouth, October 25, 1775, LAC CO42/34, 216
14 Carleton to Dartmouth, November 5, 1775, op. cit. at note 3 above
15 Carleton to Dartmouth, November 5, 1775, op. cit. at note 3 above
16 Howe to Carleton, October 12, 1775, LAC CO42/34, 233
17 November 12, 1775, reproduced in Lanctot, 259–60
18 Proclamation of November 22, 1775, LAC CO42/35, 24
19 Proclamation of May 12, 1776, LAC, CO42/35, 29
20 Proclamation of May 10, 1776, LAC CO42/35, 27
21 Cramahé to Germain, June 2, 1776, LAC CO42/35, 54
22 Cramahé to Germain, Quebec, op. cit., at note 21 above, 54
23 Carleton to Burgoyne, late October, 1776, LAC B39, 219
24 Carleton to Forster, July 19, 1776, LAC B39, 78
25 Horatio Gates to the President of the Continental Congress, Ticonderoga, November 5, 1776, Sparks ed., I, 548
26 Carleton to Germain, Chambly, September 28, 1776, LAC CO42/35, 71, italics added
27 Carleton to Germain, Crown Point, October 14, 1776, LAC CO42/35, 171
28 Carleton to Germain, Quebec, November 17, 1776, LAC CO42/35, 198
29 Germain to Carleton No.5, August 22, 1776, LAC CO42/35, 84
30 Germain to Carleton, March 26, 1777, LAC CO42/36, 51
31 Carleton to Germain, May 20, 1777, LAC CO42/36, 94 and LAC, Report on the Canadian Archives, 1885, Note D1, cxxxii
32 Germain to Carleton, July 25, 1777, LAC CO42/36, 168 and LAC, Report on the Canadian Archives, 1885, Note D2, cxxxvi
33 *Records* 1, 18
34 Sullivan to Schuyler, January 11, 1776, VSA, *Stevens Papers,* Vol. 2, 177
35 Montgomery to Schuyler, at the camp before St. John's, October 22, 1775, LAC CO42/34, 220
36 Gabriel (2), 236

CHAPTER 6: *The British Incursion into Vermont, 1777*

1 Carleton's *Memoranda,* LAC CO42/36, 4
2 Burgoyne to Germain, January 6, 1777, LAC CO42/36, 6
3 *Thoughts on Conducting the War from the Side of Canada,* LAC CO42/36, 19
4 Burgoyne to Carleton, January 1, 1777, LAC CO42/36, 1
5 Germain to Burgoyne, January 20, 1777, and Burgoyne to Germain, January 21, 1777, LAC CO42/36, 27, 29

6 quoted in Adams (2), 25
7 Germain to Carleton, March 26, 1777, LAC CO42/36, 51, also at 227; similarly, Germain to Carleton, March 24, 1777, LAC CO42/36, 235 and a memo in Germain's office, extract reproduced in Adams (2), 30
8 Howe to Carleton, April 5, 1777, LAC CO42/36, 235; Carleton to Germain, June 26, 1777, enclosing a copy of Howe's letter (itemized as No. 23), LAC CO42/36, 172
9 Howe, ibid 236, at note 8 above, italics added
10 quoted in Adams (2), 27
11 extract of Howe to Germain, August 30, 1777, reproduced in Adams (2), 33; also, similarly, Howe to Germain, New York, July 16, 1777, extract reproduced in Adams (2), 32
12 Furneaux, 47–48
13 Chipman, 44
14 UVM, EA Family Papers, Box 4, Folder 66
15 *Records* 1, 64–5
16 *Records* 1, 65
17 *Records* 1, 66
18 St Clair to Washington, Fort Edward, July 17, 1777, Sparks ed. I, 404
19 Nickerson, Vol. 1, 153
20 St Clair to Washington, Fort Edward, July 17, 1777, op. cit., at note 18 above
21 quoted in full in Nickerson, Vol. 2, 235–238, in Gabriel (3), 29 and in Stark, 51, which also reproduces the instructions to Colonel Skene at 54
22 Fryer, 56
23 Carleton to Germain, May 20, 1777, LAC CO42/36, 111
24 Petersen, 116
25 Furneaux, 120
26 Furneaux, 120
27 Schuyler to Washington, Fort Edward, July 14, 1777, Sparks ed. I, 397
28 Warner to Stark, July 24, 1777, Stark, 121
29 Schuyler to Lincoln, Saratoga, July 31, 1777, Sparks ed., II, 516; Schuyler to Lincoln, August 8, 1777, Stark, 125; Lincoln to the Council of Massachusetts, Bennington, August 10, 1777, Sparks ed. II, 516; Lincoln to Washington, Stillwater, August 12, 1777, Sparks ed., I, 423
30 Lincoln to the Massachusetts Council, August 22, 1777, Stark, 132; *Records* 1, 74–5
31 St Clair to Warner, July 3, 1777, *Records* 1, 62–4; Jones, 387
32 Congress of the Colony of New Hampshire, June 3, 1775 to John Stark, Stark, 111
33 Schuyler's Proclamation of July 13, 1777, Stark 119; Schuyler to Lincoln, Albany, August 8, 1777, Stark, 125
34 Ketchum (1), 297–8
35 *Records* 1, 135
36 *Records* 1, 64
37 Nickerson, Vol. 2, 232
38 Baum to Burgoyne, Cambridge, August 13, 1777; again on August 14 from Sancoick, Stark, 55 and 56; Furneaux, 121

39 Baum to Burgoyne, August 15, 1777, Gabriel (3), 32
40 Stark to Gates, August 23, 1777, Stark 129; Furneaux 132; Fenton, 345
41 Hancock to Stark, October 4, 1777, Stark, 138
42 Stark 128, 132
43 Lincoln to Brown, Pawlet, September 12, 1777, Sparks ed. II, 525; Lincoln to Gates, Pawlet, September 14, 1777, Sparks ed., II, 526; Nickerson, Vol. 2, 323–326
44 Brown's account of September 18, 1777, Sparks ed. II, 529; Joseph Fay, Secretary of the Vermont Council of Safety to General Wolcott, September 22, 1777, *Records* 1, 176; Chittenden to Herrick, October 3, 1777, *Records* 1, 185
45 Clinton's Report to Howe, citing Burgoyne's letter to Clinton, received on September 20, 1777, WLC, *Copies* 6; Nickerson, Vol. 2, 326
46 Clinton to Howe, n.d., WLC *Copies,* 1, italics added
47 Burgoyne to Clinton, received September 29, 1777, WLC *Copies*, 4
48 Clinton's Report to Howe, WLC *Copies*, 6
49 Henry Clinton to John Burgoyne, Fort Montgomery, October 8 and October 10, 1777, WLC *Copies,* 7, 9
50 Clinton's log, September 24, 1777, WLC *Copies,* 2
51 Riedesel, 90–91
52 Burgoyne's letter to Clinton, September 20, received October 6, 1777 and Captain Campbell's verbal report, also received October 6, WLC *Copies*, 6, 9
53 Captain Scott's verbal message from Burgoyne to Clinton, c. October 9, 1777, WLC *Copies*, 7
54 Clinton's log, entries for October 11 and 15, 1777, WLC *Copies*, 10
55 Clinton's log, October 10, 1777, verbal messages to Burgoyne via Captains Campbell and Scott, WLC *Copies*, 9
56 WLC *Copies*, 10–11; Nickerson Vol. 2, 405; Ketchum (1), 438
57 Israel Putman to George Washington, Fishkill, October 25, 1777, Sparks ed. II, 14
58 Ketchum (1), 448
59 Chittenden to Gates, November 22, 1777, Sparks ed. II, 531
60 Stark to the Council of New Hampshire, Bennington, August 18, 1777, Stark 126; *Records* 1, 144; Stark to Gates, August 23, 1777, Stark, 129
61 Petersen, 127
62 Gabriel (3), 112
63 Gabriel (3), 24, 108
64 Gabriel (3), 51, 53
65 Ketchum (1), 304
66 Gabriel (3), 28
67 Burgoyne to Germain, August 22, 1777, Gabriel (3), 95
68 Gabriel (3), 28; Resch, Tyler, Foreword, 7
69 see eg the first explanatory panel in the Bennington Battlefield exhibit, Bennington Museum
70 Burgoyne to Germain, July 11, 1777, LAC CO42/36, 360; Burgoyne to Germain, July 30, 1777, LAC CO42/36, 386; Burgoyne to Germain, August 20, 1777, CO42/37, 78

CHAPTER 7: *The Republic of Vermont*

1 *Records* 2, 490
2 VHS *Collections* 1, 22; *Records* 1, 11; IA *History*, EA-IA III, 40; Williamson (1), 55
3 IA *History*, EA-IA III, 41–42
4 Williamson (1), 6, based on VHS *Collections* 1, 22
5 *Records* 1, 16
6 Resolutions of the Continental Congress, June 4, 1776, *Records* 1, 20–22
7 Jones, 362
8 IA *History*, EA-IA III, 42; *Records* 1, 15–18
9 Petersen, 73
10 *Records,* 1, 26
11 *Records,* 1, 36
12 *Records* 1, 39; Williamson (1), 60
13 Vermont Declaration of Independence, n. d., 1777; also the similar, revised Declaration of Independence, published in the *Connecticut Courant* of March 17, 1777, *Records* 1, 50
14 EA Family Papers, Box 4, 67, signed by Jonas Fay, Thomas Chittenden, Heman Allen and Reuben Jones "in behalf of said inhabitants"; also reproduced in IA *History*, EA-IA III, 44–46
15 *Records*, 1, 373–375; Ira's letter: EA Family Papers, Box 4, 67
16 quoted in IA *History,* EA-IA III, 47–48
17 *Records* 1, 395
18 reproduced in *Records* 1, 394
19 Consideration and rejection of the petition by the Continental Congress, April 8–June 30, 1777, UVM, EA Family Papers, Box 4, 67; quoted in IA *History,* EA-IA III, 49–50; *Records* 1, 396; Samuel Adams to Richard Henry Lee, June 29, 1777, Force v7, 264, *JCC,* v8, 508
20 *Records* 1, 53–61
21 IA *History,* EA-IA III, 92
22 *Records*, 1, 59–61; IA *History,* EA-IA III, 111
23 *Records* 1, 62–64; Jones, 387
24 *Records* 1, 66
25 LAC CO42/36, 285; also reproduced (misdated) in Ethan Allen's *Narrative*
26 *Records* 1, 74; 109
27 *Records* 1, 130 ff
28 Adjourned Convention at Windsor, December 24, 1777, *Records* 1, 76
29 *Records* 1, 397
30 Williamson (1), 67
31 Declaration of Rights, Section III
32 Plan or Frame of Government, Section VI
33 Plan or Frame of Government, Section VIII
34 discussion: Watson, 227
35 Watson, 247
36 Pell, 22

37 Colonel Easton at the [Massachusetts] Provincial Congress, May 18, 1775, Force IV v2, 624

CHAPTER 8: *Defending the Republic: New York, New Hampshire and the Continental Congress*

1 e.g. EA to Meshech Weare, October 23, 1778, Duffy ed. 1, 85–86
2 Samuel Adams to Richard Henry Lee, June 29, 1777, *JCC,* v7, 264; Jellison, 183
3 *Records* 1, 137
4 reproduced in EA's *Animadversory Address to the Inhabitants of the State of Vermont* of August 9, 1778, EA-IA 1, 138 ff and in his *Vindication of the Opposition of the Inhabitants of Vermont to the Government of New-York* of August 23, 1779, EA-IA I, 181ff; *Records* 2, 486
5 quoted e.g. in EA's *Vindication,* EA-IA I, 196
6 Jellison, 205
7 Jellison, 227
8 *Records* 1, 405n and IA *History*, EA-IA III, 61
9 *Records* 2, 486
10 *Records* 1, 405
11 *Records* 1, 424
12 *Records* 1, 424–426, italics added
13 *Records* 1, 430; *Records* 3, 499; Williamson (2), 83
14 Williamson (2), 80; Daniell, 151
15 *Records* 1, 435; Williamson (2), 84, 107
16 *Records* 1, 414; the letter is reproduced in EA's *Concise Refutation* (1780), EA-IA, II, 61–62 and in IA's *Vindication* of January 9, 1779, EA-IA I,155
17 *Records,* 1, 413
18 Williamson (2), 81
19 October 10, 1778, *Records,* 1, 415
20 Report on the Proceedings of the General Assembly, October 13, 1778, *Records* 1, 423–429; Duffy ed.1, 86 n.4; IA *Vindication,* January 9, 1779, EA-IA I, 161; Pell, 155
21 IA *History*, EA-IA I, 62
22 *Records* 1, 415–6, 422, 423; IA *History,* EA-IA III, 62
23 EA to Weare, October 23, 1778, Duffy ed. 1, 85; *Records* 1, 426
24 Weare to EA, November 5, 1778, Duffy ed. 1, 86; *Records* 1, 427
25 Report on the Proceedings of the General Assembly, October 23, 1778, *Records,* 1, 423
26 *Records* 1, 430 and, especially, *Records* 3, 499; IA *Vindication,* January 9, 1779 in EA-IA I, 168–9; and IA April 19, 1779, EA-IA I, 178
27 "Resolves of a Convention held on the New Hampshire Grants," Cornish, December 9, 1778, *Records* 3, 499
28 reproduced in IA, April 19, 1779, EA-IA I, 178 and in IA, January 9, 1779, EA-IA I, 168–9
29 April 2 and April 27, 1779, *Records* 1, 435

30 IA *History,* EA-IA III, 62
31 IA, April 19, 1779, EA-IA III, 179
32 IA *Vindication,* January 9, 1779, EA-IA I, 169, 172
33 quoted in EA and Jonas Fay, 1780, EA-IA II, 63
34 EA to Weare, March 4, 1779, Duffy ed. 1, 90
35 Pell, 157; Daniell, 155
36 Chittenden to the Continental Congress, August 5, 1779, *Records* 2, 175
37 Samuel Minot to George Clinton, May 4, 1779; Petition from Cumberland County Praying Protection, quoted in Jellison, 223
38 see below, Chapter 13; Chittenden as Captain General, quoted in Jellison, 222 from *Records* 1, 299
39 *Records* 1, 442; Duffy ed.1, 93 n. 2
40 *Records* 1, 520; *Assembly Journals* III, Part I, 1778–1781, 71; Pell, 175
41 John Jay to George Clinton, June 3, 1779, *JCC* v13, 18; Clinton to Cumberland County, June 3, 1779 and Clinton to the Continental Congress, June 8, 1779, VHS *Collections* 2, 25, 27
42 Jellison, 227
43 EA and Jonas Fay to the Continental Congress, July 1, 1779, Duffy ed.1, 94; *Records* 1, 409
44 *Records* 1, 409
45 Chittenden to the Continental Congress, August 5, 1779, *Records* 2, 175
46 Chittenden to Adams, October 28, 1779, *Records* 2, 194; Adams to Chittenden n.d., *Records* 2, 195
47 *Records* 2, 197
48 Denio, *passim*
49 *Records* 1, 492; Paper A.-1 n.d.; *Records* 1, 490; see also "The Papers of Charles Phelps" in *Records* 3, 490–498
50 Hall, 681
51 *Records* 2, 197
52 *A Concise Refutation of the Claims of New-Hampshire and Massachusetts Bay to the Territory of Vermont,* by Ethan Allen and Jonas Fay Esq'rs, and published by order of the Governor and Council of Vermont, January 1, 1780, EA-IA II, 52–68, especially 52–55 on the Massachusetts claim
53 Chittenden to the Continental Congress, July 25, 1780, *Records* 2, 197
54 Chittenden to Hancock, December 12, 1780, *Records* 2, 198
55 Chittenden to Hancock, December 12, 1780, op. cit. at Note 54 above; Chittenden to Washington, January 5, 1781, *Records* 2, 198
56 Chittenden to Trumbull, December 12, 1780, *Records* 2, 84
57 *Records* 2, 199
58 quoted in Jellison, 231
59 *Records* 2, 179; *JCC* v5, 273; Cumberland County Petition, Praying for Protection and Instructions to the New York Delegates to Congress, *Documentary History* IV, 980–987
60 *JCC* v5, 276

61 *Records* 1, 413
62 *Records* 2, 183
63 John Jay, President of the Congress and delegate for New York to Governor George Clinton, June 3, 1779, *JCC* v13, 21; *Records* 2, 185
64 *JCC* V, 273–278; IA *History,* EA-IA III, 69–70
65 Jellison, 231
66 IA *History*, EA-IA III, 70–1
67 EA to the Vermont General Assembly, October 26, 1779, Duffy ed. 1, 95–96; Pell, 181–182
68 *Records* 2, 193, quoted by Jellison, 236
69 Pell, 187
70 *Records* 2, 266
71 below, Chapter 10
72 *Records* 2, 55
73 August 31, 1780, *Records* 2, 252
74 *Records* 2, 488
75 *Records* 2, 287
76 *Documentary History* IV, 1004
77 *Assembly Journals* III, Part 1, 240–242; *Records* 2, 304
78 IA *History,* EA-IA III, 93
79 *Records* 2, 320
80 Chittenden to Washington, November 14, 1781, *Records* 2, 350
81 *Records* 2, 336–341
82 *Records* 2, 335–347; Daniell, 160
83 Stark, 84
84 Stark to the President of the Congress, September 1, 1781, Stark, 231
85 Stark to Heath, December 12, 1781, Stark, 297
86 Stark to George Clinton, October 26, 1781, Stark, 279
87 Washington to Stark, June 25, 1781, Stark, 211
88 Stark to Washington, December 22, 1781, Stark, 303
89 Watt (2), 270; the Proclamation is reproduced at 214–216 and in *Records* 2, 307
90 Stark's report to Major General William Heath, December 12, 1781, Stark, 296; Robinson to Stark, October 16, 1781, Stark 275; and Safford to Stark, October 17, 1781, Stark, 277 and in Records 2, 327; Watt (2), 272
91 *Assembly Journals* III, Part 1, 244
92 *Records* 2, 327; Watt (3), 81
93 IA to the Board of War, December 8, 1781, *Stevens Papers* 4 (2), Record of the Board of War, 107
94 Watt (3), 104
95 Stark to Chittenden, August 27, 1781, Stark, 226
96 Stark to Weare, December 14, 1781, Stark, 301 and Stark to Washington, December 21, 1781, Stark, 303
97 Stark to Washington, December 21, 1781, op cit at Note 96 above
98 quoted in Duffy ed. 1, 101, n. 2

99 *Records* 1, 353
100 *Assembly Journals* III, Part 2, 67; VHS *Collections* II, 228–232
101 *Records* 2, 383
102 Chittenden to Washington, March 16, 1782, *Records* 2, 385; Sparks ed. III, 492
103 *Documentary History* IV, 1007–1012
104 Clinton to Washington, January 21, 1782, *Records* 2, 461
105 *Records* 2, 463; Williamson (1), 113
106 *Records* 1, 390
107 *Records* 2, 88
108 VHS *Collections* 2, 268; *Records* 2, 394
109 EA-IA I, 181–233
110 December 5, 1782, *Records* 3, 311

CHAPTER 9: ***Defending the Republic: The British Raids From Canada***

1 Stark, 101–102
2 Petition of Samuel Sleeper to Cramahé, circa December, 1760, LAC CO42/31,14
3 Carleton to Hillsborough, May 10, 1769 and Hillsborough to Carleton, July 25, 1769, LAC CO42/29, 53, 80
4 below, Chapter 12
5 McCorison, passim
6 Paper of Intelligence, brought by a scout to St. John's, September 16, 1779, LAC B181, 241
7 Haldimand to Christopher Carleton, November 1 and Carleton's reply of November 14, 1779, LAC B132, 28 and 30
8 Underwood, passim; Major Carleton's Report to Haldimand on Houghton's (first) raid, dated November 30, 1779, LAC B32, 36
9 Washington and Washington, 25–28; *Records* 1, 245–246; EA to Washington, May 28, 1778, Duffy ed. 1, 78 and n. 1
10 Watt (3), 383–5
11 Haldimand to Germain, July 25, 1778, LAC B42, 272
12 Haldimand to Germain, July 28, 1778, LAC B42, 27
13 Everest, 60, n. 38 and n. 39
14 Fryer, 91–92
15 Haldimand to Germain, October 15, 1778, LAC B54, 30
16 Haldimand to Carleton, October 17, 1778, LAC B132, 3
17 Washington and Washington, vii
18 Carleton's Journal, October 24 to November 13, dated November 14, 1778, LAC B132, 7, reproduced as Appendix 3 in Washington and Washington, 95; covering letter from Carleton to Haldimand, November 14, 1778, LAC B132, 18; Haldimand to Germain, November 21, 1778, LAC B54, 61
19 List of Prisoners sent to St. John's by Major Carleton, circa October, 1783, LAC B132, 96
20 Petersen, 153
21 George Clinton to George Washington, Albany, October 18, 1778

22 Warner's Report to Washington from Bennington, October 30, quoted in Petersen, 155–56; Watt (l), 109 and Appendix 5, 353–4; George Clinton to George Washington, October 30, 1780, Sparks ed. III, 130; Articles of Capitulation of Fort Anne (Adiel Sherwood to Major Carleton), October 10, 1780, LAC B132, 51
23 Watt (1), 104; Haldimand to Germain, October 25, 1780, LAC B54, 395
24 Articles of Capitulation of Fort George (John Chipman to Major Carleton), October 11, 1780, LAC B132, 51; Watt (1), Appendix 5, 354–355
25 George Clinton to George Washington, October 18, 1780, Sparks ed. III, 121
26 George Clinton to George Washington, October 30, 1780, Sparks ed. III, 130
27 Chapter 10, below
28 quoted in Petersen 156 from the Washington Papers; Watt (1), Appendix 5, 358, n. 2
29 Justus Sherwood to Robert Mathews, May 2, 1782, LAC B177–1, 132
30 Haldimand to Germain, October 25, 1780, LAC B54, 396; Watt (1), Appendix 5, 356
31 Joseph Marsh of Dresden to George Washington, November 3, 1780, VHS *Collections* 2, 74
32 Watt (1), 106, 122; Duffy ed. 1, 104, n. 1
33 Bayley, 85; Watt (1), 225
34 Watt (2), 206–209; Mathews, 73–7, 107–9; Fryer 170
35 Stark 331–334

CHAPTER **10**: ***The Haldimand Negotiations, Phase 1, July, 1780 to December, 1781***
1 DePuy, 411, 412
2 Cramahé to Dartmouth, November 9, 1775, LAC CO42/34, 229
3 Cruger to Palfrey, February 16, 1776, Force IV v6, 508
4 Coyle and Duffy, 71 and note 15; Duke of Richmond in the House of Lords, March 5 1776, Force IV v6, 294; official denials: the Earl of Suffolk's response to the Duke of Richmond, quoted in Wharton ed., v2, 289 n.
5 Montgomery to Carleton, October 22, 1775, LAC CO42/34, 220; Montgomery to Schuyler, November 24, 1775, Sparks ed. I, 491
6 Washington to Howe, December 18, 1775, VSA, *Stevens Papers* Vol. 4 (1) 203, quoted in Duffy et al. ed. (1), 56, n.1; Washington to Schuyler, December 18, 1775, *Stevens Papers* Vol. 4 (1), 205; Howe to Washington, December 21, 1775, Force IV v4, 454
7 *JCC* v1, December 2, 1775
8 Randall, 402; Jellison, 164
9 Randall, 404, citing *Stevens Papers* Vol. 5, 462; Pell, 124–5; Jellison, 164
10 EA *Narrative*, 94, 95
11 Germain to Clinton and Germain to Haldimand, March 3, 1779, LAC B43, 135; VHS *Collections* II, 59; VSA, *Stevens Papers,* Vol. 5, 517, 519; McIlwraith, 199
12 Germain to Haldimand, April 16, 1779, LAC B43, 114
13 Haldimand to Germain, September 13, 1779, LAC B54, 15
14 Germain to Clinton, September 27, 1779, VHS *Collections* II, 93 and WLC Clinton Papers, Vol. 69, 24
15 Germain to Clinton, September 27, 1779, WLC Clinton Papers, Vol. 69, 24 and

Germain to Clinton, September 27, 1779, WLC Clinton Papers, op. cit. at note 14 above

16 Germain to Clinton, December 4, 1779, WLC Clinton Papers, Vol. 79, 8

17 Germain to Haldimand and Germain to Clinton, February 7, 1781, VHS *Collections* II, 93; VSA, *Stevens Papers*, Vol. 5, 518

18 Clinton to Eden, August 21–22, 1779, WLC Clinton Papers, Vol. 66, 12; van Doren, 239

19 Clinton to Haldimand, New York, September 9, 1779, LAC B147, 85, also in Wardner (1), 61

20 Clinton to Eden, October 10, 1779, WLC Clinton Papers Vol. 71, 21

21 Clinton to Eden, December 11, 1779, WLC Clinton Papers Vol. 80, 4

22 van Doren, 240

23 Haldimand to Clinton, April 15, 1780, LAC B147, 221

24 Germain to Haldimand, April 12, 1780, LAC B44, 72

25 Ketchum (2), 366

26 Robinson to EA, March 30, 1780, VSA, *Stevens Papers* Vol. 4 (1), 327; Duffy ed.1, 108

27 Robinson to EA, February 2, 1781, *Stevens Papers* Vol. 4 (1), 345; Duffy ed.1,107

28 Pell, 210; Jellison, 267

29 *Assembly Journals* III, Part 1, 227

30 EA to Samuel Huntington, March 9, 1781, VSA, *Stevens Papers,* Vol. 5, 191; Duffy ed.1, 109

32 Stephen Bradley, *Vermont's Appeal to the Candid and Impartial World,* 1779, *Records* 2, 211; Duffy ed.1, 99n.2

33 Haldimand to Clinton, April 30, 1780, VSA *Stevens Papers* Vol. 5, 519

34 Chittenden to Huntington, July 25, 1780, LAC B175, 26, VHS *Collections* II 32, McIlwraith, 201; Chittenden to Governor George Clinton of New York, November 22, 1780 (enclosing the letter to Huntington of July 25), LAC B175, 60, VSA, *Stevens Papers* Vol. 5, 121; Chittenden to Governor Jonathan Trumbull of Connecticut and Chittenden to Governor John Hancock of Massachusetts, December 12, 1780, VSA *Stevens Papers* Vol. 5, 125, 137

35 Chittenden to Washington, November 14, 1781, Sparks ed., III, 440

36 VHS *Collections* II, 63 and 201n.

37 EA to George Washington, August 16, 1780 and George Washington to EA, August 30, 1780, Duffy ed.1, 100, 101

38 LAC B179 passim

39 Journal of Captain Sherwood, LAC B180, 42, 47

40 Sherwood to Powell, August 24, 1780, LAC B182, 245

41 Sherwood to Hawkins, August 24, 1780, LAC B182, 248

42 Paper of Intelligence, September 23, 1780, LAC B182, 271

43 S. Sherwood to J. Sherwood, September 23, 1780, LAC, B182, 264

44 Thomas Taylor, October 10, 1780, LAC B182, 278

45 Hudibras to Haldimand, September 30, 1780, LAC B182, 273

48 Carleton to EA, October 26, 1780, Duffy ed. 1, 102

49 Sherwood to Mathews, November 26, 1782, LAC B177, 604
50 Duffy ed.1,131, n.1
51 Pell, 196
52 VSA, *Stevens Papers* Vol. 4 (1), Ethan Allen, 1770–1786, 404, n.d
53 Powell to Haldimand, September 30, 1780, LAC B180, 234
54 Marsh to Haldimand, October 10, 1780, LAC B161, 150 and (misdated October 11) in Wardner (1), 63; Haldimand to Marsh, October 16, 1780, Wardner (1), 63; Mathews to Sherwood, October 16, 1780, LAC B175, 41 and LAC B179–1, 1
55 Christopher Carleton to EA, October 26, 1780, Duffy ed.1,102; Fryer 112–114; EA to Christopher Carleton, October 29, 1780, Duffy ed.1,103 and LAC B175, 46
56 Sherwood's Journal, October 28 to November 30 (mistakenly entered as November 31) 1780, LAC B180, 42–58
57 EA to Christopher Carleton, October 29, 1780 op. cit. at note 55 and EA to Christopher Carleton, November 4, 1780, Duffy ed.1, 103 and in LAC B175, 53
58 EA to Alexander Webster, from H. Q. Castleton, October 29, 1780, Duffy ed.1, 103
59 EA to Trumbull and EA to Hancock, LAC B175, 60, 61
60 Ebenezer Allen to Alexander Webster, October 30, 1780, Duffy ed.1, 104
61 *Assembly Journals* III, Part 1, 145; VHS *Collections* II, 78, 79
62 *State Papers of Vermont* Vol. 6, 38
63 LAC B175, 48; *Assembly Journals* III, Part 1, 148, November 2, 1780; *Records* 2, 49
64 *Assembly Journals* III, Part 1, 152
65 VHS *Collections* II, 73
66 Chittenden to Haldimand, LAC B175, 54
67 Chapter 8 above on the imminent armed confrontation between Vermont and New York; EA to Christopher Carleton, November 4 and November 24, 1780, Duffy ed.1, 105, 106
68 Haldimand to Germain, October 25, 1780, LAC B54, 398; Haldimand to Germain, December 16, 1780, VHS *Collections* II, 87; VSA *Stevens Papers* Vol. 5, 520
69 Bellesiles, 198
70 Haldimand to Sherwood, December 20, 1780, LAC B179-1, 2; VHS *Collections* II, 87; VSA, *Stevens Papers,* Vol. 5, 103 and *Queries to General Haldimand and Answers,* n.d., VSA, *Stevens Papers,* Vol. 5, 113
71 Haldimand to Clinton, August 13, 1780, LAC B147, 221
72 Haldimand to Dundas, December 31, 1780, LAC B132, 53
73 Chittenden to Haldimand, January 1, 1781, LAC B175, 69
74 Chittenden to Haldimand, April 26, 1781, LAC B175, 70
75 Sherwood to Mathews, Ile-aux-Noix, May 7, 1781, LAC B176, 96; Dundas to Mathews, Ile-aux-Noix, May 7, 1781, LAC B132, 79
76 Ira Allen to Frederick Haldimand, May 8, 1781, Duffy ed.1, 112
77 Haldimand to Germain, April 30, 1781, VSA *Stevens Papers* Vol. 5, 519; Sherwood Journal, May 7–25, 1781, LAC B180, 59–78, also in B176, 96, continued in B178, 76, reproduced but not identified in VSA, *Stevens Papers* Vol. 5, 67f
78 Dundas to Haldimand, May 9, 1781, LAC B132, 80
79 Sherwood to Mathews, May 7, 1781, LAC B176, 96; May 11, 1781, LAC B176,

84; May 15, 1781, LAC B176, 89
80 Haldimand to Chittenden, May 14, 1780, LAC B175, 83
81 Mathews to Sherwood, May 15, 1780, LAC B179, 32
82 Haldimand to Sherwood, May 17, 1780, LAC B179, 36
83 Haldimand to Lernoult, Dundas and Sherwood, May 11, 181, LAC B179, 30; Sherwood to Lernoult, May 12, 1781, LAC B176, 114; Sherwood's Journal, entry of May 25, LAC B180, 78
84 Sherwood to Mathews, May 20, 1781, LAC B176, 106
85 Sherwood to Mathews, May 29, 1781, LAC B176, 123
86 Sherwood to Mathews, May 23, 1781, LAC B176, 117
87 Sherwood to Mathews, May 25, 1781 (1), LAC B176, 120
88 Sherwood to Mathews, May 25, 1781 (2), LAC B176, 222
89 Sherwood to Mathews, May 19, 1781, LAC B176, 91
90 Sherwood to Mathews, May 18, 1781, LAC B176, 93
91 Mathews to Sherwood, May 28, 1781, LAC B179, 45
92 IA *History,* EA-IA III, 90
93 Haldimand to Clinton, June 6, 1781, LAC B147, 314
94 anonymous Paper of Intelligence to Haldimand, June 3, 1781, received June 16, LAC B182, 350
95 Crowfoot to Sherwood, March 3, 1781, LAC B182, 320
96 *Assembly Journals* III, Part 1, 244, 269
97 *Assembly Journals* III, Part 1, 242, 268
98 Germain to Haldimand, April 12, 1781, LAC B44, 72
99 Germain to Haldimand May 4, 1781, LAC B44, 281
100 Haldimand to Germain, July 8, 1781 (enclosing Sherwood's Journal of May, 1781), LAC B55, 58
101 Germain to Haldimand, July 26, 1781, LAC B44, 281; VHS *Collections* II, 146
102 July 7, 1781, VSA, *Stevens Papers* Vol. 5, 523
103 Haldimand to Clinton, August 2, 1781, LAC B147, 333 and 339; VSA, *Sevens Papers* Vol. 5, 305
104 Clinton to Haldimand, New York, August 2, 1781, LAC B147, 353
105 Robertson to Haldimand, July 20, 1781, LAC B74, 128
106 VHS *Collections* II, 182
107 Haldimand to Robertson, November 14, 1781, LAC B67, 45
108 Mathews to Sherwood, June 5, 1781, LAC B179-1, 72; Fryer, 134
109 Sherwood to Mathews, July 9, 1781, LAC B176, 145
110 Chittenden to Haldimand, July 15, 1781, LAC B175, 97; Joseph Fay to Sherwood, July 20, 181, LAC B176, 163
111 IA to Haldimand, Sunderland, July 10, 1781, Duffy ed. 1, 118, LAC B176, 145; Major Fay to Justus Sherwood, near Crown Point, July 24, 1781, LAC B176, 178
112 IA *History*, EA-IA 3, 86
113 IA to Alexander Dundas and Justus Sherwood, May 20, 1781, Duffy ed. 1, 115 and 113, n.1
114 Fay to Chambers, July 21, 1781, LAC B176, 166; Chambers to Fay, July 23, 1781,

LAC B176, 176
115 Joseph Fay to Frederick Haldimand, August 9, 1781, VSA *Stevens Papers* Vol. 5, 319
116 Sherwood to Mathews, August 10, 1781, LAC B176, 207
117 IA and Joseph Fay to George Smyth and Justus Sherwood, September 16, 1781, Duffy ed. 1, 121
118 Resolution of Congress of August 20, 1781, LAC B175, 118 and Chapter 7, above
119 IA and Joseph Fay to Haldimand, September 20, 1781, Duffy ed. 1, 122; VHS *Collections* II, 174
120 Haldimand to Clinton, September 13, 1781, LAC B147, 341
121 Haldimand to Clinton, September 24, 1781, LAC B147, 342; Haldimand to Clinton, September 27, 1781, LAC B147, 371; Haldimand to Clinton, September 30, 1781, LAC B147, 370
122 Haldimand to Robertson, September 30, 1781, LAC B147, 366; Haldimand to Clinton, October 1, 1781, LAC B147, 374 and VHS *Collections* II, 179, quoted by McIlwraith, 211
123 Haldimand to Germain, October 23, 1781, LAC B55, 109
124 Haldimand to Clinton, October 1, 1780, LAC B147, 374; VHS *Collections* II, 179
125 Haldimand to Germain, October 23, 1780, LAC B57-2, 372
126 Haldimand to Clinton, October 3, 1781, LAC B147, 179; VHS *Collections* II, 180
127 *A Proclamation to the Principal Men and the Inhabitants of the District of Country called Vermont,* October 5, 1781, LAC B179-1, 135
128 Clinton to Haldimand, November 12, 1781, LAC B147, 385
129 Clinton to Haldimand, October 12, 1781, VSA, *Stevens Papers* Vol. 5, 525
130 Sherwood to Mathews, October 10, 1781, St. John's, LAC B176, 303
131 Sherwood to Mathews, October 18, 1781, LAC B176, 314
132 George Smyth to Robert Mathews, October 31, 1781, LAC B176, 322
133 IA *History,* EA-IA III, 101, quoted in *Records* II, 129
134 VHS *Collections* II, 186; *Records* 2, 323
135 IA to Justus Sherwood, October 20, 1781, Duffy ed. 1, 123; LAC, B175, 152; VHS *Collections* II, 190
136 Haldimand to Germain, November 18, 1781, LAC B55, 121 and in B57, 377; Haldimand to Germain, November 26, 1781, LAC B57, 377
137 Smyth to Mathews, St. John's, October 31, 1781, op. cit. at note 132 above
138 Sherwood to Mathews, October 24, 1781, LAC B176, 316
139 Sherwood to Major Carleton, October 29, 1781, LAC B176, 320
140 Sherwood to Mathews, Ticonderoga, November 2, 1781, LAC B176, 320
141 Haldimand to Chittenden, December 30, 1781, LAC B175, 165
142 Germain to Haldimand, January 2, 1782, LAC B44, 118

CHAPTER **11**: ***The Haldimand Negotiations Phase 2, January 1782 to April 17831***
1 below, Chapter 13
2 Intelligence of Terence Smyth, February 8, 1782, LAC B177-1, 28; Smyth to Mathews, July 2, 1782, LAC B182, 551

3 Proceedings of the U.S. Congress Relative to the Proposals of Vermont, 1–17 April, 1782, LAC B177-1; 243, JCC, v22, 164–186; Jellison, 292
4 anonymous (EA) to Haldimand, via Terence Smyth, received May 8, 1782, LAC B177-1, 264; OTO (EA) to "Gentlemen," received by George Smyth and Justus Sherwood, May 8, 1782, LAC B177-1, 266; Jellison, 293
5 Justus Sherwood and George Smyth to IA and Joseph Fay, April 22, 1782, Duffy ed.1, 126; Williams (1), 268, 269
6 Sherwood to Mathews, May 9, 1782, LAC B177-1, 274
7 Ira Allen and Joseph Fay to George Smyth and Justus Sherwood, May 9 and May 19, 1782, Duffy ed.1, 128 and 129; LAC B177-1, 303 and 305
8 George Wright to Captain Mathews, July 28, 1782, LAC B182, 554
9 e.g. anonymous (EA) to Messrs Sherwood and Smyth, November 22, 1782, LAC B177-2, 598; anonymous (EA) to Captain Sherwood and Dr. George Smyth, December 20, 1782, LAC B178, 11; Sherwood to Mathews, January 8, 1783, LAC B178, 15
10 Sherwood to anonymous, May 9, 1782, LAC B177-1, 274
11 Sherwood to Mathews, May 9, 1782, LAC B177-1, 274
12 Haldimand to Clinton, June 22, 1782, LAC B182, 39
13 George Wright to Captain Mathews, July 28, 1782, LAC B182, 554
14 EA to Haldimand, June 16, 1782, Duffy ed.1, 130
15 Haldimand to Clinton, April 28, 1782, LAC B148, 24
16 Haldimand to Shelburne, July 17, 1782, LAC B55, 165
17 Haldimand to Carleton, August 11, 1782, LAC, B148, 68
18 Haldimand to Shelburne, August 15, 1782, LAC B57-2, 449
19 Haldimand to Townsend, October 25, 1782, LAC B57-2, 481 and in LAC B56, 6
20 Haldimand to Townshend, November 8, 1782, LAC B57, 499
21 Haldimand to Townshend, February 14, 1783, LAC B56, 53 and LAC B57-2, 577 (catalogued as 517)
22 Haldimand to Lord North, October 24, 1783, LAC B57-2, 574
23 *Records* 3, 248 f.; VHS *Collections* 2, 311–12, 324–326
24 Sherwood to "A," March 25, 1783, LAC B178, 151
25 anonymous (EA or Chittenden) to Haldimand, April 10, 1783, LAC B175, 188; anonymous (EA) to Justus Sherwood and Luke Knowlton, Manchester, signed with EA's cryptogram, April 18, 1783, Duffy ed.1, 138; anonymous to Sherwood, Manchester, April 19, 1783, LAC B178, 173
26 anonymous to Haldimand, April 10, 1783, LAC B175, 188; Sherwood to EA, April 10, 1783, LAC B178, 162
27 Sherwood to Mathews, April 10, 1783, LAC B178, 162
28 EA to Justus Sherwood and Luke Knowlton, April 18, 1783, op. cit. at note 25 above;
29 Smyth to Mathews, April 27, 1783, LAC B178, 85; Duffy ed.1, 138, n. 2
26 Sherwood to EA, April 10, 1783, LAC B178 162–3
27 Sherwood to Mathews, April 10, 1783, LAC B178, 162
28 EA to Justus Sherwood and Luke Knowlton, April 18, 1783, Duffy ed.1, 138 and anonymous to Sherwood, April 19, 1783, opera citata at note 25 above

29 Sherwood to Mathews, April 27, 1783, LAC B178, 85; Duffy ed.1, 138, n. 2
30 Lord North to Haldimand, August 8, 1783, LAC B50, 139
31 Haldimand to North (private), October 24, 1783, LAC B56, 149; also Haldimand to North of the same date, LAC B57, 574
32 Lord Sydney to Haldimand, April 8, 1784, LAC B50, 148
33 Haldimand to Lord Sydney, June 29, 1784, LAC B56, 237
34 e.g. Haldimand to Clinton, November 1, 1779, LAC B147, 123; Haldimand to Germain, enclosing Sherwood's Journal of May, 1781, July 8, 1781, LAC B55, 58
35 Haldimand to Clinton, August 13, 1780, LAC B147, 221
36 Morison ed., 186
37 Williamson (1), 108–9
38 VHS *Collections* 2, 89
39 Clinton to Haldimand, March 10, 1782, LAC B148, 19
40 Haldimand to Clinton, April 28, 1782, LAC B142, 24
41 Washington and Washington 7, quoting Haldimand from McIlwraith, 208
42 T. H. Breen review of Randall's *Ethan Allen: His Life and Times*, New York Review of Books, April 5, 2012
43 Wardner, Proceedings of the VHS, New Series, 1931, Vol. III, No. 13, 26
44 *Assembly Journals*, III, Part 1 (1924), 145 n.
45 e.g. William L. Stone, *Life of Joseph Brant-Thayendanegea Including the Indian Wars of the American Revolution*. Vol. 2, Chapter VI, (Buffalo: Phinney & Co., 1851)
46 Pell, 215
47 Pell, 217, 218
48 Jellison, 248
49 Jellison, 250
50 Bellesiles, 195
51 Bellesiles, 200
52 above, p.136; Bellesiles, 197, n. 35
53 Bellesiles, 199 and n. 41
54 Bellesiles, 196 and n. 33
55 Bellesiles, 198; Williams (1), 2
56 Bellesiles, 196, n. 32
57 James Madison to Edmund Pendleton, August 14, 1781, VHS *Collections* 2, 57
58 Washington to Madison, March 31, 1787, *Records* 3, 430–438
59 Williamson (1), 174–184
60 Mathews to Sherwood, November 5, 1781, LAC B179, 146
61 Haldimand to Clinton, April 28, 1782, LAC B148, 24; Haldimand to Carleton, July 28, August 11 and September 8, 1782, LAC B148, 55, 68 and 90; VHS *Collections* 2, 288, 291
62 Haldimand's three letters to Carleton, supra at note 61, and Haldimand to Guy Carleton, August 28, 1782, LAC B148, 83 and in B146, 16
63 Haldimand to Chittenden, August 8, 1782, VHS *Collections* II, 290
64 IA *History,* EA-IA 3, 101
65 EA to Guy Carleton, July 16, 1788, Duffy ed. 1, 273

66 Bellesiles, 354, n. 64; Mackintosh, 14
67 below, Chapter 12

CHAPTER 12: *The Political Philosophy of Ethan Allen*
1 *Leviathan,* Part II, Chapter 21
2 eg EA and Jonas Fay, 1780, EA-IA II, 57; EA, 1782, EA-IA II, 69
3 "Improvement": EA quoting the 1772 Report of the Lords of Trade, EA *Brief Narrative,* EA-IA I, 95; "little value": EA *Brief Narrative*, EA-IA I, 72
4 *Second Treatise of Civil Government,* Sec. 27
5 EA *Brief Narrative*, EA-IA I, 69, 73
6 c.f. *Leviathan,* Part 1, Chapter XV, "The laws of nature are immutable and eternal"
7 Continental Congress to the Inhabitants of Canada, May 29, 1775, Force IV, v2, 1838
8 EA *Brief Narrative*, EA-IA I, 11
9 *The Social Contract*, Chapters II and IV, OUP World Classics edition of *Social Contract* (1947), 241; 281
10 *Second Treatise of Civil Government,* Sec. 142
11 *Leviathan,* Part 2, Chapter XXI
12 IA *History*, EA-IA III, 43
13 EA, John Franklin and John Jenkins, An Address from the Inhabitants of Wyoming and others, September 12, 1786, EA-IA II, 101
14 Bellesiles, Appendix H, 290
15 quoted by Pell, 251
16 *contra* Bellesiles, 248–251
17 passages quoted by Pell, 251, 250 and Bellesiles, 249
18 Jellison, 317
19 Bellesiles, 253
20 quoted by Pell, 262

CHAPTER 13: *Ethan Allen: Endgame and Assessment*
1 Chapter 8, above
2 *Records* 1, 300–303
3 *Records* 2, 161–163
4 *Records* 3, 234
5 VHS *Collections* 2, 297–302; Thompson, 77; Jellison, 297
6 *Records* 3, 301–306; Thompson 78; Jellison, 300
7 EA to Carleton, July 16, 1788, Duffy ed. 1, 273
8 EA to Justus Sherwood and Luke Knowlton, April 18, 1783, Duffy ed. 1, 138
9 quoted by Pell, 127
10 Bellesiles, 128

BIBLIOGRAPHY

Archival Sources

Colonial Office Papers (British), Library and Archives Canada, Ottawa

Copies of Letters and Messages etc which passed between Lieutenant General Sir Henry Clinton and Lieutenant General Burgoyne between the 10th of September and the 23rd of October, 1777, William L. Clements Library, Ann Arbor, Michigan

Ethan Allen Family Papers, University of Vermont, Bailey/Howe Library, Special Collections, Burlington

Haldimand Papers (Haldimand Collection), B Series, Library and Archives Canada, Ottawa

Sir Henry Clinton Papers, William L. Clements Library, Ann Arbor, Michigan

Henry Stevens Papers (6 volumes) and *Henry Stevens Collection,* Vermont State Archives, Middlesex, Vermont

Collections

Abbot, W.W., ed., *The Papers of George Washington, Revolutionary War Series 2,* University Press of Virginia, Charlottesville, 1987

Barker, Sir Ernest, ed, and Introduction, *Social Contract, Essays by Locke, Hume and Rousseau, with an Introduction by Sir Ernest Barker,* London, Oxford University Press, World Classics, 1947

Crockett, Walter ed., *Journals and Proceedings of the General Assembly of Vermont,* Vol. 3, Part I, 1778–1781, Bellows Falls, Vermont, 1924;

Duffy John J. et al, ed., *Ethan Allen and Hid Kin, Correspondence, 1772–1819,* 2 volumes, University Press of New England, Hanover and London, 1998

Graffagnino J. Kevin, ed., *Ethan Allen and Ira Allen: Collected Works,* 3 volumes, Benson, Vermont, 1992

Force, Peter, *American Archives*, Documents of the American Revolution 1774–1776, 8 volumes, Washington D. C., 1837–1853

Ford, Worthington C. ed., *Journals of the Continental Congress, 1774–1789,* 34 volumes, Washington D.C., 1904–1937

O'Callaghan M.D., ed., *Documentary History of the State of New York*, Vol. IV, Albany, 1851

Shortt, Adam and Doughty eds. *Documents Relating to the Constitutional History of Canada, 1759–91,* Ottawa, 1918

Sparks Jared, ed., *Diplomatic Correspondence of the American Revolution*, Freeport, 4 volumes, New York, 1853 (reprinted 1970)

Vermont, State of, *State Papers of Vermont,* Bellows Falls, Vermont, 1918–1965

Vermont Historical Society, *Collections of the Vermont Historical Society,* 12 volumes, Montpelier, Vermont, 1870–1946

Walton E.P. ed., *Records of the Council of Safety and Governor and Council of the State of Vermont,* 8 volumes, Montpelier, Vermont, 1873–80

Wharton, Francis ed., *Diplomatic Correspondence of the United States*, six volumes, US Department of State, Washington, D.C., 1889

Articles

Bayley, Edwin A., *Brigadier-General Jacob Bayley, 1726– 1815*, (1920), Proceedings of the Vermont Historical Society, 1918–21

Burns, Brian, "*Massacre or Muster? Burgoyne's Indians and the Militia at Bennington*, Vermont History, 45, No. 3, Summer, 1977

Coyle, Eugene A., and Duffy, John H., *Ethan Allen's Irish Friends,* Vermont History, Spring 1995, Vol. 63, No. 2, Spring 1995

Denio, Herbert, *Massachusetts Land Grants in Vermont*, Colonial Society of Massachusetts Publications, XXIV, 1920–1922

Fenton, Walter S., *Seth Warner*, Vermont Historical Society Proceedings, New Series, Vol. III, No. 4, December, 1940

Graffagnino, Kevin J. *Vermont Attitudes Towards Slavery: The Need for a Closer Look, in Vermont etc,* Proceedings of the Vermont Historical Society, Vol. 45, No. 1, Winter, 1977

Howe, Archibald Murray, *Colonel John Brown of Pittsfield, Massachusetts, the Brave Accuser of Benedict Arnold*, Library of Alexandria, 1908

Mackintosh, William Alexander, *Canada and Vermont: A Study in Historical Geography,* Canadian Historical Review, VIII, I, March 1927

McCorison, Marcus A., *The Bayley-Hazen Military Road*, Vermont History, Vol. XXVII, 1959

Pemberton, Ian C., (2) *The British Secret Service in the Champlain Valley During the Haldimand Negotiations, 1780–1783*, Vermont History, Summer 1976, Vol. 44, No. 3

Underwood, Wynn, *Indian and Tory Raids on the Otter Valley, 1777–82*, Vermont Quarterly 15, October, 1947

Wardner, Henry Steele, (1), *The Journal of a Loyalist Spy*, The Vermonter, Vol. 28, 1924, Vols. 5 and 6

Wardner, Henry Steele, (2), Address to the Vermont Historical Society, Proceedings of the Vermont Historical Society, New Series, 1931, Vol. II, No. 1

Watson, Hon. John H., *In re The Vermont Constitution of 1777, as Regards its Adoption and its Declaration Forbidding Slavery* (1921), Publications of the Vermont Historical Society, 1920–21

Books

Adams, Randolph G., ed. (1), *The Headquarters Papers of the British Army in North America*, Ann Arbor, Michigan, 1926

Adams, Randolph G. ed. (2), *The Papers of Lord George Germain*, 2 volumes, Ann Arbor, Michigan, 1928

Ainslie, Thomas, *Journal of the Most Remarkable Occurrences in the Province of Quebec from the Appearance of the Rebels in 1775 Until their Retirement on the Sixth of May*, ed. Sheldon S. Cohen, Copp Clark, Toronto, 1968

Allen, Ethan, *A Narrative of the Captivity of Ethan Allen* (1779), Introduction by Brooke Hindle, Corinth Books, New York, 1961

Allen, Ethan, *Reason the Only Oracle of Man, or a Compendious System of Natural Religion*, Haswell and Russell, Bennington, Vermont, 1784

Bakeless, John, *Turncoats, Traitors and Heroes*, Lippincott, Philadelphia and New York, Philadelphia, 1959

Bellesiles, Michael L., *Revolutionary Outlaws: Ethan Allen and the Struggle for Independence on the Early American Frontier*, University Press of Virginia, Charlottesville, 1993

Berg, Fred Anderson, *Encyclopedia of Continental Army Units: Battalions, Regiments and Independent Corps*, Stackpole Press, Harrisburg, Pennsylvania, 1972

Bird, Harrison, *March to Saratoga, General Burgoyne and the American Campaign, 1777*, Oxford University Press, New York, 1963

Bradley, A.G, *Lord Dorchester*, Morang and Co., Ltd, Toronto, 1910

Burnett, Edmund Cody, *The Continental Congress,* Macmillan, New York, 1941

Burt, Alfred Leroy, *The Old Province of Quebec,* Ryerson Press, Toronto, 1933

Calloway, Colin G., *The Western Abenakis of Vermont, 1600–1800, War, Migration and the Survival of an Indian People,* University of Oklahoma Press, Norman, 1994

Chipman, Daniel, *The Life of Colonel Seth Warner,* C. Goodrich and Co., Burlington, Vermont, 1858

Clark, S.D., *Movements of Political Protest in Canada, 1640–1840,* University of Toronto Press, Toronto, 1959

Crary, Catherine S., narrative and ed., *The Price of Loyalty, Tory Writings from the Revolutionary Era,* McGraw-Hill, New York, 1973

Crockett, Walter Hill, *Vermont, Green Mountain State,* Vol. 1, Vermont Farm Bureau, Burlington, Vermont, 1921

Daniell Jere R., *Experiment in Republicanism, New Hampshire Politics and the American Revolution,* Cambridge, Harvard University Press, 1970

Dean, Leon, *Green Mountain Boy: The Story of Seth Warner,* Farrar and Reinhardt, New York

DePuy, Henry Walter, *Ethan Allen and the Green Mountain Heroes of '76* (1853), Buffalo, Phinney, 1859

Duffy, John J., Hand, Samuel B., and Orth, Ralph H., eds., *The Vermont Encyclopedia,* University Press of New England, Hanover and London, 2003

Everest, Allan S., *Moses Hazen and the Canadian Refugees in the American Revolution,* Syracuse University Press, Syracuse, New York, 1973

Fasset, John, Junior, *Diary of Captain John Fasset* in *The Follet-Dewey-Fassett-Safford Ancestry,* Henry Parker Ward, Champlin, Columbus, Ohio, 1896

Fryer, Mary Beacock, *Buckskin Pimpernel, The Exploits of Justus Sherwood, Loyalist Spy,* Dundurn Press, Toronto, 1981

Furneaux, Rupert, *Saratoga, the Decisive Battle,* London, George Allen and Unwin, 1971

Gabriel, Michael P. (1), *Major General Richard Montgomery,* The Making of an American Hero, Fairleigh Dickinson University Press, Madison, 2002.

Gabriel, Michael P., ed., (2) *Quebec During the American Invasion, 1775–1776,* Michigan State University Press, 2005

Gabriel, Michael P. (3), *The Battle of Bennington, Soldiers and Civilians,* History Press, Charleston, 2012

Gilbert, Alan, *Black Patriots and Loyalists,* University of Chicago Press, Chicago, 2012

Greene, Jack P. and Pole J.R., *A Companion to the American Revolution*, Blackwell, Oxford, 2000

Hall, Benjamin H., *History of Eastern Vermont From Its Earliest Settlement to the Close of the Eighteenth Century,* Appleton, New York, 1858

Harvey, Robert, *"A Few Bloody Noses," the Realities and the Mythologies of the American Revolution,* Overlook, New York, 2002

Haviland, William A. and Power Marjory W., *The Original Vermonters, Past and Present,* University Press of New England, revised edition, 1994

Holbrook, Stewart, *Ethan Allen,* 1940

Hoyt, Edwin, *The Damndest Yankees, Ethan Allen and His Clan,* Stephen Green Press, Brattleboro, Vermont, 1976

Jellison, Charles A., *Ethan Allen, Frontier Rebel,* Syracuse University Press, New York, 1969

Jones, Matt B., *Vermont in the Making—1750–1777*, Harvard University Press, Cambridge Mass., 1939

Ketchum, Richard M., (1), *Saratoga, Turning Point of America's Revolutionary War,* Henry Holt, New York, 1997

Ketchum, Richard M. (2), *Divided Loyalties, How the American Revolution Came to New York,* Henry Holt, New York, 2002

Lanctot, Gustave, *Canada and the American Revolution, 1774–1783,* Toronto, Clarke Irwin, 1967

Lanning, Richard Lee, *African-Americans in the Revolutionary War* (2000), Citadel Kensington, 2005

Lincoln, William ed., *Journals of Each Provincial Congress of Massachusetts in 1774 and of the Committee of Safety,* Boston, 1838

Lucas, C.P., *A History of Canada, 1763–1812*, Oxford, 1909

Morton, Doris Begor, *Philip Skene of Skenesborough,* Grastorf, Granville, New York, 1959

Mathews, Hazel C., *Frontier Spies, The British Secret Service, Northern Department, during the Revolutionary War,* Ace Press Inc., Fort Myers, Florida, 1971

McIlwraith, Jean, *Sir Frederick Haldimand,* Morang and Co. Ltd, Toronto, 1904

Nelson, Paul David, *General Sir Guy Carleton, Lord Dorchester,* Associated University Presses, Cranbury, NJ, 2000

Nickerson, Hoffman, *The Turning Point of Revolution Or Burgoyne in America,* Vols 1 and 2 (1928), Port Washington, N.Y., Kennikat Press, 1967

Nye, R.B., and Morpurgo, J.E., *A History of the United States,* 2 vols., Penguin, London, 1955

Pell, John, *Ethan Allen,* Houghton Mifflin, Cambridge, Mass., 1929
Pemberton, Ian Cleghorn Blanshard (1), *Justus Sherwood, Vermont Loyalist, 1747–1798,* PhD thesis, University of Western Ontario, London, Canada, October, 1973
Petersen, James E., *Seth Warner,* Dunmore House, Middlebury, Vermont, 2011
Pirenne, Henri, *A History of Europe,* (1938), University Book Publishers, New York, 1955
Preston, John Hyde, *Revolution 1776,* New York, 1933
Raabe, Emily, *Ethan Allen: The Green Mountain Boys and Vermont's Path to Statehood,* PowerPlus Books, New York, 2002
Randall, Willard Sterne, *Ethan Allen, His Life and Times,* Norton, New York, 2011
Rawlyk, George A., *Revolution Rejected, 1775–1776,* Prentice-Hall of Canada, Scarborough, Ontario, 1968
Reuter, Claus, *The Battle of Hubbardton, July 7, 1777, Vermont, USA,* Canadian Museum of Applied History, n.d.
Reynolds, Paul R., *Guy Carleton, A Biography,* Gage, Toronto, 1980
Riedesel, Fredericke, *Diary of Lady Riedesel (Letters and Journals Relating to the War of American Independence and the Capture of the German Troops at Saratoga),* German-Canadian Museum,n.d.
Rothbard, Murray N., *Conceived in Liberty, Volume IV, The Revolutionary War 1775–1784,* Arlington, New Rochelle, New York, 1979
Stanley, George, *Canada Invaded, 1775–1776,* Hakhart, Toronto, 1973
Stark, Caleb, *Memoir and Official Correspondence of Gen. John Stark: With Notices of Several Other Officers of the Revolution* (1860), Kessinger Reprint, n.p.,n.d
Taylor, Alan, *American Colonies and the Settling of North America,* Penguin, London, 2001
Thompson, Zadock, *History of Vermont, Natural, Civil and Statistical,* (Part II, the Civil History); Burlington, Vermont, 1842
Van Doren, Carl, *Secret History of the American Revolution,* New York: Viking Press, 1941
Van de Water, *The Reluctant Republic: Vermont, 1724–1791,* New York, John Day, 1941
Walton E. P. ed., *Records of the Council of Safety, State of Vermont,* Montpelier, VT, 1873
Ward, Christopher, *The War of the Revolution,* 2 vols, New York, 1952
Wardner, Henry Steele, *The Birthplace of Vermont, A History of Windsor to*

1781, New York, 1927

Washington, Ida H. and Paul A., *Carleton's Raid,* Phoenix, Canaan, New Hampshire, 1977

Watt, Gavin K. (1), *The Burning of the Valleys, Daring Raids From Canada Against the New York Frontier in the Fall of 1780,* Dundurn, Toronto, 1997

Watt, Gavin K., (2), *A Dirty Trifling Piece of Business, The Revolutionary War as Waged from Canada in 1781*, Dundurn, Toronto, 2009

Watt, Gavin K.,(3), *I Am Heartily Ashamed, The Revolutionary War as Waged from Canada in 1782,* Dundurn, Toronto, 2010

Wilbur, James, *Ira Allen, Founder of Vermont,* 2 volumes, Houghton Mifflin, Cambridge, Mass., 1828 (includes Ira Allen's *Autobiography*)

Wilbur, Lafayette, *Early History of Vermont,* 3 vols, Jericho, Vermont, 1899

Williams, Samuel, *The Natural and Civil History of Vermont,* Vols. 1 and 2 (1794), Samuel Mills, Burlington, 1805

Williamson, Chilton (1), *Vermont in Quandary: 1763–1825,* Vermont Historical Society, Montpelier, Vermont, 1949

Williamson, Chilton (2), *American Suffrage: From Property to Democracy, 1760–1860,* Princeton University Press, 1960

INDEX